PROMOTING HAPPINESS AMONG ADULTS WITH AUTISM AND OTHER SEVERE DISABILITIES

EVIDENCE-BASED STRATEGIES

DENNIS H. REID

Volume 5
in
The Behavior Analysis Applications in Developmental Disabilities Series

HABILITATIVE MANAGEMENT CONSULTANTS, INC.

Copyright © 2016 Dennis H. Reid
All Rights Reserved

This book may not be reproduced or transmitted in any form or by any means, electronic, mechanical, including photocopying, recording, or by any information storage and retrieval system, except in the case of reviews, without the expressed written permission of the publisher, except where permitted by law.

ISBN Number 0-9645562-6-X

Library of Congress Catalog Card Number 2015954741

Published by
Habilitative Management Consultants, Inc.
P. O. Box 2295
Morganton, North Carolina 28680

Professional Press
Chapel Hill, North Carolina 27515

Manufactured in the United States of America

DEDICATION

To Elizabeth and Cason Reid.

ACKNOWLEDGMENTS

This book would not have been possible without the collaborative and inspirational work of Carolyn Green, Marsha Parsons, and Martin Ivancic. They have each researched and practiced means of promoting happiness among adults with autism and other severe disabilities for many years and in many ways. Their work has been instrumental in forming the foundation for the book's content.

ABOUT THE AUTHOR

Dr. Dennis Reid has over 40 years of experience as a supervisor and clinician in residential, community, and educational settings for people who have intellectual and developmental disabilities. He has consulted with human service agencies in the majority of states across the United States as well as Canada, New Zealand, and Australia. Denny has published over 140 applied research articles and book chapters, and 10 books. He is the senior author of the highly acclaimed *Positive Behavior Support Training Curriculum,* sold internationally by the American Association on Intellectual and Developmental Disabilities (AAIDD), now in its 3rd Edition. His work has resulted in awards form local, state, and national organizations including the North Carolina Department of Human Resources, North Carolina Association for Behavior Analysis, Association for Behavior Analysis International, AAIDD, TASH (formerly the Association for Persons with Severe Handicaps), and the Organization for Autism Research. Denny is the founder and Director of the Carolina Behavior Analysis and Support Center in Morganton, North Carolina. His company has employed adults with autism and other severe disabilities in a supported work capacity for over 20 years.

TO CONTACT THE AUTHOR

Denny Reid can be contacted using the information provided below. Readers are invited to send comments about the book, as well as suggestions regarding future editions in the *Behavior Analysis Applications in Developmental Disabilities Series.*

> Habilitative Management Consultants, Inc.
> P. O. Box 2295
> Morganton, North Carolina 28680
> (phone: 828 432 0030)
> e-mail: drhmc@vistatech.net

PREFACE

Adult quality of life is heavily determined by the amount of happiness a person experiences on a day-to-day basis. Having a life with happiness is a desire of essentially all adults. Pursuing happiness is also considered an unalienable right of United States citizens, recognized most noticeably in the *life, liberty, and pursuit of happiness* clause in the country's Declaration of Independence. This right pertains to all Americans, including adults who have autism and other severe disabilities.

A primary determinant of the degree to which adults with autism and other severe disabilities experience daily happiness is how staff in human service agencies perform their jobs. Many of these individuals live in homes operated by human service agencies and/or attend the agencies' day support programs. Many others receive services from agency staff in a supported living, working, or recreational capacity. In short, many adults with autism and other severe disabilities spend much of their time with human service staff.

If human service staff are to promote happiness among adults with autism and other severe disabilities they support, the staff must have a sincere desire to help them have an enjoyable quality of life. However, although critical, such a desire is not enough. Staff also have to be knowledgeable about strategies specifically for helping adults with autism and other severe disabilities experience happiness, and be skilled in using the strategies. Otherwise, there is no guarantee that consumers of agency services will truly have happiness in their day-to-day lives. This is especially the case for those adults with autism and other severe disabilities whose communication and related challenges interfere with conventional expressions of their happiness and unhappiness.

Over the last two decades a considerable amount of research in applied behavior analysis has focused on the development and application of strategies for promoting happiness among people with intellectual and developmental disabilities. Such research, though by no means complete, has resulted in an impressive set of evidence-based strategies that can help adults with autism and other severe disabilities experience happiness as they go about their daily lives. The purpose of this book is to describe those strategies so staff working in human service agencies can actively and effectively promote happiness among the people they support.

In describing how staff in human service agencies can enhance happiness using evidence-based strategies, reference will often be made to agency consumers – adults with autism and other severe disabilities who receive agency supports and services. It is recognized, however, that reference to people with disabilities within human service agencies occurs in different ways around the United States as well as other countries. In some cases reference to "consumers" is the accepted nomenclature whereas in other areas this reference is not as acceptable, deferring to "clients", "residents", or just "individuals".

It is hoped that referring to "consumers" is not offensive to any reader, as that is certainly not the intent. This is just a means of conveying information in as readable a manner as possible. The essential point is that the focus is on *people* who happen to have autism and other severe disabilities. Because the focus is also on adults who are consumers of supports provided by human service agencies, reference is made to "consumers" just as people who are recipients of any type of service are considered consumers of the service.

Additionally, considering people with disabilities supported by a human service agency as "consumers" of the agency's services can help hold agency personnel accountable for their actions. The intent is to highlight the importance of agency staff ensuring that the recipients of the agency's services truly receive what they are intended to receive and what is desired. Of primary concern here is that agency staff truly promote the happiness of the adults with autism and other severe disabilities in carrying out their service delivery.

Contents

SECTION I

INTRODUCTION TO PROMOTING HAPPINESS

Chapter 1

    Introduction to Promoting Happiness Among Adults with Autism and Other Severe Disabilities 3

- The Importance of Evidence-Based Approaches for Promoting Happiness 4
- Purpose of Promoting Happiness among Adults with Autism and Other Severe Disabilities 7
- Intended Audience of Promoting Happiness among Adults with Autism and Other Severe Disabilities 8
- Organization of Promoting Happiness among Adults with Autism and Other Severe Disabilities 8
- A Special Note: Promoting Happiness And Independent Living 9
- A Quick Overview for Promoting Happiness 12

Chapter 2

    A Basic Protocol for Promoting Happiness 15

- Identify Indices of Happiness and Unhappiness 16
- Validate Identified Indices of Happiness and Unhappiness 17
- Take Action to Increase Situations Accompanied by Indices of Happiness 19
- Take Action to Decrease Situations Accompanied by Indices of Unhappiness 19
- Monitor and Evaluate Indices of Happiness and Unhappiness 20
- The Special Focus of Strategies Designed to Promote Happiness 22

Chapter 3

    Identifying Indices of Happiness and Unhappiness 25

        • Basic Indices of Happiness and Unhappiness 26

        • Using Caregiver Opinion to Identify Indices of Happiness and Unhappiness 27

        • Using Systematic Preference Assessments to Identify Indices of Happiness and Unhappiness 35

Chapter 4

    Validating Indices of Happiness and Unhappiness 39

        • Basic Steps for Validating Indices of Happiness and Unhappiness 41

        • A Final Note: Revalidation of Indices of Happiness and Unhappiness 54

SECTION II

STRATEGIES FOR INCREASING HAPPINESS

Chapter 5

    Establishing Good Relationships 59

        • Challenges Within Human Service Agencies That Impede Good Relationships 62

        • Steps for Developing Good Relationships 65

        • Maintaining Good Relationships 75

        • The Critical Role of Sincerity in Relationships 77

Chapter 6

    The Power of Social Attention 81

        • The Critical Role of Relationships on Promoting Happiness through Social Attention 83

        • Types of Social Attention 83

        • Positive Attention 84

        • Neutral Attention 87

        • Negative Attention 88

- Providing Social Attention in A Group 90
- Limits to Providing Social Attention 93
- Training Staff to Provide Social Attention for Promoting Consumer Happiness 95

Chapter 7

Promoting Consumer Choice Making During Daily Activities 99

- Qualification: A Focus on Choices During Daily Activities 101
- Ways to Provide Choice-Making Opportunities to Promote Meaningful Consumer Choices 102
- Types of Choices 116
- Special Considerations for Providing Choice-Making Opportunities to Promote Consumer Happiness 122
- A Final Note about Providing Choice-Making Opportunities: Multiple Benefits for Adults with Severe Disabilities 129

Chapter 8

Accessing Preferences 133

- Ensuring Consumers Access Their Preferences: A Two-Step Process 134
- Special Note: The Relationship Between Consumer Access to Preferences and Stereotypic Behavior 153

Chapter 9

Personal Goal Planning 159

- Preparing for Major Lifestyle Changes: Person-Centered Planning 161
- Additional Concerns with Person-Centered Goal Planning 171

Chapter 10

Promoting Happiness By Reducing Unhappiness 179

- Identifying Sources of Unhappiness 180
- Changing Sources of Unhappiness to Promote Happiness 181
- Importance of Routine Monitoring and Evaluation 197

SECTION III

PROMOTING HAPPINESS THROUGH INDEPENDENCE

Chapter 11

Preference-Based Teaching: Promoting Happiness While Learning 203

- A Pre-Requisite for Making Teaching Enjoyable: Good Instructor-Learner Relationships 206
- The ABC Model of Preference-Based Teaching 207
- The Important Role of Learner Choice in Promoting Happiness During Teaching 219
- Some Special Concerns with Preference-Based Teaching 222

Chapter 12

Teaching Naturalistically to Increase Independence and Promote Happiness 227

- When Naturalistic Teaching is Most Applicable 229
- A Naturalistic Teaching Protocol 232
- Key Situations for Naturalistic Teaching 238
- Naturalistic Teaching in Community Settings and Activities 239
- Teaching When Consumers are Naturally Motivated to Learn 240
- Teaching Typical Instruction Following 241
- Promoting Staff Application of Naturalistic Teaching 245
- A Final Note on Naturalistic Teaching and Happiness 246

Chapter 13

Working With Staff to Promote Consumer Happiness 249

- Importance of Working with Staff to Promote Work Quality and Work Enjoyment 250
- An Evidence-Based Protocol for Supervising Staff Work Performance .. 252
- Special Supervisory Actions for Promoting Staff Work Enjoyment 272

SECTION IV

APPENDIX AND SELECTED READINGS

Appendix 281

Selected Readings 293

Index 301

SECTION I

INTRODUCTION TO PROMOTING HAPPINESS

CHAPTER 1

INTRODUCTION TO
PROMOTING HAPPINESS AMONG
ADULTS WITH AUTISM AND
OTHER SEVERE DISABILITIES

A primary purpose of agencies that provide services for adults with autism and other severe disabilities is to promote a desirable quality of life. Although many factors affect life quality, one of the most important is the amount of happiness individuals experience on a day-to-day basis. The pursuit of happiness is a fundamental right of all citizens, including people with severe disabilities. Along with health and safety, happiness also is arguably the most important concern parents have for their adult sons and daughters who are the recipients of agency services.

Essentially all human service agencies acknowledge the importance of an enjoyable quality of life for the people with disabilities they support. However, truly promoting happiness among adults with autism and other severe disabilities can be difficult. Whereas most people can readily express when they are happy, the latter individuals often have communication challenges that interfere with conventional expressions of happiness. Consequently, agency staff must take certain steps to accurately identify when the people they support are truly happy.

Promoting happiness is also difficult because of varying types of supports provided in human service agencies for adults with autism and other severe disabilities. Such agencies usually have a number of purposes. Sometimes fulfilling those purposes can impede or reduce happiness among the people with disabilities they support. To illustrate, programs may be implemented to help individuals learn useful skills or overcome challenging behavior. Various teaching and behavior-reduction programs can be effortful or otherwise disliked by consumers of agency services, resulting in their unhappiness when the programs are in effect. Similarly, staff attempts to promote participation in certain activities of daily living can be accompanied by discontent or resistance among some consumers. Hence, procedures to enhance happiness must occur in conjunction with other types of supports provided within human service agencies.

Another reason promoting happiness is difficult is the manner in which human service agencies operate. Although agencies frequently espouse an enjoyable quality of life for the adults with disabilities they support, often there is little formal attention directed to enjoyment or happiness relative to other outcomes. Agency staff usually develop specific procedures for assisting individuals in attaining outcomes such as increased independence or community participation. Implementation of those procedures is monitored and records are maintained on consumer responses to the procedures. In contrast, few agencies have formal procedures specifically for ensuring happiness, and individual happiness is not formally monitored or assessed on a regular basis.

> **The pursuit of happiness is a fundamental right of all people; human service agencies must act to ensure adults with autism and other severe disabilities experience that right.**

THE IMPORTANCE OF EVIDENCE-BASED APPROACHES FOR PROMOTING HAPPINESS

For reasons just noted, as well as others to be discussed later, happiness among adults with autism and other severe disabilities should not be taken for granted within human service agencies. Human service staff must actively strive to ensure these consumers of agency services experience happiness on a regular basis. Further, to maximize the likelihood that actions taken by staff will truly promote happiness, the actions should be *evidence-based*. Evidence-based means that actions taken to identify and enhance happiness have been developed and evaluated through scientific research to document the effectiveness of the actions. Most importantly, the actions should have been shown to reliably increase happiness when applied within the conditions typically operating in human service agencies.

When procedures used to promote happiness among people with severe disabilities are not evidence-based, multiple problems exist. Most notably, the likelihood that the strategies will effectively increase happiness is reduced significantly. Without reliance on evidence-based means of increasing happiness, support staff must rely on their own ideas or intuition about how to promote happiness among adults with severe disabilities. Sometimes personal ideas and intuition are accurate and effective, but often they are not.

Different support staff also have varying ideas about how to assist a given individual in being happy and the ideas sometimes conflict across staff. Additionally, some staff project their own experiences regarding what makes them happy to the people they support. However, happiness is an individual experience; what makes a given staff person happy will not necessarily have the same effect on a person with autism or other severe disability.

Due to recognition of the need for effective means of enhancing happiness among adults with autism and other severe disabilities, a considerable amount of research has focused on how to promote happiness among this population. Although the research is by no means complete, investigations to date have resulted in a significant amount of useful information for practitioners.

A number of evidence-based strategies have been developed for promoting happiness in human service agencies for adults with autism and other severe disabilities. The strategies include general approaches that agencies can adopt overall to increase the likelihood that recipients of their services will routinely experience happiness. The strategies also include ways to promote happiness that are highly tailored for certain individuals based on their existing skills, preferences, and challenges.

> **Actions taken to promote happiness are most likely to be effective if those actions are *evidence-based*.**

Research on promoting happiness among people with autism and other severe disabilities has not only resulted in effective strategies for increasing happiness, it has further emphasized the importance of actively helping individuals experience happiness. In particular, investigations have demonstrated that increasing happiness can have a therapeutic effect on challenging behavior. Almost every human service agency is faced with assisting some people in overcoming various types of challenging behavior, such as aggression toward others or disruptive social activities. When individuals are effectively supported in being happy, challenging behavior is frequently prevented or reduced.

Challenging behavior usually occurs because a person is displeased or unhappy with something in the immediate environment. The problem behavior occurs in an attempt by the individual to change whatever is causing the discontent. If, however, the person is pleased or otherwise happy with an ongoing situation, then there is no reason to engage in challenging behavior. How promoting happiness can help overcome problem behavior will be addressed more specifically later in this book. The point here is that happiness and problem behavior frequently occur in an inverse relationship: the happier an individual is, the less likely the person is to display challenging behavior.

> **Using evidence-based means to promote happiness can reduce problem behavior among adults with autism and other severe disabilities; generally the more happiness individuals experience on a daily basis, the less likely they are to engage in problem behavior.**

PURPOSE OF *PROMOTING HAPPINESS AMONG ADULTS WITH AUTISM AND OTHER SEVERE DISABILITIES*

The purpose of this book is to describe evidence-based strategies that human service staff can use to enhance day-to-day happiness among adults with severe disabilities they support. The intent is to describe tried and tested means of promoting happiness among people with disabilities whose communication and related challenges interfere with conventional expressions of this emotional experience. The procedures to be described have been shown to effectively enhance happiness among adults with a variety of disabilities and of particular concern here, autism and intellectual disabilities.

The evidence-based procedures to be presented for increasing happiness are applicable for people with the full range of intellectual disabilities and autism. However, the primary emphasis is on those adults who have more significant disabilities and especially severe or profound intellectual disabilities as well as autism on the severe end of the spectrum of autism disorders. Because the latter individuals often cannot describe emotions such as happiness in the same manner as people who do not have disabilities as noted earlier (or people with less significant disabilities), special attention is warranted to assessing and promoting their happiness.

The emphasis here is also on *adults* with autism and other severe disabilities. Human service agencies have unique challenges when serving adults with disabilities relative to settings for children. To illustrate, the primary service settings for most children with disabilities are schools. A primary function of schools is to prepare students for their future lives as adults. In contrast, agencies that support adults focus more heavily on maximizing the current quality of life among their consumers (though continued preparation for future lives is also relevant). This is particularly the case in residential agencies, as those agencies represent the homes for many adults with autism and other severe disabilities.

Intended Audience of *Promoting Happiness among Adults with Autism and Other Severe Disabilities*

The primary audience of this book is personnel working in human service agencies providing supports for adults with autism and other severe disabilities. The content is particularly directed to supervisors of direct support staff, clinicians, administrators, and executive personnel. Many direct support staff should also find the information relevant.

The content of this book is most applicable for personnel working in residential agencies (e.g., group homes, center-based living, supported living) and day support sites such as adult education programs, day activity centers, and sheltered and supported work situations. The content is likewise relevant for people aspiring to work with adults with disabilities, such as students in university and community college programs. Finally, family members and professional advocates should find the information useful in their attempts to advocate for an enjoyable quality of life for adults with autism and other severe disabilities.

Organization of *Promoting Happiness among Adults with Autism and Other Severe Disabilities*

This book consists of four sections. **Section I: Introduction** includes this and the following three chapters that focus on an overall approach to promoting happiness and how to accurately identify happiness and unhappiness. **Section II: Strategies for Increasing Happiness consists of **Chapters 5–10** that describe specific procedures support staff can use on a daily basis to promote happiness and decrease unhappiness. **Section III: Promoting Happiness Through Independence** includes **Chapters 11** and **12** that pertain to increasing happiness while simultaneously supporting adults with autism and other severe disabilities in living their lives as independently as possible. Additionally, **Chapter 13** in this section describes managing human service agencies in a manner that facilitates application of previously presented information for consistently promoting happiness among consumers of agency services. Finally, **Section IV: Appendix** and **Selected Readings** provides more detailed information for using some of the strategies discussed in preceding chapters. It also provides references to background material upon which the information in preceding chapters is based. The articles, chapters, and books referenced provide the interested reader with access to the research that forms the evidence base for specific topics covered in respective chapters.

A Special Note:
Promoting Happiness *And* Independent Living

Throughout the following chapters there is a basic premise that underlies the information presented about promoting happiness among adults with autism and other severe disabilities. The premise is that happiness should be promoted *in conjunction with promoting skill development and maintenance.* Happiness among people with autism and other severe disabilities, just like with everybody else, is closely linked to the degree to which they possess the skills to live their lives independently. Specifically, the more independent skills they have and apply to everyday life, the greater the degree of happiness they will usually experience.

A defining characteristic of severe intellectual disabilities and autism is the need for assistance in learning meaningful skills to function independently. Teaching skills to promote independent functioning allows individuals to have personal control over their lives. In turn, having personal control allows people to do things that are desired and in ways that are desired – ways that enhance personal happiness.

If adults with autism and other severe disabilities are not effectively supported in learning and using skills necessary to function independently, then they are heavily dependent on staff for meeting their needs. Although in many cases staff help meet those needs in ways an individual desires, in other cases staff attempt to meet those needs in ways that the person does not like. In other cases, a person's needs simply will not be met, either because a staff person is not immediately present or the staff person does not exert the effort to ensure the individual's needs are met. In the latter situations, the individual's immediate happiness is almost always compromised.

> **Happiness and independence are closely aligned; the more independently an individual functions day-to-day, generally the more happiness the person experiences.**

Because of the relationship between independent functioning and happiness, special concern is directed throughout this book to promoting happiness while simultaneously teaching and otherwise supporting independence among adults with autism and other severe disabilities (see in particular **Section III**). Although special cases will be highlighted in which the promotion of happiness sometimes overrides concerns for increasing independent functioning at a given point in time—and vice versa—these cases are exceptions. Again, happiness generally should be promoted in conjunction with enhancing an individual's acquisition and application of skills necessary to function in an independent manner.

Concerns over promoting independence while enhancing happiness are also warranted due to some misconceptions about how certain strategies to promote happiness should be applied. To illustrate, one means of promoting happiness to be discussed is incorporating choices into the daily routines of a person with a severe disability **(Chapter 7)**. At times, some support staff allow an individual to repeatedly engage in an activity that over time is detrimental to the person's overall well being, such as eating only one type of food item every day or consistently staying in one's bedroom throughout the major portion of the day. The rationale provided by certain staff for the repeated occurrence of such activities is that the activities represent the individual's preference or choice.

Supporting an individual to repeatedly engage in activities that are detrimental to the person's overall well being may seem at first glance to represent a means of promoting the person's immediate happiness (i.e., if the activities represent an individual's preference). On closer examination though, it usually becomes clear that the person engages in one or a small set of activities because: (1) either the person has not been taught skills necessary to enjoy other activities or, (2) the individual is not effectively supported in using existing skills to engage in other activities. The end result is that the person's happiness is compromised over the long run due to having limited skills for engaging in varied activities that are accompanied by happiness.

People generally experience an enjoyable quality of life when they have many options for doing things that make them happy. To do many things though, people must have many skills. When adults with autism and other severe disabilities repeatedly engage in only one or a few activities, they are not learning or applying skills to participate in other activities that can expand opportunities to experience happiness.

In short, happiness should be promoted with concerns both for immediate happiness of an individual as well as the person's future happiness. Considerations for effectively enhancing happiness on a short- *and* long-term basis will be addressed where relevant in subsequent chapters. Such considerations almost always involve concerns for promoting happiness in conjunction with teaching meaningful skills and enhancing independent functioning.

A Quick Overview for Promoting Happiness

This book is intended to provide readers with evidence-based strategies for promoting happiness on an *individual* basis. As summarized in the next chapter, there is an overall protocol for using the strategies with individual adults with autism and other severe disabilities who have varying challenges. That protocol involves (1) identifying when an individual appears happy and unhappy, or *indices* of happiness and unhappiness, (2) taking steps to ensure the identified indices accurately represent when the person experiences happiness and unhappiness, or *validating* the reported indices, (3) taking action to increase situations accompanied by the person's happiness, (4) taking action to decrease situations accompanied by unhappiness and, (5) routinely monitoring the indices to evaluate the effectiveness of whatever actions are taken.

To effectively use the evidence-based approach for increasing happiness, steps constituting the protocol must be applied with each individual of concern within a human service agency. Of course, human service agencies typically serve groups of people with disabilities. Consequently, because the procedures must be implemented *individually*, the evidence-based approach to promoting happiness can be time consuming when considering an agency's entire consumer population.

Additionally, some procedures described in the initial chapters (**Chapters 2-4**) are rather technical in nature. This is particularly the case with those procedures necessary to *validate* indicators of when an adult with autism or another severe disability is truly happy and unhappy (**Chapter 4**). It can take a degree of effort to acquire a good understanding of the procedures and apply them appropriately.

> **Evidence-based procedures for promoting happiness must be implemented on an *individual* basis with each adult with autism or another severe disability.**

Due to the technical nature of information presented in the initial chapters, readers may find it somewhat cumbersome to progress through these chapters. Nonetheless, information in this first section is necessary to establish the foundation for using procedures in subsequent chapters in an evidence-based manner to effectively increase happiness. Upon completing the first section, readers should find information in the following chapters—that describe in detail evidence-based ways to promote happiness—much less cumbersome.

Chapter Summary: Key Points

1. *Happiness is a fundamental right of adults with autism and other severe disabilities just as with all citizens; human service agencies have the responsibility to act specifically to ensure the people they support experience that right.*

2. *Actions taken to promote happiness are most likely to be effective if the actions are evidence-based.*

3. *Promoting happiness often prevents or reduces challenging behavior among adults with autism and other severe disabilities.*

4. *Happiness should be promoted in conjunction with enhancement of independent functioning.*

5. *Evidence-based procedures for promoting happiness must be carried out on an individual basis with each adult who has autism or other severe disability.*

CHAPTER 2

A Basic Protocol for Promoting Happiness

As indicated in **Chapter 1**, a variety of evidence-based strategies exists for human service agencies to promote daily happiness among adults with autism and other severe disabilities. As also noted, there is an overall framework for guiding efforts in using the various strategies to promote happiness. This framework, involving a systematic and step-wise approach, is illustrated below. The key steps of the framework are summarized in the remainder of this chapter. Subsequent chapters discuss each step more in-depth along with variations for applying respective steps in situations with special circumstances.

FRAMEWORK FOR PROMOTING HAPPINESS

Step 1: **Identify indices of happiness and unhappiness.**

Step 2: **Validate identified indices of happiness and unhappiness.**

Step 3: **Take action to increase situations accompanied by happiness indices.**

Step 4: **Take action to decrease situations accompanied by unhappiness indices.**

Step 5: **Routinely monitor and evaluate occurrence of happiness and unhappiness indices.**

IDENTIFY INDICES OF HAPPINESS AND UNHAPPINESS

A major obstacle to promoting happiness among adults with autism and other severe disabilities is knowing when they are truly happy. Many of these individuals do not have the communication skills to readily tell people what they are experiencing emotionally. Other individuals may demonstrate good communication skills in specific or familiar situations, whether by speaking, signing, or using various assistive means. However, even in the latter situations the communication skills often are not sufficient to adequately describe emotional experiences in ways that are easily understood by human service staff. Consequently, the first step for promoting happiness is to identify when individuals are happy and unhappy.

Happiness is a private event or experience. As such, happiness cannot be directly observed per se. Judging whether someone is happy or not must be based on what the person is doing. People tend to do certain things when they are happy, and other things when they are not happy. Determining whether an adult with autism or other severe disability is happy or unhappy involves initially identifying what the person usually *does* when happy and unhappy, respectively.

Because a person's happiness and unhappiness are private experiences and can only be judged by others based on what the person does when happy and unhappy, these emotional experiences are observed indirectly. More specifically, only *indices* of happiness and unhappiness can be observed, not the private experiences of happiness and unhappiness. When such indices are carefully identified and then validated as discussed later, they can be a very good reflection of the happiness and unhappiness of a person with autism or other severe disability. As will also be discussed, however, it is always important to remember that judgments about someone's happiness and unhappiness are based on *indices* of these emotional experiences.

Making decisions about whether someone is happy or not based on what the person does pertains to everybody, not just adults who have autism and other severe disabilities. Although making such decisions is usually easier with people who can clearly talk about how they feel, the decisions are still based on indices of happiness and unhappiness in terms of what the person does—in this case, what the person says. What a person says about feeling happy is a common indicator or index of the person's happiness, but is not the same as the actual experience of happiness.

> **Happiness and unhappiness are private emotional experiences and cannot be observed directly; only *indices* of happiness and unhappiness can be observed.**

VALIDATE IDENTIFIED INDICES OF HAPPINESS AND UNHAPPINESS

Because only indices of happiness and unhappiness can be directly observed, care must be taken to ensure the indices accurately reflect someone's experiences of happiness and unhappiness. Hence, the second step of the protocol for promoting happiness is to *validate* the identified indices. Evidence must be obtained to support the accuracy of specific indices as truly reflecting a person's private emotional state.

The importance of taking steps to validate indices of happiness and unhappiness is well illustrated with people who can readily describe these private experiences. Again, although determining when someone is happy or unhappy is easier with people who do not have disabilities that impede their communication, such determinations are still based indirectly on indices of their experiences. It is usually assumed, for example, that if people say they are happy, they really are happy. This assumption is not always accurate.

To illustrate, a husband may believe his wife is unhappy with him because she refrains from interacting with him, slams a door or an object on a table in his presence, etc. However, when the husband asks his wife if something is wrong (and she really is unhappy with her husband at that point in time), she says that everything is "fine". In this case, the vocal indicator of happiness is not accurate but the other behavior (refraining from interactions, slamming things) is accurate.

Taking action to validate identified indices of happiness and unhappiness is more important with adults who have autism and other severe disabilities relative to people who have typical communication skills. The importance exists for several reasons. Most apparently, individuals with autism and other severe disabilities often lack the most common means of expressing their happiness and unhappiness to other people—that of vocally describing their private experiences.

Additionally, many adults with autism and other severe disabilities do rather unusual things when they are happy and unhappy, or at least unusual in regard to what people without disabilities do when experiencing these emotions. For example, one adult with autism and other severe disabilities has been known to make a high-pitched sound when happy and spin in circles when unhappy. Another person would lightly pat a support staff on the back when happy and bite his wrist when unhappy.

Because of the somewhat unusual indicators of happiness and unhappiness, support staff frequently have difficulty knowing when an adult with autism or other severe disability is happy or not. Unless specific actions are taken to clearly identify and validate individual indices of happiness and unhappiness for each person they support, agency staff will not be in a position to effectively increase happiness among respective individuals.

> **Before happiness can be effectively promoted, *valid* indicators of happiness must be identified.**

TAKE ACTION TO INCREASE SITUATIONS ACCOMPANIED BY INDICES OF HAPPINESS

Once indices of happiness have been identified and validated, then actions can be taken to increase happiness among agency consumers with autism and other severe disabilities. This is the step of the overall protocol that entails routine implementation of evidence-based strategies to increase individual happiness. The first five chapters in **Section II** describe these strategies in-depth.

Strategies for increasing happiness presented in later chapters each have varying degrees of applicability across different situations. To illustrate, in many situations happiness can be promoted by offering people choices during their daily activities, such as how or with whom to do an activity. In other cases, choice opportunities may be limited because, for example, an activity must be done in a certain way (e.g., how a work task must be completed in a supported job). In the latter situation, other strategies to increase happiness may be implemented such as by incorporating an individual's preferences within the job task itself. Again, detailed descriptions of evidence-based strategies for promoting happiness, including when different strategies are most applicable, are described in **Section II**.

TAKE ACTION TO DECREASE SITUATIONS ACCOMPANIED BY INDICES OF UNHAPPINESS

Happiness and unhappiness can be conceptualized as representing a continuum of emotional experiences. On one end of the continuum is happiness at its most significant level and on the other end is the most significant unhappiness. A person's quality of life is enhanced the most when experiencing emotions toward the former end of the continuum much more often than emotions toward the latter end. The strategies to increase happiness exemplified in the previous section are intended to help an individual experience emotions on the happiness part of the continuum.

Strategies to decrease unhappiness are intended to reduce how often a person experiences emotions characteristic of the unhappiness end of the continuum. These strategies do not necessarily promote significant happiness. However, they still enhance quality of life overall by reducing unpleasant experiences that are accompanied by unhappiness. People usually enjoy their day more when they are not unhappy, even if they are not particularly happy. That is, their emotional experiences move away from the unhappiness end of the continuum, though not all the way to the most significant level of happiness.

The nature of actions taken to reduce unhappiness is somewhat different than actions directed to increase happiness. Increasing happiness usually entails support staff incorporating various strategies within the ongoing routine of adults with autism and other severe disabilities they support; certain things are added to the daily environment. In contrast, decreasing unhappiness often involves removing certain activities that are ongoing, or altering how those activities occur. To effectively decrease unhappiness, indices of a person's unhappiness must be observed during the daily routine with the intent of identifying when unhappiness occurs. Those routines are then discontinued or otherwise altered where possible such that they are no longer accompanied by the individual's indications of being unhappy. Specific strategies for decreasing unhappiness in this manner are discussed in **Chapter 10** in **Section II**.

MONITOR AND EVALUATE INDICES OF HAPPINESS AND UNHAPPINESS

The fifth step of the evidence-based protocol for promoting happiness involves monitoring and evaluating indices of happiness and unhappiness. As indices are identified and validated and then strategies to increase happiness and decrease unhappiness are implemented, the occurrence of the identified indicators should be simultaneously monitored. Such indices must be monitored to identify situations accompanied by happiness and unhappiness indices, to ensure strategies to promote happiness are having the desired effect and if not, to revise the strategies to more effectively enhance happiness.

As indicated in **Chapter 1**, the importance of identifying desired outcomes among people with disabilities and regularly monitoring attainment of those outcomes is well accepted in most human service agencies. Again, agencies typically have systems in place to monitor, for example, how well people they support are acquiring skills targeted in teaching programs and changes in challenging behavior as a result of implementing behavior support plans. Results of the monitoring are used to document progress of respective consumers in attaining desired outcomes and to revise supports and services if adequate progress is not observed.

There is a common view among supervisors in human service agencies that the job duties agency staff perform most proficiently generally coincide with those duties that are most frequently monitored. That is, performance areas of staff that are routinely monitored by management tend to be completed more often and more appropriately than those areas that are not regularly monitored. This view is generally accurate but incomplete.

Research has repeatedly shown that staff tend to do not just what is monitored, but what is also systematically attended to by supervisors in other ways. Specifically, staff usually perform those aspects of their jobs most proficiently for which they are well trained and for which they receive frequent feedback from supervisors regarding the quality of their performance.

Given that human service agencies typically report the importance of promoting life quality for people with disabilities they support, it is somewhat disconcerting that systems are usually lacking for monitoring and providing feedback to staff based on the observed happiness of agency consumers. If happiness as a reflection of quality of life is valued within an agency, then it should be regularly monitored and attended to just like more traditional types of consumer outcomes. Otherwise, there is no guarantee that happiness will be effectively promoted.

Indices of individual happiness should be regularly monitored within human service agencies just like other desired consumer outcomes.

THE SPECIAL FOCUS OF STRATEGIES DESIGNED TO PROMOTE HAPPINESS

In considering the protocol just summarized for promoting happiness, special concern is warranted regarding the specific focus of strategies designed to increase happiness and decrease unhappiness. The concern is that the strategies must focus on situations that are accompanied by indices of happiness and unhappiness. The intent is to increase activities and events that are accompanied by happiness indices and decrease activities and events accompanied by indices of unhappiness. The focus should not be on increasing or decreasing the respective *indices themselves* without addressing the situations in which the indices are observed.

Indices of private emotional experiences such as happiness and unhappiness, or what a person usually does when experiencing the emotions, are observable behaviors. The occurrence of those behaviors is usually affected by changes in private emotional experiences such as happiness, but also by environmental events independent of an existing emotional experience. Implementing interventions just to change the frequency of behavioral indices without attending to ongoing situations that are accompanied by respective indices is unlikely to affect a person's private emotional experience.

To illustrate, a common indicator of happiness among most people is smiling; people often smile when they are happy. Smiling is an observable behavior though and can also occur in response to environmental events that actually *reduce* a person's happiness. For example, a person may not be happy when a certain (disliked) individual approaches and initiates a social greeting. However, the former person believes that it is polite to smile when greeted by another individual even though the person is not happy to see the latter individual. In this case, smiling is not a valid indicator of the person's happiness. Interventions developed to increase how often a person smiles when greeted by someone may affect how polite the person appears, but would not likely be affecting the person's private experience of happiness.

The concern over focusing interventions on situations accompanied by happiness indices and not exclusively on the indices themselves will be discussed more in-depth later. The point of concern here is that the intent is to structure the daily routines of adults with autism and other severe disabilities such that indices of happiness are frequently observed and unhappiness indices are infrequently observed. Situations constituting various routines represent the focus of the interventions, and changes in indices serve as an *indirect* means of assessing whether individuals are experiencing happiness or unhappiness within the situations.

CHAPTER SUMMARY: KEY POINTS

1. *A basic protocol for promoting happiness among adults with autism and other severe disabilities in human service agencies involves: (1) identifying indices of happiness and unhappiness, (2) validating the identified indices, (3) taking action to increase situations accompanied by happiness indices, (4) taking action to decrease situations accompanied by unhappiness indices and, (5) monitoring the occurrence of happiness and unhappiness indices.*

2. *Happiness is a private emotional experience for each person and cannot be observed directly; only indices of happiness can be observed.*

3. Indices of happiness and unhappiness must be validated for each consumer who has autism or other severe disability.

4. If happiness is to be consistently promoted, indices of happiness must be regularly monitored.

5. Interventions designed to increase happiness and decrease unhappiness must focus on situations accompanied by indices of happiness and unhappiness, not exclusively on the indices.

CHAPTER 3

IDENTIFYING INDICES OF HAPPINESS AND UNHAPPINESS

As indicated in the preceding chapter, the evidence-based process for promoting happiness among adults with autism and other severe disabilities begins by identifying what individuals do when happy and unhappy. Clear indicators of a person's happiness and unhappiness need to be accurately specified before happiness can be consistently promoted. It was also indicated that human service agencies typically have systems in place to support people with disabilities in attaining certain outcomes such as learning new skills, but rarely have systems specifically for promoting happiness as a desired outcome. Clearly identifying indices of happiness and unhappiness begins the process for agency personnel to specifically address happiness as a valued outcome.

Promoting consumer outcome attainment through agency supports and services is initiated by establishing goals related to achieving desired outcomes. Corresponding behavioral objectives that need to be sequentially met to achieve the goals are likewise established. From the perspective of promoting happiness, relevant goals usually pertain to increasing or maintaining happiness and decreasing unhappiness on a general or overall basis. Behavioral objectives typically relate to bringing about more measurable, desired changes in specified indices of happiness and unhappiness that are observed. This chapter describes how indices of happiness and unhappiness can be accurately specified.

BASIC INDICES OF HAPPINESS AND UNHAPPINESS

In **Chapter 2** it was noted that a number of adults who have autism and other severe disabilities engage in somewhat unusual behavior when they are happy and unhappy relative to how people without disabilities show these emotions. However, many adults with autism and other severe disabilities also display the behaviors that other people typically display when happy and unhappy. Research has indicated, for example, that a number of adults with autism and other severe disabilities often smile or laugh when they are happy just as people without disabilities frequently smile or laugh when happy. Investigations have also shown that many adults with autism and other severe disabilities frown, grimace, or cry when they are unhappy, which are also typical indicators of unhappiness among the general populace.

BASIC INDICES OF HAPPINESS AND UNHAPPINESS

(observed among many adults with autism and other severe disabilities as well as most people in general)

Happiness: smiling, laughing, yelling while smiling

Unhappiness: frowning, grimacing, crying, yelling without smiling

---

Because basic indices of happiness and unhappiness among people in general are displayed by many adults with autism and other severe disabilities, the indicators just illustrated represent an initial basis for identifying what the latter population does when happy and unhappy. These are also the most common indicators that human service staff rely on to judge if a given consumer is happy or not. However, these typical indices should not be relied on exclusively to identify happiness and unhappiness among adults with autism and other severe disabilities; they represent only a starting point.

The basic indices of happiness and unhappiness should not be relied on exclusively for people with autism and other severe disabilities because as previously noted, many of these individuals also display other indicators of their emotional states. Additionally, some adults with autism at the severe end of the spectrum rarely or never display the basic indices—their emotional experiences of happiness and unhappiness are reflected in highly idiosyncratic ways. A number of adults with profound intellectual and physical disabilities likewise do not display the typical indicators of happiness and unhappiness very frequently, or at all. Consequently, certain strategies are necessary to ensure that what adults with autism and other severe disabilities do when they are happy and unhappy—their indices of happiness and unhappiness—are accurately identified.

> **Many adults with autism and other severe disabilities display the same indicators of happiness and unhappiness as other people; however, some do not and some display indicators that are not usually observed among the common populace.**

USING CAREGIVER OPINION TO IDENTIFY INDICES OF HAPPINESS AND UNHAPPINESS

The most common way indices of happiness and unhappiness among adults with autism and other severe disabilities are identified in human service agencies is through assessment of caregiver opinion. Agency staff who work with a given individual are simply asked their opinion regarding what the person does to show happiness and unhappiness. In this respect, a considerable amount of research has evaluated the utility of caregiver opinion for accurately identifying happiness indices among people with autism and other severe disabilities. Such research has indicated that there are both advantages and disadvantages of relying on caregiver opinion as a means of identifying these indices.

ADVANTAGES AND DISADVANTAGES OF RELYING ON CAREGIVER OPINION TO IDENTIFY INDICES OF HAPPINESS AND UNHAPPINESS

The most notable advantage of using caregiver opinion to determine indications that an adult with autism or other severe disability is happy or not is *time efficiency*; it takes minimal time to query caregivers about how a person they support displays happiness and unhappiness. Another advantage is that in certain situations, caregiver opinion has been demonstrated to be a rather accurate means of identifying valid indices of happiness and unhappiness. In particular, caregivers often are accurate in identifying what an adult who has a severe disability does when *very happy* and *very unhappy*.

The most common disadvantage of using caregiver opinion to identify happiness indices is that such opinion is not consistently accurate. Although caregiver opinion is frequently accurate for identifying what a person with a severe disability does when very happy and very unhappy as just indicated, generally caregivers are not as accurate in identifying what the person does when experiencing these emotions at less significant levels. The relative inaccuracy of caregiver opinion in the latter situations is important to consider because being very happy or very unhappy is not as common for most people relative to experiencing happiness and unhappiness at less significant levels.

As most people go about their daily routines they may experience a degree of happiness or unhappiness associated with certain activities that constitute the routines. More significant levels of happiness and unhappiness are usually associated with special types of events that do not occur as frequently or routinely. For example, people may experience a rather mild degree of happiness at various times as they go about their daily jobs. More significant levels of happiness at work tend to occur when something special happens such as attaining a highly desired work goal, receiving a pay raise, or being specially recognized by management or peers for a job well done.

Because of the relative infrequency of situations that result in a person being very happy or unhappy, these types of situations have an important but circumscribed effect on one's daily quality of life. In contrast, frequent situations during the daily routine that are accompanied by some happiness or unhappiness, albeit not on a highly significant level, usually have a much more important effect on daily quality of life. People tend to enjoy their day when they experience some happiness frequently during the day and rarely experience any unhappiness.

Due to the importance on life quality of experiencing some happiness frequently during the day and rarely experiencing any unhappiness, indicators of varying levels of happiness and unhappiness are important to identify. As just noted, caregiver opinion is not consistently accurate in identifying varying levels of happiness beyond the most significant levels of happiness. Consequently, relying on caregiver opinion to identify indices of happiness and unhappiness among adults with autism and other severe disabilities should be done cautiously. Most importantly, when caregiver opinion is used to identify such indices, additional steps should be taken to verify or validate the accuracy of the reported indices as truly representing happiness and unhappiness, respectively. **Chapter 4** describes how identified indices can be validated.

> **Caregiver opinion is usually accurate for identifying what adults with autism and other severe disabilities do when very happy and very unhappy, but less accurate for identifying when they experience these emotions at less significant levels.**

ENHANCING THE ACCURACY OF CAREGIVER OPINION FOR IDENTIFYING INDICES OF HAPPINESS AND UNHAPPINESS

The precise conditions in which caregiver opinion accurately identifies happiness and unhappiness indices among adults with autism and other severe disabilities have not been delineated. However, research has indicated three general situations in which such accuracy is likely to be enhanced. The first condition has already been noted: caregiver opinion is more likely to accurately identify when a person with a severe disability is very happy and very unhappy than when the individual experiences these emotions at less significant levels. Even in this situation though, the opinion of caregivers such as agency staff should be considered cautiously. Caregiver opinion is not *always* accurate for identifying indices of happiness and unhappiness even at the most significant levels.

A second condition in which the accuracy of caregiver reports of indices of happiness is likely to be enhanced is when the caregivers are *very familiar* with a person they support. An exact definition of what constitutes "very familiar" in this regard has not resulted from research to date. However, investigations have shown that when a caregiver has worked at least weekly with an adult with autism or another severe disability for at least six months, the accuracy of that caregiver's opinion of what the individual does when happy and unhappy is likely to be enhanced.

At this point, the weekly contact for at least six months can be a guide for determining if a caregiver has sufficient familiarity with a person s/he supports to initially rely on the caregiver's description of happiness indices. If there are no caregivers with that degree of familiarity with a given consumer of agency services, then caregivers should be selected who have the most familiarity with the person relative to all other caregivers.

The issue of caregiver familiarity with an adult who has a severe disability for identifying happiness indices warrants attention beyond the degree of familiarity of staff working in a human service agency. When agencies desire to identify happiness indices, a useful resource is a consumer's family members. Parents and other family members who have lived with a person with a severe disability usually are very familiar with how the individual acts in different situations. Family members also are often astute at determining if their relative with autism or other severe disability is happy when they visit the individual in an agency. Hence, whenever possible agency personnel should solicit the opinions of family members when identifying happiness and unhappiness indices for an agency consumer.

A third condition in which the accuracy of caregiver opinion is likely to be enhanced for identifying indices of happiness and unhappiness is when there is *caregiver agreement.* Some research suggests when two staff in an agency agree on a specific indicator of happiness or unhappiness, the indicator is more likely to accurately reflect a person's happiness or unhappiness than if only one staff person identifies the particular indicator. Consequently, it is recommended when initially identifying happiness indices, the opinions of several support staff be solicited. The independent reports of these staff should then be reviewed to determine what specific indices are agreed on by two different staff.

The accuracy of caregiver opinion for identifying indices of happiness and unhappiness can be enhanced by ensuring the caregivers are very familiar with respective consumers and by obtaining caregiver agreement regarding the indices.

An Evidence-Based Protocol for Assessing Caregiver Opinion of Indices of Happiness and Unhappiness

Assessing caregiver opinion generally is the easiest way to initially identify indices of happiness and unhappiness among adults with autism and other severe disabilities. Assessing caregiver opinion requires little time and can result in accurate indicators of the emotional states of happiness and unhappiness. This is especially the case when assessing caregiver reports of what an individual does when very happy and very unhappy as indicated previously.

Caregiver reports of indices of less significant levels of happiness and unhappiness for a consumer can also be accurate in many cases. Accuracy in this regard is most likely to result if care is taken to attend to the conditions that research has identified as supporting the accuracy of caregiver opinion. Again, those conditions include assessing the opinion of caregivers *very familiar* with a respective adult with a severe disability and obtaining *agreement* between two familiar caregivers.

Generally the most effective way to solicit caregiver opinion to identify happiness and unhappiness indices is to use a systematic and consistent assessment process. The process should result in records of indices reported by caregivers so that alterations can be made with the indices if necessary following a verification or validation of the indices (see **Chapter 4**). Conducting a systematic and consistent process with written records of identified indices is facilitated if an assessment form is developed to be completed by each caregiver who participates in the assessment. The following illustrates a form that has been used to systematically assess caregiver opinion in a number of cases.

FORM FOR ASSESSING CAREGIVER OPINION OF INDICES OF HAPPINESS AND UNHAPPINESS

Consumer name:_____

Date of assessment:_____

Name of caregiver completing the form:_____

Length of time caregiver has worked with the person at least weekly (at least six months where possible):_____

Questions to be completed by caregiver:

1. What does *(consumer name)* do when s/he is happy (list specific behaviors)?_____

   _____

2. What does *(consumer name)* do when s/he is unhappy (list specific behaviors)?_____

   _____

To administer the form for assessing caregiver opinion regarding indices of happiness and unhappiness for an adult with autism or another severe disability, the following steps should be taken. First, the rationale for administering the form should be explained. It can be discussed that the intent is to determine what the consumer does to indicate happiness and unhappiness. It can be further explained that this represents the first of several actions to be taken to promote the person's happiness during daily routines. Finally, it should be noted that the caregiver's opinion is particularly valued as part of the overall endeavor because of the caregiver's familiarity with the individual.

The second step is to review the information on the form and answer any questions the caregiver may pose. In reviewing each part of the form special attention should be directed to questions one and two. It should be emphasized that what is desired is specifically what the consumer *does* when happy and unhappy, respectively. The caregiver should be instructed to note *specific behaviors* the consumer displays when happy and unhappy. Particular emphasis should be directed to requesting specific behaviors because some caregivers will otherwise be overly general or vague in their descriptions such that individual indices will not be clearly identified.

For example, in one situation an agency staff member reported that a man with autism she supported became very active when happy. When questioned further, the staff person then specified that the gentleman would run around the room when he was happy. In another case, a staff member reported a man with severe intellectual disabilities was noncompliant when unhappy. When asked for more specifics, the staff member indicated that he would shake his head "no" or yell "no" in response to an instruction when he was not happy.

The third step in the assessment process is to leave the form with the caregiver with an instruction to fill in each blank on the form and return it to the assessor within a specified time period. Alternatively, the caregiver can complete the form immediately after step two above and then give it to the assessor. If the assessor is concerned that the caregiver may have difficulty with reading or writing sufficiently, then the assessor can read each part of the form and write down what the caregiver says in response to each part.

The fourth step with the assessment process involves soliciting the responses from three or four familiar caregivers. Next, the fifth step involves reviewing the forms containing the information from each caregiver and recording those indices of happiness and unhappiness that were provided by at least two of the caregivers. Each indicator that was listed on at least two forms should then be used as the initial indices of happiness and unhappiness, respectively.

There is another consideration when reviewing information provided by different caregivers. Sometimes caregivers will report similar things that a person they support does when happy or unhappy but not identical things. For example, one staff member may report that a particular adult with autism engages in a high-pitched whine when unhappy whereas another staff person reports the individual yells when unhappy. When this situation results it is helpful to prompt caregivers to provide more specificity, such as asking the latter caregiver the exact sound the person makes when yelling. The intent is to determine if the caregivers are referring to the same behavior but describing it somewhat differently. However, the assessor should be careful not to lead a caregiver into providing certain answers, only to request more specificity.

It should also be noted that sometimes special circumstances arise that present obstacles with caregiver identification of happiness and unhappiness indices. In particular, at times no caregiver agreement is reached regarding any of the initially identified indices. In other cases, caregivers have difficulty identifying *any* specific indices, and especially with indices of unhappiness for some adults with severe disabilities. Other actions are necessary when these types of special circumstances arise. Because the required actions are closely tied to subsequent steps necessary to validate the reported indices, the necessary actions are described in the next chapter that focuses on validating indices of happiness and unhappiness (see in particular the **Special Circumstances** section of **Chapter 4**).

Using Systematic Preference Assessments to Identify Indices of Happiness and Unhappiness

A second way to identify indices of happiness and unhappiness among adults with autism and other severe disabilities is through *systematic preference assessments.* There are a number of evidence-based ways of systematically assessing the preferences among people with disabilities. These are discussed in-depth in **Chapter 8**.

Systematically identifying individually preferred activities and items is almost always a critical step in the promotion of happiness among adults with autism and other severe disabilities. The various ways systematic preference assessments relate to promoting happiness will be discussed in **Chapter 8**. Of concern here is using systematic preference assessments as a means of initially identifying indices of happiness and unhappiness.

Most preference assessment procedures involve providing repeated choices to an individual regarding various items and events. Those items and events that are chosen most often represent the most preferred items and events among all the options assessed. When adults with autism and other severe disabilities subsequently access preferred items and events, such access is often accompanied by indices of happiness. An individual's behavior can be observed and compared between situations involving engagement with something highly preferred versus engagement with something that is nonpreferred. Certain behaviors observed in the former situations but not in the latter often are valid indicators of happiness.

The primary advantage of using systematic preference assessments to identify indices of happiness is that there is a good evidence base to support their accuracy in identifying valid indices. The main disadvantage is that such assessment processes usually require a certain time investment among support staff to conduct. Although there are some preference assessment procedures that have been streamlined to increase their time efficiency, they essentially always require more time than assessing caregiver opinion of happiness indices. Additionally, a relatively considerable degree of skill is required of staff to conduct preference assessment procedures in the appropriate manner. Many human service agencies do not have ready access to staff with the training and skills to conduct systematic preference assessments with people who have autism and other severe disabilities.

Although systematic preference assessments have been effectively used to identify happiness indices among a number of adults with autism and other severe disabilities, the identified indices still warrant subsequent verification. Preference assessment procedures, though very useful, are not a foolproof way of identifying indicators of happiness. Therefore, as with reliance on caregiver opinion to identify indices of happiness, indices identified through preference assessments should always be subsequently validated.

CHAPTER SUMMARY: KEY POINTS

1. *Promoting happiness among adults with autism and other severe disabilities begins with identifying indices of happiness and unhappiness.*

2. *Although many adults with autism and other severe disabilities engage in the same behaviors as other people when they are happy and unhappy, some do not and some engage in very idiosyncratic behaviors when experiencing these emotions.*

3. *Caregiver opinion is often accurate for identifying happiness indices of individuals when: (1) focusing on when the individuals are very happy and very unhappy, (2) the caregivers are very familiar with respective individuals and, (3) there is agreement between two caregivers regarding specific indices.*

4. *Indices of happiness and unhappiness can often be identified by conducting systematic preference assessments with adults who have autism and other severe disabilities.*

5. *Regardless of how indices of happiness and unhappiness are initially identified, the indices subsequently should be validated as truly representing the respective emotions of happiness and unhappiness.*

CHAPTER 4

VALIDATING INDICES OF HAPPINESS AND UNHAPPINESS

Once indicators of happiness and unhappiness have been identified as described in **Chapter 3**, the next step in the evidence-based process for promoting happiness is to *validate* the identified indices. As previously emphasized, indices must be validated because they are only *indirect* representations of the private experiences of happiness and unhappiness. Care must be taken to ensure the indices accurately represent an individual's ongoing emotional experience before implementing strategies to increase happiness or decrease unhappiness.

A basic protocol for validating indicators of happiness and unhappiness among adults with autism and other severe disabilities in human service agencies is presented on the following page. This protocol builds on the approach summarized earlier for initially identifying happiness and unhappiness indices by assessing the opinion of caregivers. However, the protocol is applicable whether the indices have been identified previously through caregiver opinion or systematic preference assessments as also discussed in the preceding chapter.

The protocol for validating indices of happiness and unhappiness involves a basic, step-by-step process. Each step in the process is described in the following chapter sections. In most cases, following steps of the protocol will result in verification that specific indicators accurately represent an individual's experiences of happiness or unhappiness, respectively.

There are also some special circumstances that arise from time to time in human service agencies that affect how certain steps of the validation process should be completed. Each of these circumstances requires specific alterations with parts of the validation process. The special circumstances and corresponding alterations are detailed in the **Appendix**.

BASIC PROTOCOL FOR VALIDATING INDICES OF HAPPINESS AND UNHAPPINESS AMONG ADULTS WITH AUTISM AND OTHER SEVERE DISABILITIES

Step 1. Identify situations in which a person usually experiences happiness and unhappiness.

Step 2. Observe previously identified indices while the person participates in situations specified in Step 1.

Step 3. Compare the occurrence of happiness and unhappiness indices across situations to determine those specific situations in which the person displays the most happiness and unhappiness indices.

Step 4. Provide the person with repeated choices of the two types of situations resulting from Step 3.

In **Chapter 1** it was noted that because evidence-based processes for identifying and validating indices of happiness and unhappiness can be somewhat technical or detailed, reviewing the procedures can be cumbersome. This is especially the case with the information in the current chapter. Nonetheless, if happiness of adults with autism and other severe disabilities is to be effectively promoted in human service agencies, it is important to understand and apply evidence-based means of identifying when they are truly happy and unhappy. Upon completion of this chapter readers should find information in subsequent chapters regarding increasing happiness and decreasing unhappiness much less cumbersome to review.

Basic Steps for Validating Indices of Happiness and Unhappiness

Step 1: Identify Situations in Which a Person Usually Experiences Happiness and Unhappiness

The first step in the process of validating reported indices of happiness and unhappiness is to identify situations in which an adult with a severe disability usually experiences these emotions. This step can be most readily accomplished by relying on caregiver opinion in a manner similar to that discussed in **Chapter 3** for initially identifying indices. In this case however, caregivers are questioned regarding respective *situations* in which a person they support is typically happy and unhappy.

Identifying situations in which an adult with autism or other severe disability usually experiences happiness and unhappiness is best accomplished by using a prepared assessment form. The same type of form described in the previous chapter can be used with one specific change: the two main questions posed to the caregiver completing the form are altered. Instead of asking *what* the person does when happy and unhappy, respectively, the questions ask *in what situations* the individual is usually happy and unhappy.

Alternatively, one form can be used to identify both indices of happiness/unhappiness and situations in which a person experiences these emotions. Using one form can expedite these initial steps of the evidence-based process for promoting happiness. A general assessment form that has been used in this manner is presented on page 43.

Similar to caregiver reports regarding indices of happiness and unhappiness, the accuracy of reported situations in which an adult with a severe disability experiences happiness and unhappiness is usually enhanced if two conditions are met. First, questions about the situations should only be addressed to caregivers who are very familiar with a given individual (i.e., a caregiver has worked with the person at least weekly for a minimum of six months if possible). Second, the reported situations are most likely to be accurate if there is agreement between two caregivers regarding the identified situations.

It is also helpful from a practical perspective if caregivers are instructed to think about situations in which a person they support is usually happy and unhappy that occur relatively frequently, such as daily or weekly. The practical issue becomes relevant when considering subsequent steps in the validation protocol. Specifically, the person will need to be observed participating in the identified situations. If the situations reported by caregivers involve events that happen infrequently, then observing the individual's participation in those situations will encompass a lengthy time period.

When questioning caregivers about when a person they support is happy it may be necessary to provide the caregivers with some general situations to consider. For example, leisure activities are helpful situations to think about regarding when individuals are likely to be happy. Other situations to consider include when a person engages in activities with favorite staff and when consuming a desired snack. The intent is to offer assistance if caregivers have difficulty identifying situations in which a person they support is usually happy. However, care should be taken to avoid leading caregivers to certain answers about when a consumer experiences happiness; only general types of situations should be provided as examples.

GENERAL HAPPINESS ASSESSMENT FORM
(CAREGIVER OPINION)

Consumer name:_____

Date of assessment:_____

Name of caregiver completing the form:_____

Length of time caregiver has worked with the person at least weekly (at least six months where possible):_____

Questions to be completed by caregiver:

1. What does (*consumer name*) do when s/he is happy (list specific behaviors)?_____

    _____

2. What does (*consumer name*) do when s/he is unhappy (list specific behaviors)?_____

    _____

3. In what situations is (*consumer name*) usually happy?

    _____

    _____

4. In what situations is (*consumer name*) usually unhappy?

    _____

    _____

Care is also warranted when questioning caregivers about situations in which a person is likely to experience unhappiness. The focus of the questioning should be on ongoing situations that an individual does not like. Caregivers should not be asked to identify *possible* situations in which they think a person would be unhappy.

Usually there are some activities ongoing within human service agencies that consumers tend not to prefer and result in them being unhappy. For example, a number of people with severe disabilities often are unhappy when required by staff to respond to certain instructional programs, and particularly those that are difficult for a given person. Other individuals frequently are unhappy when instructed to discontinue a highly preferred activity such as playing a favorite computer game. These types of existing situations should be considered by staff as activities when people they support are likely to be unhappy in contrast to creating new situations deemed likely to be unwanted by consumers.

Questioning familiar caregivers about situations in which a person with a severe disability is usually happy and unhappy typically results in identification of several situations to allow the validation process to proceed. However, in some cases caregiver opinion will not be successful and particularly in regard to different caregivers identifying the same situations—that is, agreement will not be reached. Although this outcome is relatively rare, alternative actions need to be taken to continue the process of validating indices of happiness and unhappiness. These actions are discussed in the **Appendix**.

When identifying situations in which a person with a severe disability is unhappy, *new* **activities should not be created in an attempt to assess unhappiness; the focus should be on** *ongoing* **activities within the regular routine that an individual does not seem to like.**

STEP 2: OBSERVE REPORTED SITUATIONS IN WHICH A PERSON IS USUALLY HAPPY AND UNHAPPY

Once situations are identified in which a person is usually happy and unhappy, the next step in the validation process is to observe the individual in each situation. The focus of the observations is the identified happiness and unhappiness indices. The intent is to gather objective information to eventually determine if: (1) more happiness indices occur in the identified happiness situations than the unhappiness situations and, (2) more unhappiness indices occur in the reported unhappiness situations than the happiness situations.

If results of the observations reveal more happiness indices in the happiness situations and more unhappiness indices in the unhappiness situations, then *initial validation* is obtained regarding the identified indices. This initial validation process stems from basic logic: it is logical a person would display more happiness indices in situations that familiar caregivers report the person is usually happy relative to situations in which the individual is reported to be unhappy. Such logic requires of course that indices and situations are accurately identified. Otherwise, validation support will not be obtained.

It is likewise logical that the person would demonstrate more unhappiness indices in situations in which familiar caregivers report the person is unhappy, again assuming that caregiver reports of respective indices and situations are accurate. If this outcome does not result from the observations, such as an individual not showing any indices of happiness or unhappiness during the situations, then other actions are needed to continue the validation process (see subsequent section on **Comparing Indices of Happiness and Unhappiness**).

The specific situations observed will of course have to be tailored for each person with autism or other severe disability based on the situations agreed upon by caregivers. Correspondingly, the types of situations in which each person will need to be observed will vary considerably. Examples of situations in which different adults with severe disabilities have been observed as part of the validation process for reported happiness and unhappiness indices are provided in the illustration on the following page.

Typically each reported situation requires only a brief period of observation, such as five or ten minutes. However, to obtain a sufficient sample of happiness and unhappiness indices, each situation will need to be observed on at least three different occasions (typically a maximum of five separate observations). For each situation, observations must be conducted in a systematic and consistent manner to accurately assess how frequently the indices are exhibited.

There are two general ways for observing happiness and unhappiness indices during specific situations. One way is to simply count and record how often each indicator is observed during a set time period. Again, the period of time usually only needs to encompass five to ten minutes. Whatever time period is determined, it must remain consistent throughout all observations to allow an accurate comparison of how often specific indices occur across the separate observations.

Counting the occurrence of respective indicators is the recommended observation process if each indicator occurs for a brief period of time—generally no longer than a few seconds—and it is easy to determine when each behavioral indicator begins and ends. For example, it would be easy to count how often an individual gently pats a staff person on the back (an indicator of happiness reported for one particular adult with autism). Patting someone on the back usually encompasses only a few seconds of time. It is also easy to observe when the patting begins and ends.

A second way to systematically observe indices of happiness and unhappiness is to watch and record whether or not each indicator occurs during a brief time interval. For example, if reported happiness and unhappiness situations are observed for a five-minute period, the five minutes can be divided into consecutive 15-second intervals. At the end of each 15-second interval, recordings are then made regarding whether each indicator was observed to occur for any length of time during the respective interval.

EXAMPLES OF TYPES OF HAPPINESS (H) AND UNHAPPINESS (U) SITUATIONS IDENTIFIED BY CAREGIVERS FOR ADULTS WITH AUTISM AND OTHER SEVERE DISABILITIES

PERSON	H SITUATION	U SITUATION
adult with severe autism at work	*drawing on a sketch pad during work break*	*waiting (with no other activity) for a job task to be assigned*
adult with profound multiple disabilities at home	*being rocked back and forth in a hammock*	*staff performing range of motion exercises*
adult with severe intellectual disabilities in a day program	*drinking a soda during break time*	*being prompted by staff to finish the soda and clean up*

An interval recording process is the most common way to observe indices of happiness and unhappiness. The process is usually easier than counting each indicator because many indices do not have an easily determined beginning and end. To illustrate, a happiness indicator for one adult with severe intellectual disabilities was running around a room. However, when he ran there were brief interruptions with his running such as when he changed the direction he was running. It was difficult to count how often he ran because it was not clear what constituted the end of one running episode and the beginning of another versus a continuous running episode. In contrast, it was very easy to record if any running occurred during a 15-second interval.

As indicated earlier, observations of happiness and unhappiness indices must be conducted in a systematic and consistent manner to accurately assess how often the indices occur. This is particularly the case when using an interval observation process as just described. To facilitate conducting observations systematically and consistently, a formally prepared observation form is recommended. A sample form for observing happiness and unhappiness indices using an interval process is illustrated on the following page.

The sample observation form was prepared to observe Mr. Johns' indices of happiness and unhappiness during the situation in which he was swinging on a porch swing at his group home. Swinging represented a situation reported by two staff in which Mr. Johns was often happy. As indicated by information written on the sample form, the observation was designed to be conducted for 5 minutes at 6:00 in the evening during Mr. Johns' leisure time, which was when he usually chose to swing on the porch. Staff person Randy (indicated as "Observer" on the form) was identified as being responsible for conducting the observation.

Using the sample observation form, the observer watched Mr. Johns' behavior for five consecutive minutes while he was swinging, with each minute divided into 15-second intervals. At the end of the first 15 seconds, the observer marked with a slash (/) through any indicator of happiness on the form (smile and/or pat his leg) that was observed during the 15 seconds as well as any unhappiness indicators (frown and/or bite his hand). The marking was recorded on the form in the interval under "1st 15 sec." on the line identified as "Min. 1". The observer then continued observing and recording at the end of each of the three remaining 15-second intervals for the first minute. The entire process was then repeated for four more minutes.

Upon completion of the five minutes of observation, the observer determined the percentage of intervals in which any happiness indices were recorded. Likewise, the percentage of intervals in which any unhappiness indices were recorded was determined. The resulting percentages indicated the general frequency with which Mr. Johns displayed indices of happiness and unhappiness while swinging on the porch swing. The entire process of observing and determining the frequency of happiness and unhappiness indices was then repeated for four more observation periods across four days.

**OBSERVATION FORM FOR
HAPPINESS AND UNHAPPINESS INDICES**

Consumer: *Mr. Johns*　　　　　　　　　　Date: *Oct. 4*
Situation: *Swinging on porch*
Time of Observation: *6:00 – 6:05*　　　　Observer: *Randy*

Happiness indicators (H): smile, patting leg
Unhappiness indicators (U): frown, bite hand

	1st 15 sec.		2nd 15 sec.		3rd 15 sec.		4th 15 sec.	
	H	U	H	U	H	U	H	U
Min 1	smile pat	frown bite	smile pat	frown bite	smile pat	frown bite	smile pat	frown bite
Min 2	smile pat	frown bite	smile pat	frown bite	smile pat	frown bite	smile pat	frown bite
Min 3	smile pat	frown bite	smile pat	frown bite	smile pat	frown bite	smile pat	frown bite
Min 4	smile pat	frown bite	smile pat	frown bite	smile pat	frown bite	smile pat	frown bite
Min 5	smile pat	frown bite	smile pat	frown bite	smile pat	frown bite	smile pat	frown bite

Percentage of intervals with any happiness indices: _____
Percentage of intervals with any unhappiness indices: _____

Step 3: Compare Results of Observations Across Happiness and Unhappiness Situations

Once a person has been observed in reported happiness and unhappiness situations on at least three occasions, the next step in the validation process is to compare the summaries of each observation. The comparison involves the following process. First, for both the happiness and unhappiness situations, the percentage of observation intervals with *happiness* indices is averaged across the situations.

If, for example, an individual was observed three times in the happiness situation of playing a computer game, the percentage of intervals with happiness indices would be averaged across all three observations. The resulting figure would provide an overall score for happiness indices during the happiness situation. Similarly, if the individual was observed three times in the unhappiness situation of being instructed to print his name, the percentage of intervals with happiness indices would be averaged across all observations of that situation. The latter figure would provide an overall score for happiness indices during the unhappiness situation.

The second step of the comparison process involves averaging the percentage of *unhappiness* indices across all respective situations in the same manner as with the happiness indices. Using the illustration just described, unhappiness indices would be averaged across all observations of the individual playing the computer game to determine an overall score of unhappiness indices during the happiness situation. An average also would be calculated across all observations of the printing-instruction activity to determine an overall score of unhappiness indices during the unhappiness situation. Upon completion of this step there would be an overall score for both happiness and unhappiness indices during both the happiness and unhappiness situations.

To further illustrate these two steps of the comparison process, consider the earlier example with Mr. Johns. He was observed during his happiness situation of swinging on the porch on five occasions.

Across the five observations, his happiness indices (in this case, smiling) averaged 35% of observation intervals and his unhappiness indices averaged 0%. Mr. Johns was also observed on five occasions during an unhappiness situation that involved being instructed to perform an unfamiliar task during his supported job. Across five observations of the unhappiness situation, his happiness indices (again, smiling) averaged 4% and his unhappiness indices (frowning in this case) averaged 39%.

Once overall scores for happiness and unhappiness indices are obtained for both the happiness and unhappiness situations, the next step is to determine if the resulting data offer support for the validity of the identified indices. The strongest support in this regard would occur if: (1) in the happiness situation there were more happiness indices than unhappiness indices and more happiness indices than in the unhappiness situation and, (2) in the unhappiness situation there were more unhappiness indices than happiness indices and more unhappiness indices than in the happiness situation. This type of support occurred with the observations of Mr. Johns just summarized.

RESULTS OF OBSERVATIONS OF REPORTED HAPPINESS AND UNHAPPINESS SITUATIONS THAT OFFER SUPPORT FOR THE VALIDITY OF OBSERVED INDICES OF HAPPINESS AND UNHAPPINESS*

During Happiness Situation	During Unhappiness Situation
More happiness indices	Less (or no) happiness indices
Less (or no) unhappiness indices	More unhappiness indices

* more versus less refers to the relative differences between the two types of situations

If steps described to this point are followed for identifying indices and then identifying and observing situations in which an individual is usually happy and unhappy, then results of observations frequently support the validity of the indices as just described. That is, the individual will show more happiness indices in the happiness situation than the unhappiness situation, and more unhappiness indices in the unhappiness situation than the happiness situation. There will also be more happiness indices than unhappiness indices in the happiness situation, and more unhappiness indices than happiness indices in the unhappiness situation.

However, sometimes special circumstances affect results of the observations. For example, a person may be happy but show no apparent indicators of being happy, such as when listening to a favorite song. Again, the most common types of special circumstances that occur with adults with autism and other severe disabilities are summarized in the **Appendix**. How the validation process should continue in the various circumstances is also described in the **Appendix**.

Assuming that support for the validity of happiness and unhappiness indices is obtained through the observation and comparison process, then the final step for validating the indices can be undertaken. This step involves providing choices to a person of different situations.

STEP 4: PROVIDE CHOICES OF HAPPINESS AND UNHAPPINESS SITUATIONS

The choice step of the validation process involves providing a person with a choice of situations that have been observed to be accompanied by different frequencies of happiness and unhappiness indices. The most common choice involves providing an individual with a choice of two situations: (1) the situation in which the previous observations revealed the highest level of happiness indices and lowest level of unhappiness indices and, (2) the situation in which previous observations revealed the highest level of unhappiness indices and the lowest level of happiness indices.

A choice of the two types of situations should be provided repeatedly until the person demonstrates a clear pattern of choosing one situation more often than the other situation. More often in this regard typically means the individual chooses to access one situation on at least 75% of the choice opportunities. Usually at least four choice opportunities should be offered at different times to provide an adequate sample of the person's preference for one situation versus the other.

If a person chooses the situation accompanied by the most happiness indices and least unhappiness indices on at least 75% of the choice opportunities, then support for the validity of the indices is obtained. Validity is obtained because the person is demonstrating a strong preference for a situation in which s/he has displayed the most happiness indices and least unhappiness indices. By definition, engaging in a preferred situation means a person likes that situation. In turn, liking something is closely associated with happiness. Because the preferred, chosen situation previously has been shown to be accompanied by happiness indices it can be reasonably concluded that those specific indices are a representation of a person's happiness.

Similar reasoning, which also supports the validity of the identified indices, pertains to the person's lack of choice for the situation previously to be accompanied by the highest level of unhappiness indices (and lowest level of happiness indices). When a person does not choose something, it means the individual does not like that option. Not liking something is closely associated with unhappiness. Because the situation that was not chosen, and hence at least relatively disliked, was previously shown to be accompanied by unhappiness indices then the indices likely represent when the individual is experiencing unhappiness.

When special circumstances arise that affect the outcome of the observation steps of the validation process, then the types of situational choices provided may need to be modified (see **Appendix**). Additionally, **Chapter 7** summarizes ways choices can be presented based on the skills and challenges of respective adults with autism and other severe disabilities to ensure the choices are understood and result in meaningful choice responses. The information provided in **Chapter 7** can be helpful for determining how best to provide a choice of different situations as part of the validation of reported happiness and unhappiness indices.

A Final Note: Revalidation of Indices of Happiness and Unhappiness

If the procedures described in this and the preceding chapter are carried out, valid indicators of the happiness and unhappiness of adults with autism and other severe disabilities will usually be identified. Accurate identification of a person's happiness and unhappiness sets the foundation for then promoting the person's happiness in an evidence-based manner. However, one question that arises once valid indices of happiness and unhappiness are identified is how often do the indices remain valid? That is, do adults with autism and other severe disabilities continue to display the same indicators of happiness and unhappiness over time?

Research to date suggests that once validated, specific indices of an individual's happiness and unhappiness tend to remain rather consistent. However, this issue has not been sufficiently investigated to allow definitive conclusions. Hence, it is recommended that a person's indices of happiness and unhappiness be reassessed and revalidated from time to time.

Generally it is recommended that indices of happiness and unhappiness be assessed and validated at least annually. Most human service agencies have annual assessment procedures in place as part of the development of treatment or service plans for the people they support. Assessing and validating happiness and unhappiness indices can be incorporated within yearly assessment and planning processes.

A more conservative approach would be to revisit existing indices of happiness and unhappiness at least every six months. The primary point is that valid indices of happiness and unhappiness must be reassessed periodically.

CHAPTER SUMMARY: KEY POINTS

1. *Because indices of happiness and unhappiness are indirect representations of the private experiences of happiness and unhappiness, the indices must be validated to ensure they accurately reflect those experiences.*

2. *A basic protocol for validating happiness and unhappiness indices involves: (1) identifying several situations in which a person with a severe disability usually seems happy and unhappy, (2) observe the indices as the person participates in the situations specified in Step #1, (3) compare the occurrence of the indices across situations to determine in which situations the person displays the most happiness and unhappiness indices and, (4) provide the person with repeated choices of the two types of situations resulting from Step #3.*

3. *Identifying situations in which a person is usually unhappy should focus on existing activities in the individual's regular routine, not on creating new situations that may be unwanted by the person.*

4. *Observations of a person's happiness and unhappiness indices in different situations must be conducted in a consistent and systematic manner.*

5. *Happiness and unhappiness indices are considered valid representation of the happiness and unhappiness of an adult with a severe disability, respectively, if the person consistently chooses to participate in a situation previously observed to have more happiness indices and less unhappiness indices*

versus a situation with less happiness indices and more unhappiness indices.

6. *Special circumstances arise periodically that require alterations in the validation process, with specific action steps for continuing the validation process in each respective situation.*

7. *Indices of happiness and unhappiness for an adult with a severe disability should be reassessed and revalidated at least annually.*

SECTION II

STRATEGIES FOR INCREASING HAPPINESS

CHAPTER 5

ESTABLISHING GOOD RELATIONSHIPS

A primary source of happiness for most people is social relationships. Having good relationships with other people is a well-established indicator of life quality. When an individual has a good relationship with someone the individual usually enjoys interacting with the person. The individual also typically enjoys simply having the person present in the immediate environment.

Many adults with autism and other severe disabilities experience challenges in developing and maintaining social relationships. Personal relationships nevertheless represent a critical source of potential happiness within their day-to-day lives, just like with everybody else. Hence, one important means of enhancing happiness among consumers with autism and other severe disabilities is to help them establish personal relationships.

> **An important source of happiness among adults with autism and other severe disabilities in human service agencies is the existence of a good relationship with their support staff.**

An individual's relationships often involve a variety of people. Relationships for most people exist, for example, among family members, social acquaintances or friends, and co-workers. For adults with autism and other severe disabilities, there is another potential type of relationship that can be of significant importance—the relationship between a consumer and staff in human service agencies.

Most adults with autism and other severe disabilities spend very considerable amounts of time with support personnel in human service agencies. This is particularly the case in residential agencies in which many adults with severe disabilities reside. In these settings, such as center-based living and group homes, support staff are almost continuously present with consumers. Similarly, in day support sites such as adult education programs, agency staff and the people they support spend time with each other essentially every weekday. The type of relationship that consumers have with agency staff with whom they spend their time can significantly affect their day-to-day happiness.

The importance of a good relationship between an agency staff member and an individual with a severe disability is well illustrated by a situation many human service staff have experienced with challenging behavior among certain individuals. For many adults with severe disabilities who engage in problem behavior, such behavior does not occur when a particular staff member is on duty and interacts with a respective individual. Problem behavior does not occur in this situation because the individual has a good relationship with the staff member, and vice versa. In contrast, when that particular staff member is not present, the individual's problem behavior is much more likely to occur.

In **Chapter 1** it was noted that when an adult with autism or other severe disability is experiencing happiness, the individual is not very likely to engage in problem behavior. In contrast, when the individual is discontented or unhappy, problem behavior is likely to occur in an attempt to alter or escape from the source of the discontent. Being around a staff member with whom an individual has a good relationship enhances the individual's happiness. Such happiness reduces the individual's reason or need for challenging behavior.

> **When a staff person has a good relationship with an adult with autism or other severe disability who engages in challenging behavior, often the individual will not display the behavior when that staff person is immediately present.**

As indicated previously, an individual's relationships typically involve other people in a variety of ways, including within a familial context, social encounters, and work situations. The focus here, however, is on the relationships that exist within human service agencies between agency staff and the people they support. The emphasis is on this specific type of relationship because of the amount of time these people spend together. The time spent together is much more enjoyable for adults with autism and other severe disabilities if they have good relationships with their support staff.

The emphasis on the relationships between consumers of agency services and staff who work in the agencies is not meant to diminish the importance of other types of relationships. Adults with autism and other severe disabilities benefit from relationships with family members, friends, and co-workers just like everybody else. The focus here exists primarily because of the overall intent of this book: to describe how to promote happiness among adults with autism and other severe disabilities in human service agencies.

Another reason for focusing on the relationships between support staff and consumers with whom they work is because of the way human service agencies often operate. There are several ways such agencies typically function that impede good relationships between people with severe disabilities and agency staff, and correspondingly reduce consumer happiness during daily activities. The most common features of human service agencies that interfere with relationship development are highlighted in the next section.

CHALLENGES WITHIN HUMAN SERVICE AGENCIES THAT IMPEDE GOOD RELATIONSHIPS

A prerequisite for developing a relationship with someone is *familiarity*; people have to become familiar with each other before a relationship can develop. In many cases agency staff and consumers with autism and other severe disabilities are very familiar with each other because they interact on a daily or weekly basis. However, there are also common situations in human service agencies in which such familiarity is not consistently present. The lack of consistent familiarity in this respect impedes relationship development and corresponding happiness among consumers.

One situation that results in consumers and support staff lacking familiarity with each other occurs in essentially every human service agency to some degree: staff absenteeism. When support staff do not report for a scheduled work day, agency management must make arrangements to fulfill the duties expected to be performed by the absent staff. Those arrangements frequently result in a staff member being assigned to work with one or more individuals whom the staff member does not know very well—the staff member and the people with disabilities lack familiarity with each other.

To illustrate, in residential settings such as group homes, if a staff member does not report to work then another staff member often is reassigned or "pulled" from another home to work in the home of the absent staff member. The staff member who is reassigned frequently is not familiar with the people residing in the latter home and vice versa. A similar situation occurs when "substitute" staff are called in to work for an absent staff member in day program settings.

A related situation that frequently results in lack of familiarity between staff and consumers of agency services is staff turnover. When a staff member leaves a job there is often a period of time before a new staff person can be hired. During that time period the same situation basically occurs as when a staff member fails to report to work. Agency management must reassign staff to fulfill the duties of the staff member who has left the agency or hire temporary staff. In both situations there is likely to be a lack of familiarity between consumers and certain staff.

> **A prerequisite for good relationships between staff in human service agencies and adults with autism and other severe disabilities is *familiarity*; consumers and staff who work with them should be very familiar with each other.**

The lack of familiarity between support staff and consumers in human service agencies impacts the development of positive relationships and consumer happiness in several ways. Most apparently, desirable relationships that promote happiness cannot develop if people do not have opportunities to get to know each other well. If agency operations frequently involve unfamiliar staff working with people the agency supports, then opportunities for good relationships to develop are significantly reduced.

Lack of familiarity also impedes happiness because it can cause significant *unhappiness* among consumers. Unhappiness occurs due to the nature of the work performed by direct support staff with individuals who have disabilities. Such work often involves staff being in close physical proximity with individuals for supervision purposes and assistance with activities of daily living. Direct support work also frequently involves physical contact between staff and consumers such as, for example, when a staff member assists a person in getting dressed, carries out a teaching plan that includes physical prompting, or implements a behavior support plan that involves physically redirecting a person's ongoing activity.

Most people do not mind when certain individuals get in close proximity or have physical contact with them. However, most people also do not like it when other individuals get in their physical space or initiate physical contact. This is especially the case when a stranger or otherwise unfamiliar person gets in close proximity or touches them. The same situation arises for an adult with a severe disability when an unfamiliar staff member begins to provide direct support that involves close physical proximity or contact.

In the situation just noted, the physical proximity and contact by the unfamiliar staff member can cause anxiety or other discontent for an individual. The individual is unhappy with the activity and often will act to avoid or escape the situation. Frequently such actions involve various types of challenging behavior such as aggression, property disruption, or even self-injury in an attempt to discontinue the activity.

Because of the detrimental effects of unfamiliar staff working with adults with autism and other severe disabilities, this type of situation should be avoided in human service agencies. Unfortunately, events that often result in lack of familiarity between staff and the people they support exist in every human service agency to at least some degree as noted previously. It is beyond the scope of this text to address how agencies can alter major aspects of their operations to prevent such events as frequent absenteeism and turnover that result in unfamiliar staff working with consumers. However, there are steps that agency supervisors can take to maintain as much familiarity as possible between support staff and the people they support when routine operations are disrupted.

> **A common source of unhappiness among adults who have autism or other severe disabilities is unfamiliar staff working with them in a manner that involves close physical proximity or contact; it is a supervisory responsibility to arrange staff work assignments to prevent such situations.**

Supervisory personnel must be aware that when unfamiliar staff work with agency consumers in ways that involve close physical proximity or contact, problems are likely to develop. Supervisors have the responsibility to recognize when such a situation is likely (e.g., a staff person calls in sick to work) and to review the assignments of staff who will be present. The review should focus on how specific work responsibilities can be reassigned among staff to ensure only familiar staff work closely with respective individuals with disabilities.

In short, supervisors should alter job assignments when necessary to prevent situations in which unfamiliar staff work closely with consumers. When this type of situation appears essentially unavoidable (e.g., several staff are absent from work), then supervisors should alter the duty schedule to allow an unfamiliar staff member some initial time to interact with an individual in an enjoyable manner. This basic action allows the staff member and the person with a severe disability to get to know each other at least somewhat before the staff person is expected to fulfill duties involving close physical proximity or contact. The intent is to promote at least initial familiarity between a staff person and an individual within a pleasant context, and perhaps the beginning of a good relationship.

STEPS FOR DEVELOPING GOOD RELATIONSHIPS

Earlier it was noted that adults with autism and other severe disabilities frequently experience challenges in developing relationships with other people. This is especially the case with adults who have autism on the severe end of the spectrum of autism disorders. The disability of autism is heavily characterized by difficulties in interacting with people. Relatedly, adults with autism as well as those with severe intellectual disabilities usually have challenges communicating or conversing with people, which can significantly impede relationship development.

In light of the importance of relationships and the challenges that many adults with autism and other severe disabilities experience in this area, relationships between human service staff and consumers of agency services should not be taken for granted. Rather, specific steps should be carried out to promote good relationships. Although much is yet to be learned about relationship development, research has indicated three important actions staff can take to develop a good relationship with an adult who has a severe disability. These actions involve three steps: (1) spending time with an individual doing things that the person enjoys, (2) helping the person avoid situations that are disliked and, (3) learning how to effectively communicate with the individual.

The steps for establishing a good relationship should be taken whenever possible before an unfamiliar staff member begins working with a consumer in a manner involving close physical proximity or contact. The steps are most relevant in this respect when a new staff member is hired within an agency or a staff member from another location in the agency is reassigned to work with a given individual. The steps are also relevant when people initially volunteer within an agency if the volunteer activities involve interacting with one or more consumers.

The steps for establishing a good relationship are also most relevant when an adult with autism or another severe disability initially begins receiving supports within an agency. When an individual moves into a group home or enrolls in a new day program, for example, steps should be initiated immediately to promote relationships between the person and agency staff. To successfully carry out the steps for establishing a good relationship in these cases, information about the person must be obtained by agency staff from people who already know the individual well (e.g., family members, staff from other agencies who have worked with the person). The most relevant information to be obtained is summarized in the following description of the three basic steps for developing good relationships.

Step 1: Spend Time With the Person Doing Things the Person Enjoys

The first step for a staff member to develop a good relationship with a consumer is for the staff member to spend time with the person doing things the individual enjoys. When an unfamiliar staff member repeatedly engages an individual who has a severe disability in enjoyable activities, the person begins to associate the staff member with enjoyment. In essence, the staff member's immediate presence indicates that good things are about to happen for the individual.

The time the staff member spends with the individual doing enjoyable activities also allows them to become familiar with each other. As indicated earlier, gaining familiarity is necessary for establishing a good relationship. In the process described here, such familiarity is also associated with enjoyment for the individual because s/he and the staff member are doing things together that the individual enjoys.

Whenever possible, the initial time the staff member spends with the person with a disability doing things the person enjoys should represent the only time the staff person interacts with the individual (see Step 2 of the relationship-development process for an exception). Typically such times should be specifically scheduled each day. How this process can occur is exemplified in the case illustration on the following page.

The time the staff member spends doing things with a consumer should continue until the individual is consistently enjoying the time with the staff member. Such enjoyment will be apparent when the individual shows indices of happiness while with the staff member. Once such indices are observed, then a good relationship can be considered to be developing. At that point, the staff member can begin fulfilling other duties with the person beyond the designated "fun" time activities.

CASE ILLUSTRATION
First Step for Developing A Good Relationship

Background: Mr. Givens, an adult who has autism and is non-vocal, was beginning a new placement in an adult education program. Ms. Johnson, a staff person who was unfamiliar with Mr. Givens, was assigned to work with him. Ms. Johnson's duties included carrying out individualized teaching programs with Mr. Givens and assisting him in completing assigned tasks as well as transitioning between daily activities. Results of previous preference assessments and reports of staff familiar with Mr. Givens had indicated he particularly liked to draw on a sketch pad, consume sodas and crackers, and swing on a porch swing.

Activities to begin establishing a good relationship: Ms. Johnson was assigned to spend one hour in the morning and one hour in the afternoon to work individually with Mr. Givens. During the one-hour periods, Ms. Johnson spent alternate amounts of "fun" time providing the sketch pad for Mr. Givens to use, having a soda and eating crackers with him, and swinging on the porch swing with him. During each activity Ms. Johnson interacted socially with Mr. Givens and provided frequent praise (e.g., complimenting his drawing on the sketch pad, thanking him for sharing the snack time). Ms. Johnson had no other formally scheduled time periods to work with Mr. Givens beyond the designated "fun" activities.

The amount of time an unfamiliar staff member spends with an individual helping the person experience enjoyment will vary across staff and adults with severe disabilities. Frequently though, only a week or so of the specially assigned "fun" activities is required before an individual begins to show consistent indices of happiness during the time spent with the staff member. However, a staff member spending time helping an individual have fun is only one part of establishing a good relationship. The other two steps of the relationship-building process should likewise be undertaken.

Before describing the remaining steps of establishing a good relationship, a point of caution is warranted. Specifically, while a staff member is initially interacting with a person who has a severe disability in the manner just described, the staff member has to establish some boundaries. The staff member should not allow the individual to engage in challenging behavior or other inappropriate activities during the designated "fun" time periods. Otherwise, the person may begin to associate time with the staff member as opportunities to do whatever is desired, including engaging in behavior that is inappropriate.

Prior to the unfamiliar staff member spending time with an individual to promote enjoyment, the staff member should be informed by people familiar with the person about inappropriate behavior s/he may display. The unfamiliar staff member should likewise be informed regarding what should be done to prevent or interrupt such behavior. For example, in the case illustration involving Mr. Givens, the staff person (Ms. Johnson) was informed that Mr. Givens periodically engaged in stereotypic behavior in which he stared at his fingers in front of his face. Ms. Johnson was further informed that when this happened, she should instruct him to engage in another activity such as a familiar task that he knew how to perform.

In some cases, such as with serious challenging behavior for which a consumer has a specific behavior support plan, preventing or interrupting inappropriate behavior may be difficult. The difficulty can be due to the individual physically resisting a staff member's implementation of the support plan, or refusing to comply with instructions to discontinue a certain activity. When this type of situation is likely, it can be helpful to have a familiar staff member present in the same location while the other (unfamiliar) staff member is interacting with the individual to promote his/her enjoyment.

In the type of situation just noted, the familiar staff member should have the primary responsibility of carrying out the behavior support plan or otherwise intervening if the person engages in inappropriate behavior. The unfamiliar staff member can subsequently assume responsibility for intervening with undesired behavior after it becomes apparent that a good relationship is developing between the individual and that staff member.

STEP 2: HELP THE PERSON AVOID DISLIKED SITUATIONS

Similar to the purpose of the first step of the relationship-development process, the purpose of the second step is to enhance an individual's enjoyment associated with a respective staff member. However, the purpose is fulfilled with the second step in a more indirect manner relative to the first step. Instead of promoting the person's happiness by helping him/her enjoy doing things with the staff member, Step 2 involves enhancing happiness by decreasing unhappiness experienced by the individual.

There are often certain activities or situations within the daily routines of human service agencies that are at least somewhat disliked by adults with autism or other severe disabilities. If a staff member can effectively help an individual avoid those situations, the person will experience less unhappiness during the day. In turn, reduction of unhappiness results in more happiness on an overall basis.

Additionally, the reduction in unhappiness and increase in overall happiness represents another means through which an individual begins to associate a staff member with enjoyment. An example of how this step can be carried out is presented in the scenario on the following page involving the same adult with a severe disability and staff member represented in the previous case illustration.

To successfully carry out Step 2 of the relationship-building process, the unfamiliar staff member who is attempting to develop a good relationship must be provided with information about what the individual does not like. Such information usually has to be provided by other people who are very familiar with the individual and are aware of the person's common dislikes. They can also provide suggestions for what the staff person can do to prevent the individual from experiencing the disliked situations.

Often a person with a severe disability can be assisted in avoiding a situation that is disliked by presenting an alternative, more preferred situation. This was the action represented in the case illustration in which Ms. Johnson provided Mr. Givens with one of his preferred activities (drawing on a sketch pad) in lieu of him sitting with no activity in which to engage. In other cases, a staff member may need to escort the person away from an immediate situation to avoid it altogether.

CASE ILLUSTRATION
SECOND STEP FOR DEVELOPING A GOOD RELATIONSHIP

Background: The same situation illustrated previously involving a consumer, Mr. Givens, beginning a new placement in an adult education program with an unfamiliar staff person, Ms. Johnson. People familiar with Mr. Givens had informed Ms. Johnson that he disliked situations in which he is instructed to sit in a chair without anything to do while waiting for an activity to be presented. Mr. Givens often became upset when sitting with no apparent activity and began to repeatedly wave his fingers and turn over furniture.

Activities to begin establishing a good relationship: Ms. Johnson was instructed to stand away from Mr. Givens and just observe him when she was not interacting with him during the designated "fun" time activities described previously. When Ms. Johnson saw that Mr. Givens had just finished an assigned task and was likely to have to wait for the next assignment with no intervening activity, she approached him and provided him with something that he liked to do such as drawing on his sketch pad. In this manner, Ms. Johnson helped Mr. Givens avoid his disliked situation of sitting with nothing to do.

For example, again with Mr. Givens, it was known that he disliked being in a room when the usual routine was disrupted and unfamiliar people entered the immediate environment (e.g., a tour group entered the adult education classroom). The staff member could be informed of this particular dislike as well as when a tour group was scheduled to enter Mr. Givens' room. Subsequently, when the tour group began to enter the room, the staff member could ask Mr. Givens to go with her to swing on the porch outside of the classroom (representing an alternative, more preferred situation).

There are of course likely to be situations that a person dislikes that cannot be realistically avoided, such as implementation of a teaching program that is disliked by an individual because of its apparent difficulty. It may be undesirable to allow the person to totally avoid the teaching program because it is necessary to enhance the individual's independent functioning. However, there is usually little detriment in *temporarily* postponing a disliked activity such as a teaching program by having a new staff member do something else with the individual in lieu of the undesired activity.

Once the new staff member begins to establish a good relationship with the person, then the staff member can reinitiate the disliked yet important activity with the individual. At that point, the person's dislike of the activity is likely to be decreased at least somewhat. The activity usually will be less unpleasant for the person because s/he will be participating in the activity with a staff member with whom the person enjoys interacting.

STEP 3: LEARN TO EFFECTIVELY COMMUNICATE WITH THE PERSON

Having a relationship requires people to interact with each other: people must be able to communicate well with each other. Most people who work in the human services fully understand the importance of being able to communicate well with individual consumers with whom they work. However, effectively communicating with adults with autism and other severe disabilities can be difficult for support personnel, and especially for staff who have minimal familiarity with a given consumer.

Human service staff often have difficulty communicating with adults with autism and other severe disabilities because of their communication challenges. This is especially the case for adults who have autism on the severe end of the spectrum and adults who have more severe intellectual disabilities. These individuals rarely communicate fully in conventional ways—ways in which support staff are accustomed to communicating with other people. Essentially every adult with autism or other severe disability relies to some degree on idiosyncratic ways of communicating including, for example, unique gestures, nonword vocalizations, and various body movements.

Staff in human service agencies must become very familiar with the individualized ways that consumers communicate. Otherwise they will not be able to effectively communicate with respective consumers which in turn prohibits good relationships from developing. Learning to communicate with individuals who have severe disabilities represents the third step necessary for developing good relationships between staff and the people they support.

Although learning to communicate effectively constitutes the third step in the three-step process for developing good relationships, it should not be considered as the last step per se. Human service staff should take specific actions to learn to communicate with an individual *prior to* and *during* implementation of the first two steps for building good relationships. In particular, before spending time with a person doing things the person likes (Step 1) and helping a person avoid disliked situations (Step 2), an unfamiliar staff member should learn as much as possible about how the individual typically communicates.

To learn how a person with a severe disability communicates, an unfamiliar staff member should first talk to people who know the individual well and query them about how the person interacts with others. The staff member also should study any available written descriptions about the individual's communication skills and challenges. Such descriptions may involve formal assessment instruments that have been completed and individualized support plans. Available person-centered plans should especially be studied as these can provide particularly helpful information about a consumer's communication style (see **Chapter 9** for detailed information about person-centered plans).

In addition to talking with people who are familiar with an individual and reviewing relevant documents, often an unfamiliar staff member will need to learn about assistive communication processes. Many adults with autism and other severe disabilities rely at least in part on assistive communication tools for interacting with other people. Assistive communication may involve use of pictures, writing materials, Voice Output Communication Aides, and other various types of computer-based technology. New or unfamiliar staff frequently have minimal experience with how someone uses assistive communication to interact.

Unfamiliar staff may also have to become knowledgeable about manual sign language. A number of adults with autism and other severe disabilities supplement other communication means with manual signing, or rely exclusively on signing for communication. A staff member must learn how to produce relevant signs as well as to interpret signs expressed by a person. Many staff have experienced the situation in which an adult with a severe disability signs to them but they do not know what the signs mean. Such a situation can be very frustrating for the person with a disability and staff, and clearly does not constitute effective communication.

The procedures just noted for acquiring information about how a person communicates can be helpful for a new or unfamiliar staff member. However, talking to people familiar with an individual, reviewing relevant documents, and learning about assistive communication are not sufficient in this regard. The best way for a staff member to learn how to communicate with a person with a severe disability is to spend time with the individual.

Earlier it was emphasized that the primary goal of Step 1 of the relationship-building process is for a consumer to begin associating an unfamiliar staff member with enjoyment. There is also another beneficial outcome of this initial step. The time spent helping an individual experience enjoyment requires a staff member to interact with the person. Such interaction represents an opportune way to learn how the individual communicates.

Another helpful way for an unfamiliar staff member to learn to communicate with an adult with autism or other severe disability is to observe the individual during interactions with other people. Whenever possible, an unfamiliar staff member should be allotted time to watch such interactions prior to initiating interactions with the individual. Hence, before a staff member is expected to spend specific time periods with an individual for the purpose of enhancing the person's enjoyment (again, Step 1), the staff member should spend time observing other people interacting with the individual.

KEY STEPS FOR A STAFF MEMBER TO DEVELOP A GOOD RELATIONSHIP WITH A PERSON WHO HAS AUTISM OR OTHER SEVERE DISABILITY

1. **Spend time with the person doing things the person enjoys.**
2. **Help the person avoid disliked situations.**
3. **Learn to communicate effectively with the person.**

MAINTAINING GOOD RELATIONSHIPS

Earlier it was stressed that good relationships between agency staff and consumers should not be taken for granted. Similarly, *maintaining* good relationships once established should not be assumed to occur automatically. Staff should continuously strive to actively promote good relationships with the people they support.

The degree to which good relationships are maintained once developed is closely related to the extent to which staff effectively enhance happiness among consumers on a day-to-day basis. As discussed in subsequent chapters, there are a number of evidence-based ways to promote the happiness an adult with a severe disability experiences during daily routines. By implementing the procedures discussed in remaining chapters to increase happiness, staff will also be actively working to maintain good relationships that have been established.

There are also times when more attention than usual should be directed to the existing relationships between agency staff and people they support. In particular, when a given individual appears to be experiencing unusually frequent or serious unhappiness, the person's relationships with support staff should be scrutinized. Significant unhappiness is typically apparent by frequent occurrence of identified indices of unhappiness or an apparent decrease in happiness indices relative to what is usually observed. Staff relationships with a consumer should likewise be carefully attended to when an individual is engaging in more problem behavior than usual.

When unhappiness or problem behavior is more prevalent than typical, or happiness is less apparent than what is usually observed, the source of the person's discontent should be assessed and remedied. As emphasized in this chapter, one likely source of discontent to consider is unfamiliar staff working with an individual in ways that involve close proximity or physical contact. Subsequent chapters illustrate other likely sources of discontent, including such events as a consumer's physical discomfort or illness, an abrupt change in usual daily routines, or a significant increase in instructional and related demands placed on an individual. The latter chapters also provide suggested strategies for alleviating specific sources of discontent among adults with autism and other severe disabilities.

Sometimes, despite conscientious effort by support staff and other agency personnel, removing or altering sources of a person's unhappiness are prohibited or unsuccessful. At these times, it is sometimes helpful to temporarily change major aspects of the person's daily routine. For example, demands placed on the individual or certain daily activities may be discontinued for a period of time. Correspondingly, an emphasis should be placed on reestablishing or further enhancing staffs' relationships with the person, and especially by conducting more "fun" time periods as described with Step 1 of the relationship-building process.

Once the actions just illustrated have been taken and a person begins to display more happiness and less unhappiness then the daily routine can be gradually phased back to the original schedule. At that point, if the attempts to reestablish or strengthen staff relationships with an individual have been successful, it is likely the person will experience less unhappiness during routine activities. However, attempts to specifically address the exact sources of the person's discontent should be continued as well.

THE CRITICAL ROLE OF SINCERITY IN RELATIONSHIPS

The procedures discussed in this chapter represent the most established, evidence-based means of developing good relationships between human service staff and adults with autism and other severe disabilities. However, there is another critical aspect underlying relationship development that has not been discussed: ensuring *personal sincerity*. For truly good relationships to develop between human service staff and the people they support, staff must be sincerely concerned about individual consumer welfare.

Despite the importance of sincerity in establishing relationships, there is no readily apparent means for ensuring support staff are sincerely concerned about the happiness of people they support. For many staff, sincerity seems to develop over time as they interact with and generally get to know individuals. The development of sincere concern for consumer welfare in this respect is something that is clearly desired as staff become familiar with respective adults with autism and other severe disabilities.

There is also no precise way to determine the exact degree of sincerity a staff member has for the well being of people the staff member supports. There are, however, clear indications when there is a serious lack of sincerity, such as persistent negative interactions with an individual or evidence of neglect or abuse. When such situations are apparent it is incumbent upon staff supervisors and agency executive personnel to take action to discontinue the staff member's work with the consumer or remove the staff person from the agency altogether.

CHAPTER SUMMARY: KEY POINTS

1. *An important source of happiness among adults with autism and other severe disabilities in human service agencies is the existence of a good relationship with their support staff.*

2. *A prerequisite for establishing good relationships between adults with severe disabilities and agency staff is familiarity; consumers and staff must have opportunities to get to know each other.*

3. *Consumer happiness is often impeded when unfamiliar staff work in a manner that involves close proximity or physical contact with the consumers; agency supervisors should strive to prevent such situations from occurring.*

4. *The development of good relationships between agency staff and the people they support should not be taken for granted; staff should take specific action to establish good relationships.*

5. *Three steps for developing a good relationship between an agency staff member and an adult with autism or other severe disability is for the staff member to: (1) spend specific time periods with the person doing things the person enjoys, (2) help the person avoid situations that are disliked and, (3) learn to effectively communicate with the person.*

6. *Agency staff can learn to effectively communicate with an adult with a severe disability by: (1) questioning other staff who are familiar with the person's style of communicating, (2) observing interactions between other staff and the person, (3) reviewing relevant documents that describe the individual's communication skills and challenges and most importantly, (4) spending time doing things with the person.*

7. *Once a good relationship is established between an agency staff member and a consumer, the staff person should actively strive to maintain the relationship.*

8. *A critical factor underlying the development of a good relationship between staff and the people they support is personal sincerity; staff must be sincerely concerned about individual consumer happiness.*

CHAPTER 6

THE POWER OF SOCIAL ATTENTION

A fundamental source of happiness for most people is social attention that comes from interacting with other individuals. Although people vary widely in how much they like to interact with others, as well as with whom they want to interact, everybody enjoys social attention to some degree. The same is true for adults with autism and other severe disabilities.

The importance of social attention is sometimes overlooked during the daily routines of human service agencies, and particularly in regard to consumers with autism. A defining characteristic of autism is difficulties with social interactions. A primary reason for the difficulties is that many adults with autism do not respond to social attention in ways that most people respond.

In essence, social attention does not always seem to be very important to some adults with autism. Consequently, providing social attention to adults with autism sometimes is not viewed as important as it is with other people supported within human service agencies. Some staff also refrain from interacting with certain individuals with autism because the individuals do not readily respond when the staff do attempt to interact.

Difficulties in responding to attention or generally interacting with people does not mean that social attention is not important or desired by individuals with autism. This is especially the case for *adults* with autism. Whether due to relationship development or formal teaching by caregivers, adults with autism usually show a desire for social attention at least in some form.

To illustrate, an adult with autism may rarely approach or initiate interactions with support staff or peers in a group home. The lack of attention directed to other people suggests that social attention is not important to the individual. However, when a family member of the consumer visits the group home, the consumer immediately approaches the person and readily interacts.

In the illustration just noted, it is apparent that the person with autism does like social attention, but not necessarily attention from all people. The person has a special relationship with the family member, which makes that individual's attention important and desirable for the person. There are many other cases in which a particular adult with autism enjoys social attention from some people but not others, be they certain staff in human service agencies, peers, or simply familiar acquaintances.

In short, social attention *is* important for adults with autism and should never be overlooked as a source of happiness. Human service staff should be cognizant of the importance of social attention on the day-to-day happiness of all people they support. However, because of difficulties many adults with autism and other severe disabilities experience interacting socially, agency staff also must take care to provide attention in a manner that respective individuals desire. Of particular concern here, social attention should be provided in a manner that promotes consumer happiness. This chapter describes how human service staff can provide attention specifically in ways that enhance happiness among adults with autism and other severe disabilities.

A basic source of happiness for adults with autism and other severe disabilities in human service agencies is social attention provided by agency staff.

THE CRITICAL ROLE OF RELATIONSHIPS ON PROMOTING HAPPINESS THROUGH SOCIAL ATTENTION

Chapter 5 emphasized the importance of human service staff actively striving to develop a good relationship with people they support. One important outcome of establishing a good relationship is that it enhances the desirability of a staff person's attention for a given consumer. When a good relationship develops between a staff member and a person with a severe disability, the person typically enjoys interacting with the staff member and the accompanying attention from the staff member. Such enjoyment enhances the immediate happiness of the person.

Developing a good relationship is particularly important when considering the effects of social attention for adults with autism on the severe end of the spectrum. These individuals usually have the most difficulty interacting with support staff (as well as other people) and responding to attention that is provided. Consequently, for human service staff to interact with adults who have more severe autism in ways that promote happiness, staff must be especially concerned about establishing good relationships with these individuals.

REVIEW OF KEY STEPS FOR A STAFF MEMBER TO DEVELOP A GOOD RELATIONSHIP WITH A PERSON WHO HAS AUTISM OR OTHER SEVERE DISABILITY

1. **Spend time with the person doing things the person enjoys.**
2. **Help the person avoid disliked situations.**
3. **Learn to communicate effectively with the person.**

TYPES OF SOCIAL ATTENTION

Human service staff can provide attention to adults with autism and other severe disabilities by interacting with them in many ways. Most apparently, attention is provided when staff speak directly to consumers. Attention is also provided when staff gesture to individuals such as by waving or showing a "thumbs up" movement. More subtle forms of attention involve simply looking at a person while smiling and lightly patting an individual on the back when walking by the person.

From the perspective of promoting consumer happiness, each of the various ways staff interact with consumers generally represents one of three types of attention. Each type is differentiated based on the meaning that the staff member's interaction conveys to the individual. Specifically, interactions can involve: (1) positive attention, (2) neutral attention or, (3) negative attention.

Positive Attention

Positive attention refers to any interaction a staff member has with a consumer that includes an expression of approval. The most common types of positive attention often involve praising a person's action. Typical examples include saying "Good job", "Awesome", "Well done", etc., following an individual's completion of an assigned task. Other common types of positive attention include verbally thanking a person for complying with a request and explicitly complimenting something associated with an individual (e.g., saying how nicely a person looks in a particular outfit).

There are also a number of nonvocal means of providing positive attention. Frequent examples include head nodding following an individual's initiation of a desired behavior, providing an "OK" gesture following a person's completion of a task, and manually signing "thank you" when an individual complies with a staff request. Other nonvocal expressions of positive attention include various greetings such as shaking an individual's hand and providing a brief hug.

Interacting to express approval is generally viewed as the most apparent way to provide social attention as a means of promoting consumer happiness. Most people experience enjoyment when someone expresses approval to them, and such enjoyment is closely associated with a degree of happiness. However, to ensure that positive attention is favorably received by an adult with autism or other severe disability and truly promotes the person's happiness, expressions of approval must be provided in certain ways.

Positive Attention Must Be Sincere. The importance of sincerity was stressed heavily in the previous chapter on developing good relationships. Sincerity is likewise important when providing positive attention to a person who has a severe disability. In particular, staff should not praise consumer actions unless the staff are sincerely pleased with what the person has done. Otherwise, the praise statements are not likely to be favorably received by respective consumers and have any impact on their immediate happiness.

For example, many human service staff are trained to praise appropriate learner responses to teaching programs. Sometimes, however, certain staff are not really concerned about how well a learner performed but know they are expected to praise appropriate responses. In such cases, the praise statements tend to be repetitive and appear rote or mechanical, often without a staff person even looking at the learner while offering praise. The lack of staff sincerity becomes apparent in the way praise is provided, which does little if anything to impact consumer happiness.

> **Support staff must be sincere in their praise for consumer behavior; otherwise the praise is not likely to represent positive attention for the person.**

As also indicated in **Chapter 5**, sincerity about consumer happiness or general welfare cannot be specifically taught to support staff. It is simply desired that staff in human service agencies will be sincerely concerned about the people they support. As also noted previously, staff often do develop sincere concern about consumer welfare as they get to know individuals. Nonetheless, it is generally wise to emphasize to staff that praise and other expressions of approval should only be provided when they are sincere in what they express.

Positive Attention Must Be Interactive. Positive attention must also be provided in a way that is *interactive*. Interactive means that both the staff member who provides attention and the consumer recipient actively engage in the respective interaction. To illustrate, in many cases a staff member will need to evoke a consumer's attention such as by obtaining the individual's eye contact with the staff member before providing positive attention. Otherwise staff attempts to praise or compliment an individual could be unheeded by the person and have no impact on his or her immediate happiness.

It is likewise important for a staff member to carefully observe for any response a consumer might make to the staff member's attention. A response such as a quick smile or brief eye contact with the staff member would suggest that the individual did indeed attend to the staff member's expression of approval. If no response is observed, then the staff member may need to more actively strive to evoke the individual's attention prior to providing approval the next time.

Ensuring a consumer attends to a praise statement or other expression of approval is especially important with individuals who do not readily interact with others, such as adults with autism on the severe end of the spectrum. The latter individuals often appear unaware of what other people are doing or saying. Hence, unless specific efforts are made to obtain the attention of individuals with more significant challenges prior to expressing some type of approval, it is unlikely they will be responsive to the interaction.

An Extra Benefit of Positive Attention. The primary benefit of providing positive attention to adults with autism and other severe disabilities is that it often helps them feel good about themselves and experience a degree of happiness. There is also another benefit of providing positive attention that impacts happiness more indirectly. Specifically, receiving frequent positive attention from staff during daily routines prevents challenging behavior that is associated with unhappiness among a number of adults who have severe disabilities.

Some adults with autism and other severe disabilities engage in challenging behavior to obtain staff attention. As discussed in previous chapters, challenging behavior usually occurs because a consumer is unhappy with something in the immediate environment. In the situation addressed here, an individual is unhappy because the person desires attention but no one has been interacting with him/her. The individual then acts to resolve the unhappiness by engaging in challenging behavior because the individual has learned that such behavior results in attention from staff.

If, however, staff provide frequent positive attention, the individual does not experience unhappiness due to lack of attention—the unhappiness is prevented. In turn, the individual does not need to engage in problem behavior to decrease unhappiness. As noted repeatedly, preventing unhappiness has the effect of promoting happiness on an overall basis.

Neutral Attention

Although explicitly expressing approval is generally the most recognized way to provide social attention to enhance consumer happiness, it is not the only way. Social attention of a *neutral* nature from support staff can also promote consumer happiness. Neutral attention actually represents the most common type of attention involved in interactions between people. Neutral attention involves any social exchange between two or more people that does not explicitly express approval (or disapproval; see next chapter section). Greeting someone, asking questions, responding to questions, and generally conversing all involve neutral attention.

People often enjoy interacting socially with others, and most of those interactions are primarily neutral in nature. Hence, simply interacting with an adult with autism or other severe disability represents a means through which human service staff can enhance the individual's happiness. Happiness is most likely to result in this situation if the individual has a good relationship with the staff member who is interacting with the individual; the individual enjoys the staff person's attention even if there is no explicit expression of approval.

> **Simply interacting socially with adults with autism and other severe disabilities can promote their happiness.**

There is of course a limit to how much social attention a person receives that is desired by the person and results in the individual's immediate happiness. Although people enjoy social interactions in general that do not necessarily involve explicit expressions of approval, people also like different amounts of attention at various times. Everybody prefers to limit interactions with other people at times, or to avoid attention from others altogether. Ways to avoid providing attention that is unwanted by an adult with a severe disability in certain situations are discussed later in the section on **Limits to Providing Social Attention**.

NEGATIVE ATTENTION

The final type of social attention is *negative* attention. Negative attention involves a staff person interacting with a consumer in a way that includes an explicit expression of disapproval. Common types of negative attention include a staff person criticizing what an individual is doing or has done, telling a person to stop doing something in a disapproving manner, and warning an individual about doing something in the future.

Negative attention generally has the opposite effect of positive attention in regard to a consumer's happiness. Whereas positive attention can promote happiness, negative attention is more likely to result in unhappiness for a consumer. Hence, staff provision of negative attention should be limited.

Notice that the emphasis is on *limiting* the amount of negative attention directed to consumers. It is not implied that negative attention should never be provided. Adults with autism and other severe disabilities warrant correction or negative feedback for their actions at times, just like everybody else. This type of attention is sometimes necessary to help individuals engage in appropriate activities in lieu of problem behavior and at times, to protect them or others from harm. Nonetheless, because negative attention is usually unpleasant to receive and can result in immediate unhappiness, staff should provide negative attention judiciously.

Additionally, negative attention does not mean that interactions should be overly critical or harsh. Negative attention necessary to prevent problem behavior or potential harm can be very mild, such as simply saying something like "I don't think that's a good idea" or "We probably don't need to do that" when re-directing an individual's behavior from something inappropriate to something more acceptable. Likewise, the interaction can be provided in normal conversational tones in contrast to raising one's voice.

A general guideline regarding negative attention is that on a day-to-day basis, there should be much less negative attention provided to individual consumers than positive attention. A number of human service agencies also have endorsed more specific guidelines for providing negative attention. Probably the most common is the 4:1 rule: for every occurrence of negative attention directed to a consumer there should be at least four occurrences of positive attention.

Establishing guidelines regarding provision of positive versus negative attention to agency consumers can help staff in limiting their negative interactions. A number of people, including those who obtain jobs in human service agencies, commonly engage in negative interactions with others. To illustrate, it is relatively common to observe some adults repeatedly providing disapproving statements to their children while waiting at the checkout line at a grocery store. Negative interactions are also frequently observed between various human service staff during meetings, upon receiving directions from supervisors, and when informed of unexpected duties that need to be completed.

Although frequent negative interactions may be common place for some people, such interactions should not be common between support staff and adults with autism and other severe disabilities in human service agencies. Agency staff should be explicitly informed that negative interactions with people they support must be limited. Most importantly, if negative attention is observed being provided by staff to consumers at approximately the same frequency as positive attention or even more, then supervisors should take immediate action to change staff interaction styles. Additional information regarding what supervisors should do in such cases is provided in **Chapter 13** on supervisory responsibilities for working with staff to promote consumer happiness.

> **Staff attention provided to adults with autism and other severe disabilities can be positive, neutral, or negative; positive and neutral attention can promote happiness whereas negative attention usually promotes unhappiness.**

Providing Social Attention in A Group

The discussion on providing social attention as a means of promoting happiness among adults with autism and other severe disabilities has focused on situations in which a staff person interacts individually with a consumer. However, in most human service agencies the majority of support staff are usually responsible for *groups* of people with disabilities. Special considerations are warranted when staff are working with groups of people in regard to providing social attention.

The primary consideration for interacting in a group situation is to ensure each individual receives social attention. This requires a staff person to actively move about to interact with each individual in the group. That is, the staff person's attention must be distributed among all individuals present.

Distributing attention within a group situation typically requires a staff person to interact only briefly with each individual, usually for less than a minute or so. Brief interactions can involve providing positive attention such as praising what a person is doing or complimenting something about the individual. Neutral attention can also be briefly provided such as, for example, asking an individual if everything is alright or informing a person about a forthcoming activity.

Brief distribution of social attention among all individuals in a group is particularly important when only one staff person is working with a respective group. There is a tendency for many staff to attend to some individuals more than others in regard to their social interactions. When this happens, some consumers receive little if any attention from staff, which in essence results in lost opportunities to affect the latter individuals' happiness.

Even when there are several staff present with a consumer group, it is helpful if at least one staff member has the assigned responsibility of moving among individuals to ensure each person receives social attention. The other staff present can spend time interacting with certain individuals for longer periods of time or completing other duties. The primary point is that at least one staff member should continuously rotate among all consumers to provide social attention to each individual.

The main reason for distributing attention among all individuals in a group is to enhance the likelihood that each person will experience enjoyment or happiness that often accompanies social attention. There is also another benefit of distributing attention among all individuals present. When a staff member interacts directly with an individual it essentially allows the staff member to briefly assess the indivdual's immediate situation and appropriately respond if something needs to be changed.

Sometimes a person who has a severe disability may be experiencing some discontent such as difficulty in performing a certain task. When the staff member interacts with the person, the individual's discontent will likely become apparent and the staff member can help resolve the source of the discontent (e.g., assist an individual in completing a task). In this manner, the staff member is functionally reducing a consumer's immediate unhappiness. In contrast, if no staff member interacts with an individual for a long time period, the person's discontent will not be readily apparent and cannot be quickly resolved.

Another consideration when staff work with groups of people with disabilities pertains to the importance of focusing on positive (or neutral) attention and not negative attention. When staff do not actively distribute their attention among all individuals, certain consumers who do not receive attention may act out to solicit staff attention. The inappropriate behavior evokes staff responses that frequently involve negative attention in an attempt to stop or correct the undesired behavior.

The pattern just noted can escalate as other individuals begin to act out for attention. The end result is a rather negative social environment involving frequent expressions of disapproval. If staff frequently interact with all consumers in a positive or neutral manner though, there is reduced likelihood that individuals will engage in inappropriate behavior to obtain staff attention. In turn, the negative staff attention that often follows inappropriate behavior will be avoided.

Concerns over distribution of staff attention within group situations are especially relevant during leisure times such as late afternoon in residential settings and break times in educational and vocational settings. Leisure times are generally when people interact socially with others and agency consumers should have similar opportunities for socialization. In contrast, during more structured or goal-oriented activities, it is not always desirable for staff to distribute their attention among all individuals in a group.

> **When staff are working with a group of individuals, at least one staff member usually should have the assigned role of rotating among all persons to interact briefly with each individual to provide social attention.**

To illustrate, when consumers are working at a job or performing educational tasks there are usually specific staff assignments regarding their interactions with individual consumers (e.g., when, how, and with whom to provide assistance or instruction). It may not be beneficial for staff to frequently rotate among all individuals to provide brief social attention during these types of activities. For example, frequently interacting socially with individuals while they are working or engaged in an academic task may interfere with their progress on learning to work independently.

Staff should be explicitly informed when it is not desired to provide frequent social attention to all people they support. Again, such situations usually involve formally structured activities for which staff have specific responsibilities regarding how they should interact with respective individuals. Otherwise, providing social attention to all individuals should generally be an ongoing performance expectation of staff (see the following chapter section for additional considerations in this regard).

LIMITS TO PROVIDING SOCIAL ATTENTION

A basic premise of this chapter is that people, including adults who have autism and other severe disabilities, like attention from others. People frequently enjoy social attention and such enjoyment increases their immediate happiness. However, it has also been noted that at times people do not want to interact with others, or they become discontented with an ongoing interaction and want to discontinue the activity. Staff in human service agencies must be sensitive to individual consumer preferences regarding when attention is and is not desired.

There is no hard and fast rule regarding how often attention should be provided for individuals with autism and other severe disabilities, nor how much attention should be provided at a given point in time. Sometimes formal assessments, such as those completed when developing certain behavior support plans, provide information about providing attention based on an individual's social likes and dislikes. In most cases though, staff have to decide for themselves when an individual consumer does not want their attention.

The best way to determine whether attention is desired by a consumer is to judge the person's response when an interaction is initiated. If the individual responds in an interactive manner as described earlier or shows indices of happiness, then generally staff can be assured that their attention is desired by the person. In contrast, if an individual does not reciprocate in any manner or shows indices of unhappiness, it is usually beneficial to discontinue the interaction at that time (assuming the individual has the skills to reciprocate as evidenced by the person's history of actively responding to previous interactions).

When staff observe indications that a person they support does not want their attention as just illustrated, it should not imply that staff should decrease their attention directed to the individual in the future. It just means that at that point in time the person does not want attention from respective staff. It may also mean that *how* the attention is being provided in that immediate situation is not desired. For example, some people with autism dislike loud or overly effusive talking, preferring quiter or less exuberant interaction styles.

In essence, as long as staff base their continuation or discontinuation of attention on a consumer's response to their interaction *at that moment*, there is really no serious detriment in providing frequent attention. More pointedly, problematic issues with social attention provided to adults with autism and other severe disabilities in human service agencies rarely relate to *too much* attention from staff. Most problems in this respect pertain to consumers not receiving enough attention from staff. Human service staff should be well trained in specific ways of providing social attention that promote consumer happiness as described in this chapter.

Training Staff to Provide Social Attention for Promoting Consumer Happiness

The quality of an agency's supports and services, including the degree to which an agency promotes consumer happiness, is heavily dependent on the quality with which agency staff perform their work. For staff to perform job duties in a quality manner, they must have the necessary skills to complete their work duties proficiently. Because most people begin their direct support jobs in human service agencies with no prior training in how to work with adults with severe disabilities, agencies must train their staff in relevant work skills.

The importance of training staff how to perform job duties associated with promoting consumer happiness is discussed in **Chapter 13**. The latter chapter also describes well-established, evidence-based ways of effectively training work skills to human service staff. The role of staff training is noted here because of its particular importance for ensuring staff know how to provide social attention in specific ways for promoting happiness among adults with autism and other severe disabilities.

Human service agencies must ensure staff are trained how to interact with adults with autism and other severe disabilities in ways that promote individual happiness.

There are three reasons why staff training is especially important in regard to staffs' provision of social attention for promoting consumer happiness. The first reason is most basic: when people are hired into a direct support role, they usually do not know how to interact with adults with autism and other severe disabilities who have communication challenges. Because these individuals often do not interact in the same way most people engage in social exchanges, new support staff may find it difficult to interact with them. Such difficulty results in many staff avoiding interactions with certain individuals because they are not sure what to do and are uncomfortable trying to interact with them.

The situation just illustrated represents an experience that a number of readers probably encountered early in their human service careers. Many readers will likely remember feeling unsure of how to interact with individuals who had autism or other severe disabilities and perhaps a degree of anxiety when they attempted to interact. Readers also will likely recall how they gained confidence in interacting with the individuals and overcame their anxiety as they became more familiar with each person. The latter experiences can be facilitated for new staff if they are effectively trained how to interact with adults with autism and other severe disabilities when initially employed.

A second reason for the importance of training staff how to provide social attention to the individuals they support pertains to a phenomenon noted previously. That is, some people begin their roles as direct support staff with a history of negative interaction styles with other persons, such as their own children. As also discussed earlier, negative interactions of staff with agency consumers must be limited if their social attention is to promote consumer happiness. Staff must receive training early in their employment to ensure they understand the importance of limiting negative attention. Such training often must involve explicitly informing staff that negative interactions that may be normal for them with other people are not acceptable with individuals in their agency.

A third reason for the need for training staff how to provide social attention is that such attention must be provided in certain ways (beyond limiting negative interactions) if the attention is to promote consumer happiness. To review briefly, these ways include ensuring praise and other expressions of approval are provided sincerely, individuals are attentive and respond to interaction attempts, attention is routinely provided to all individuals a staff person is supporting, and the continuation of interactions is based on an individual's apparent desire for attention at that moment.

In short, staff skills in interacting with adults with autism and other severe disabilities should not be taken for granted. This is especially the case for ensuring staff have the skills to provide social attention in a manner that promotes consumer happiness. It is incumbent upon agency executive personnel to ensure staff are provided with the necessary training to learn how to appropriately interact with individuals with whom they will be working. Again, ways of training staff how to provide social attention as well as other important skills for promoting happiness among adults with autism and other severe disabilities are discussed in **Chapter 13**.

Chapter Summary: Key Points

1. *A basic source of happiness for adults with autism and other severe disabilities in human service agencies is social attention from agency staff.*

2. *Social attention can be positive, neutral, or negative; positive and neutral attention from staff can promote consumer happiness whereas negative attention usually promotes unhappiness.*

3. *For attention to be received as positive, it must be presented sincerely and evoke an attentive response by the recipient of the attention.*

4. *Routinely providing positive attention can prevent challenging behavior among many adults with severe disabilities; receiving frequent positive attention reduces an individual's need to act out to gain staff attention.*

5. *Negative attention sometimes needs to be provided to adults with severe disabilities just like everybody else, but it should occur much less often than positive social attention.*

6. *When staff work with groups of adults with severe disabilities, special concern should be directed to providing attention to all individuals in the group.*

7. *Staff should base the amount of social attention provided to individuals on observed indications of individual desires for attention at that moment.*

8. *Human service staff must be effectively trained in ways to provide social attention that promote happiness among adults with autism and other severe disabilities.*

CHAPTER 7

PROMOTING CONSUMER CHOICE MAKING DURING DAILY ACTIVITIES

In the introductory comments to this text it was emphasized that happiness among adults with autism and other severe disabilities should be promoted within human service agencies in conjunction with promoting their independence. Effectively supporting people to be increasingly independent enhances the personal control they have over their lives. When individuals have personal control they do more things that they desire and more things in ways that are desired – ways that enhance individual happiness.

There is another way human service staff can help adults with autism and other severe disabilities have personal control: ensure they have frequent *choices* regarding how they live their lives each day. Generally the more choices people make during daily activities, the more they will do things that they want and enjoy. In turn, enjoyment during routine activities enhances their day-to-day happiness.

Most people make numerous choices during the day that affects their enjoyment. People often choose, for example, what time they will get up in the morning, what they will eat for breakfast or whether they will have breakfast or not, and with whom they will spend their day. These choices, which represent only a fraction of typical choices people make on a daily basis, are essentially taken for granted among the general populace. In contrast, these types of choices are frequently lacking in the daily routines of adults with severe disabilities in human service agencies. The relative lack of choice making impedes the amount of happiness they experience each day.

There are a number of reasons why consumer choice is often limited in human service agencies relative to the amount of choices most people make. The majority of the reasons relate to a basic way that human service agencies typically operate. Specifically, human service agencies are *schedule-oriented*.

To illustrate, in residential settings there usually are schedules regarding when consumers must get up in the morning, when breakfast will occur, when bathing will take place, etc. There are likewise schedules in day program settings, such as when individual and group instruction will occur, when break times will happen, etc. The schedule-based routines often restrict consumer choices regarding how they spend their day.

Human service agencies generally must have schedules to function effectively. Schedules are necessary for agency staff to know what their expected performance duties entail as well as when respective duties should be completed. In essence, human service agencies rely on daily schedules to help ensure services that are expected to be provided for individuals they support are indeed provided.

People in general follow certain schedules during the day, such as those associated with maintaining their jobs, fulfilling family responsibilities, and ensuring bills are paid on time, just to name a few. However, people also usually make many choices in regard to establishing their schedules as well as precisely how they will comply with their schedules once established. Again though, such choices are often lacking among adults with autism and other severe disabilities in human service agencies.

The schedule-based routines typical of most human service agencies do not have to negate daily choices by the people they support. Consumer choices can be incorporated within the schedules and routines just like other people make choices during their daily activities.

When consumer choice is built into agency routines, they are much more likely to experience happiness as they go about daily activities.

> **Daily choice making is closely associated with happiness; the more one chooses how to spend one's day, the more happiness the person usually experiences.**

There is also another reason consumers in human service agencies typically have far fewer choices than the general populace. This reason relates to the intellectual and related challenges among adults with autism and other severe disabilities. Such challenges impact their skills necessary to make informed choices.

Adults who have severe disabilities usually need active support from staff in human service agencies to make meaningful choices. This chapter describes how human service staff can provide choice-making opportunities that help individuals with disabilities make informed choices during the typical, daily operations of human service agencies. Providing frequent choice opportunities is one of the most well-established, evidence-based means of promoting happiness among adults with autism and other severe disabilities.

QUALIFICATION: A FOCUS ON CHOICES DURING DAILY ACTIVITIES

The focus of this chapter is on supporting consumers of agency services in making choices on a *daily* basis. There are numerous choice opportunities that usually can be provided to consumers throughout the course of the day such as, for example, what to wear, with whom to sit during activities, and what to do during leisure time. Again, these types of daily choices are usually taken for granted among most people but are often lacking in the daily routines of adults with severe disabilities in human service agencies.

Before describing how consumer choice-making opportunities can be routinely provided in human service agencies, another type of choice making warrants mention that also has a major impact on individual happiness. This type of choice making pertains to major lifestyle changes. The latter choices involve such decisions as where to live, with whom to live, and what type of job to seek.

Choices associated with major lifestyle changes have a very significant and long-term effect on the happiness of adults with severe disabilities, just like they do for everybody else. However, helping consumers make choices that significantly affect their lives for extended time periods involve different procedures relative to assisting them in making choices during daily routines. Strategies for assisting consumers of agency services in making more life-altering choices will be discussed in **Chapter 9** on **Personal Goal Planning**.

> **Providing frequent choice opportunities during daily routines in human service agencies is one of the most well-established, evidence-based means of promoting happiness among adults with autism and other severe disabilities.**

WAYS TO PROVIDE CHOICE-MAKING OPPORTUNITIES TO PROMOTE MEANINGFUL CONSUMER CHOICES

Providing a choice-making opportunity to someone basically involves presenting the person with an option of doing something or not, or with two or more options associated with doing something. The focus here is on the latter process: providing a person who has a severe disability with at least two options about doing something. Providing several options increases the likelihood that a person will choose something that the individual enjoys. Providing an option of doing one particular thing or not will be addressed later in the chapter.

There are a number of ways staff in human service agencies can provide choice-making opportunities to adults with autism and other severe disabilities. The precise way a choice is presented to a given individual must be based on the person's specific skills and challenges. Otherwise, the choice presentation is not likely to result in a meaningful choice response by the individual. To illustrate, it would be essentially meaningless to ask what someone would like to do on the forthcoming weekend if the person does not speak or have other means of verbal expression (e.g., writing skills, sign language, use of a voice output communication aide).

Across all ways of providing choice-making opportunities, there is a basic protocol for presenting choices that increases the likelihood an adult with a severe disability will respond to a choice opportunity in a meaningful manner. The protocol was designed through research and application for providing a choice involving two options. However, the same basic process is relevant when providing more than two options.

BASIC PROTOCOL FOR PROVIDING CHOICE-MAKING OPPORTUNITIES FOR ADULTS WITH AUTISM AND OTHER SEVERE DISABILITIES

1. **Present a request for the person to choose between two options.**
2. **If the person chooses one of the options, honor the choice.**
3. **If the person does not choose one of the options, provide the individual with assistance to understand the options being presented.**
4. **Repeat the request for the person to choose between the two options.**

The basic protocol for providing a choice opportunity begins with requesting the consumer to choose one of two presented options. If the person chooses one of the options, it is critical that the selection be *honored*. Honoring a person's choice response means that s/he is provided access to what was chosen. If, for example, a person expresses a desire to go to a store to purchase a soda when a staff member asks what the person would like to do after supper, then it must be ensured that the individual gets to the store to buy the soda.

If staff do not honor what a consumer chooses, then there is in essence no choice. Such a process also is likely to decrease future choice making by the individual. The person's choice-making behavior is not reinforced and s/he is less likely to respond to choice opportunities in the future.

In most cases, providing an adult who has a severe disability with a request to choose one of two options will result in the person making a choice. In some cases though, an individual will not respond to the staff member's request and not make a selection. When this happens, a staff member cannot be certain that the person understood the choice that was being provided. Hence, the staff member should assist the individual in understanding the choice opportunity (see following discussion). Subsequently, the choice presentation should be repeated and the person's choice response honored at that time.

How to apply the choice-presentation protocol is best illustrated when considering the different ways in which choices can be presented, again based on individual consumer skills and challenges. How to use the protocol with the most common ways to present choice opportunities to adults with autism and other severe disabilities is described in the following chapter sections. Special circumstances that can arise in which alterations with the protocol are necessary are discussed in a later section.

PROVIDING AN OPEN-ENDED CHOICE

A common type of choice presentation involves an *open-ended choice* presented to a person with a severe disability. An open-ended choice presentation allows an individual to select one of a number of options of which the person is aware. Examples of this type of choice include such questions as "What would you like to wear today?", "Whom do you want to go with you to the store?", and "Where do you want to go for supper?". An open-ended choice is usually easy for staff to provide because this is a way of providing choice opportunities to people in general with which staff are usually familiar.

Although open-ended choice presentations are easy for staff to provide, they can be difficult for many adults with autism and other severe disabilities to respond to in a meaningful manner. Whereas some individuals have the verbal and related intellectual skills to answer these types of questions, many do not. Hence, open-ended choice presentations are usually only appropriate for people with less significant disabilities.

Even when consumers have the prerequisite skills to respond meaningfully to an open-ended choice presentation, some will not respond to this type of choice in certain situations. Usually the lack of a consumer response is due to the person not attending to or otherwise understanding the choice opportunity being presented. When an individual does not respond to an initial choice request, then the remaining steps of the choice-presentation protocol should be implemented by the staff member offering the choice.

Specifically, if an individual does not make an apparent choice following an open-ended choice presentation, the staff member should provide more assistance to the person. More assistance can be provided by offering the person two specific options relevant to the initial choice presentation. For example, if an individual does not respond to a question such as "What do you want to do after supper?", the staff member could then ask "Do you want to play on your computer or go to the ball game?"

Providing specific options generally makes it easier for a consumer to make a choice response relative to responding to an open-ended choice presentation. The former type of choice opportunity requires only that the person name one of the suggested options. In contrast, responding to the open-ended choice presentation requires the person to be aware of and mentally consider all potential options, and then adequately describe the option that is most desired. When adults with autism and other severe disabilities do not respond to an open-ended choice presentation, often they subsequently respond to one of the options specifically named by the staff member.

If a person does not respond by naming one of the subsequent options provided by a staff member, then the staff member can present other available options. To illustrate, in the example just noted, the staff member could ask "Would you like to watch a movie or sit on the porch swing after supper?". If the person does not make an apparent choice response after several different options are presented, it may be that the person is not interested in making a choice at that time. Hence, the staff member should discontinue the choice presentations. The staff member can approach the individual at a later time to provide additional choice opportunities.

If, however, a person fails to make a choice response to repeated presentations of open-ended choices and specific options subsequently provided, then it is likely the individual lacks the skills to respond to this type of choice opportunity. For these individuals, efforts could be undertaken to begin teaching necessary choice-making skills to them. How to teach such skills is addressed in **Chapter 11**.

> **The more effectively adults with autism and other severe disabilities are taught functional communication skills, the easier it is for agency staff to provide frequent choice-making opportunities for them.**

It should also be noted though that a prerequisite for successfully teaching adults with autism and other severe disabilities how to respond to open-ended choice presentations is an existing verbal repertoire—the individuals must have the verbal skills to effectively express their choice. Teaching functional verbal skills can take a considerable amount of time. Hence, if consumers do not already communicate verbally, then usually staff should provide choice opportunities in a manner more commensurate with a consumer's existing skills (see following chapter sections). As the person learns more advanced verbal skills, then staff can begin providing choice opportunities in a manner that corresponds to the individual's newly acquired communication skills.

Providing a Two-Item Choice

For people who do not readily demonstrate the skills to respond to open-ended choice opportunities presented vocally, the most common means of providing choice opportunities is a *two-item choice.* Research has indicated that most adults with autism and other severe disabilities usually respond to a two-item choice presentation with a meaningful choice response. A two-item choice involves providing two specific options while presenting a visual referent for each option.

The most typical referents used in two-item choice presentations are actual items that directly pertain to accessing the options presented. To illustrate, a two-item choice presentation for what to do during leisure time might involve asking if a consumer would like to play on the computer or watch television while simultaneously pointing to each item as it is named. Similarly, a two-item choice involving what an individual would like for snack might involve asking if s/he would like an apple or some chips while pointing to each item in sequence.

> **A means of providing a choice-making opportunity that usually results in a meaningful choice response by most adults with autism and other severe disabilities is a two-item choice; a caregiver asks an individual which of two options is desired while showing a visual referent for each option.**

Typically when two items are offered for choice a consumer readily chooses one of the options represented by the items. The choice response may involve pointing or reaching for a specific item or naming one of the items. In some cases though, a response will not be forthcoming following the choice presentation. In these cases the subsequent steps of the basic choice-presentation protocol should then be implemented.

The choice-presentation protocol is used with a two-item choice in the following manner. First, a staff member shows both items to the consumer, points to one of the items and asks if the individual would like that item while naming the item, and then points to the other item while asking if the person would like that item (while again naming the item). The staff member then allows the individual time to indicate a preference by pointing toward, reaching for, or naming one of the items. If the person chooses one of the items, then the item is presented to the individual or s/he is assisted in accessing the activity that the item represents.

If an individual does not make a choice response to the initial two-item presentation, then more assistance should be provided. More assistance means the staff member provides additional information about the options presented to help the person understand what is being offered. For example, when providing a choice of watching a DVD or looking at a magazine, the staff member could describe something about the movie on the DVD and show the individual some of the pages in the magazine. After providing increased assistance, the staff member should then repeat the original choice presentation.

Most adults with severe disabilities who do not respond to an initial two-item choice presentation usually make a choice for one of the items following the increased staff assistance. Regardless of which choice presentation a person responds to by selecting one of the options, the choice response should be honored as discussed previously. If, however, a person does not make a choice response even after increased assistance is provided, then the staff member could provide other options in a two-item format.

If an individual does not respond to repeated presentations of different two-item choice opportunities, then usually a staff member should discontinue the choice presentation and come back later to offer specific choices. Typically when a consumer does not respond to repeated two-item presentations it means the person is not interested in making a choice at that time. However, it may also mean that the two-item presentation format is too difficult for the individual to understand. In the latter case, future choices should be offered in a way that is easier for the person to make a meaningful choice response.

Before describing an alternative choice-presentation process that requires less skills on the part of people with severe disabilities, variations with the two-item process that are relevant for some individuals warrant mention. The variations pertain to the visual referents used within the two-item presentation. Earlier it was noted that the most common referents in this type of choice presentation involve items that are directly used by a person following his/her choice.

Although providing specific items that pertain to choice options represents a way of providing choice opportunities that most adults with autism and other severe disabilities usually respond to in a meaningful manner, this process has a notable shortcoming. Specifically, although the types of choices that can be provided are important, they are limited. The limitation exists because the items must be available in the person's immediate environment.

In many cases, items to include in respective choice presentations are not immediately available. To illustrate, if a consumer in a group home is offered a choice of two specific restaurants regarding where to have supper, the two restaurants would of course not be present in the residence. In such cases other visual referents could be used within the two-item choice presentation, depending again on a given consumer's skills and challenges.

For some individuals with severe disabilities, the referents used in two-item choice presentations can involve pictures that relate to the choice options. In the situation just noted for example, the person could be shown a picture of each of two favorite restaurants during the choice presentation. Other individuals may be able to read two options printed on cards or a piece of paper and point to the desired option if they lack the skills to say what they prefer. Still other people may be skilled in using assistive communication devices that allow them to express a preference when provided a two-item choice.

The types of choices agency staff can provide to consumers are noticeably expanded if consumers have the skills to respond to a choice presentation without specific objects being present that pertain to the available options. Of course, being able to make a choice based on pictorial or written representations of the choice options requires more advanced consumer skills than making a choice with two specific items being presented. This is another reason that promoting happiness among adults with autism and other severe disabilities should occur in conjunction with promoting adaptive skill development. In this case, teaching more advanced communication skills to consumers expands the number and types of choices that can be readily provided by agency staff.

Providing a One-Item Choice

For a small but very important minority of adults who have autism or other severe disabilities, responding to a two-item choice presentation is beyond their existing skill level. This is especially the case for people who have profound intellectual and physical disabilities. Physical challenges of the latter individuals often prohibit speaking, independent ambulation, and fulfillment of basic needs without essentially total assistance from support staff. From the perspective of meaningfully responding to choice presentations to express their preferences, many are unable to reach for or point to presented items.

Due in large part to the profound nature of their disabilities, these individuals usually have very few if any choice opportunities during typical routines in human service agencies. Essentially everything is done for them by agency staff. They are dressed, bathed, and fed by support staff, usually on a schedule over which they have no personal control. Agency staff likewise decide their leisure activities, or what entertainment will be provided.

Despite the challenges faced by adults with profound multiple disabilities, individual choice is as important for their happiness just as much as it is with everybody else. Although it can take relatively significant amounts of staff time to provide choice opportunities to these consumers during daily routines, as well as a certain degree of skill on the part of staff, meaningful choices *can be provided*. In one sense, providing people with profound multiple disabilities with meaningful choice opportunities is more important than with most people because they rarely if ever have opportunities to make choices during their typical days.

> **Providing choice opportunities for adults who have the most significant disabilities is especially important because these individuals usually have far fewer opportunities to make choices during daily routines than everybody else.**

There is a well-established, evidence-based means of providing choice opportunities for people who have profound multiple disabilities: a *one-item choice* presentation. A one-item choice presentation is designed to allow individuals with the most significant disabilities personal control over key aspects of their daily activities. This type of choice presentation pertains to the situation noted early in this chapter in which a consumer is provided a choice of whether to do something or not.

The same basic protocol is used with a one-item choice presentation as with providing individuals a choice involving two or more options, although there are necessary alterations. The most common alteration pertains to staff determining what an individual's choice response could involve prior to providing a choice opportunity. Generally, responses to a choice presentation among adults with profound multiple disabilities fall within one of three categories: *approach, avoidance,* or *neutral.*

When an item is presented to an individual, an *approach* response represents an indication that the person desires the item. Approach responses usually entail a person looking at the item for at least several continuous seconds, leaning toward the item, or if possible reaching for the item. In other words, the person approaches the presented item in any way possible for the individual. Approach responses can also involve indices of happiness such as a person smiling while looking at an item that is presented.

In contrast, an *avoidance* response represents an indication that an individual does not want an item that is presented. Avoidance responses typically involve a person turning away from the item, leaning back from the item, or possibly pushing the item away. The individual avoids the item in whatever way is possible for him/her. Avoidance responses also can include indices of unhappiness, such as frowning or grimacing when an item is presented.

The general definitions of approach and avoidance responses are well-established guides for determining whether an adult with profound multiple disabilities desires an item that is presented. However, because of the idiosyncratic nature of the disabilities of these individuals, at times agency staff will have to revise the general definitions of approach and avoidance responses somewhat for certain individuals. Such revisions usually require some trial-and-error practice observing individual responses to items that are presented.

From the perspective of promoting choice making among adults with profound multiple disabilities, approach and avoidance behaviors are the desired responses when an item is presented for a choice. Such responses indicate either the person wants (approaches) or does not want (avoids) the item; hence the individual is making an observable choice. However, quite commonly approach or avoidance responses are not observed when providing a one-item choice opportunity to these individuals. People with profound multiple disabilities frequently will respond in a manner that is considered *neutral*.

A neutral response to a choice presentation is defined by the absence of either approach or avoidance behavior. Such a response can mean that the person is neither interested nor disinterested in whatever is presented. Frequently though, a neutral response is an indication that the individual does not understand or is otherwise inattentive to the choice presentation.

Once the precise definitions of approach and avoidance responses are established for an individual, with all other responses being considered neutral, then a one-item choice can be presented using the basic choice protocol. The item is presented while simultaneously asking if the person wants the item. For example, a staff member could present a CD player with music playing in front of the individual. If the person approaches the CD player, such as by leaning toward it and looking at it, then the choice (approach) response should be honored by leaving the player with the person. In contrast, if the person displays an avoidance response, such as turning away from the CD player, then the avoidance response should be honored and the CD player removed.

If, however, the person makes no approach or avoidance response (i.e., a neutral response), then the next steps of the protocol should be implemented. The staff member should assist the individual in understanding what is presented such as by holding the CD player next to the person's ear and describing what music is playing. Next, the staff member should repeat the first step of the protocol by presenting the CD player and asking if the individual wants to listen to the music. Attention should be directed to whether the person then approaches or avoids the item and the staff member should act accordingly based on the individual's response as just described.

If the second presentation of the item for the person's choice still results in a neutral response (or an avoidance response), then the staff member should offer another item for the individual's choice. The intent is to find something that the person desires at that moment. If no approach responses are observed following several item presentations, the staff member usually should discontinue the choice-presentation process and return to offer choice opportunities at another time.

The description to this point of a one-item choice presentation for a person with profound multiple disabilities has focused on presenting an item for an individual to access if s/he so desires. The same process can be used with various activities. To illustrate, a staff member may be happy to see a consumer when first arriving at work and desire to greet the person with a brief hug. The consumer, however, may or may not want to be hugged by the staff person. The staff member could give the individual a choice of being hugged or not by using the choice-presentation protocol.

Specifically, instead of proceeding with hugging the person, the staff member could begin to provide a hug and then momentarily stop—such as by leaning toward the individual with arms out wide as the first indication of providing a hug. At that point the staff member should observe whether the individual approaches or avoids the staff member's movements. If the person approaches the staff member, then it would suggest s/he desires to be hugged and the staff member could proceed with the hug. In contrast, an avoidance response would indicate the person does not want to be hugged and the staff member should not proceed with hugging the individual.

There are many things that staff in human service agencies do with or for consumers with profound multiple disabilities during the day that could be altered in the manner just noted. The simple act of temporarily stopping an action once initiated and then continuing only if a consumer approaches the staff person's action gives the consumer personal control over what is happening. When staff provide these types of choices frequently during the day, adults who have very significant disabilities will be exercising more control over their daily activities. Consumers will be experiencing things they desire and avoiding things that are unwanted. Such a process can have a significant impact on their daily happiness.

> **Adults with the most profound, multiple disabilities can make meaningful choices if support staff initiate an action with an individual and then carefully observe the person's response before proceeding with the action.**

Previously it was noted that a number of adults with profound multiple disabilities frequently do not respond to a one-item choice presentation in a manner involving apparent approach or avoidance. It was also noted that a primary reason for the absence of such responses is a lack of understanding that a choice opportunity is being provided. The lack of understanding often occurs because many of these individuals have no history of being provided choice opportunities and being expected to make a choice.

In short, many people with profound multiple disabilities have had no opportunities to learn how to make choices and exert control over what happens to them during daily routines. They can, however, usually *be taught* basic choice-making skills. In this regard, the protocol for providing a one-item choice-making opportunity has a teaching component built into it.

When an individual repeatedly fails to make approach responses when choice opportunities are presented, staff should not abandon attempts to offer choices. Rather, presentations of a variety of one-item choices should continue at different times. When choice opportunities involving various items or activities are provided repeatedly, often an individual will eventually show some type of approach response.

When a person does approach an item or activity and a staff member then responds to the approach behavior by providing the desired item or activity, the consumer's approach response will be reinforced. The more often this happens, the more likely the person will be to make approach responses to desired items or activities in the future. The individual essentially learns how to exert some control over staff actions and access things that are desired.

The same basic process occurs with avoidance responses. If one-item choice opportunities are presented frequently, eventually most adults with profound multiple disabilities will display an avoidance response to a given item or activity that is not desired. When the staff member subsequently withdraws what is presented, that act can reinforce the person's avoidance behavior. The individual is learning how to express a desire to avoid an unwanted item or activity.

TYPES OF CHOICES

The daily choices people routinely make, as well as choices that can be provided to adults with severe disabilities in human service agencies, have been exemplified in previous sections. Each choice a person makes on a daily basis usually represents one of five different *types* of choices. Staff awareness of the different types can facilitate their provision of choice opportunities for people they support during routine activities.

TYPES OF CHOICES

Type	Example
What	watch a movie or look at a book
How	bathe by taking a bath or a shower
Where	eat in the living room or the dining room
When	do laundry before or after lunch
With whom	which staff person to help with a chore

Probably the most common type of choice is a "*what*" choice. A "what" choice involves providing a consumer with options regarding what to do during a certain time period. Particularly opportune times to offer "what" choices involve leisure activities.

Leisure time is especially relevant for offering "what" choices because "leisure" by definition is characterized by an individual choosing what to do at that time. Examples of common types of "what" choices provided during leisure times include a staff member asking what a consumer would like to do after supper, whether an individual would like to draw on a sketch pad or play on the computer on a weekend afternoon, and whether a person would like to listen to music or watch television while waiting for supper.

There are also routine situations in human service agencies in addition to leisure activities for which staff can provide "what" types of choices. For example, a number of "what" choices can be incorporated into self-help routines. Such choices may involve what outfit to put on when getting dressed, what to eat for lunch, and what to take to a day program to engage with during break time.

Another common type of choice that can be incorporated into many routines is a *"how"* choice. A "how" choice pertains to how something is performed. This is a good way to present a choice when something has to be done, but can be done in different ways. If a consumer has to take a medication, for example, a choice could be offered regarding whether the person takes the pill with a glass of water or in a dish of ice cream (i.e., *how* the individual wants to ingest the pill). Other common types of "how" choices include how to dry one's hair by using a towel or a hair dryer, how to get to work by taking a cab or the bus, and how to complete an academic assignment by writing the answers or typing them on a computer.

Providing consumers with "what" types of choices is especially appropriate during leisure times whereas "how" choices are advantageous when presenting individuals with tasks that they are expected to complete.

A somewhat less common but still important type of choice is a *"where"* choice that involves an option of where to do something. Common examples of "where" choices include whether to eat a snack at one's desk or in the break area of a classroom, to play on an iPad in the living room or bedroom, and to read on the couch or on the porch. Still another type of choice involves *when* to do something. Whether to work on a writing assignment in the morning or afternoon, to take a bath before or after supper, and to phone a friend before or after work represent "when" types of choices.

In some situations concern is warranted with offering certain individuals "when" types of choices. In particular, if a choice is offered regarding when to complete an undesired but necessary task, some consumers will always choose to do the task later rather than immediately (e.g., cleaning one's room later after lunch rather than in the morning when the choice is presented). Subsequently, when it becomes time to perform the undesired task, individuals again express a preference to perform the task at a later time. In essence, they are really attempting to avoid performing the task altogether.

If this choice-making pattern appears with a consumer, it is usually best not to provide a "when" type of choice for an undesired but necessary task. Providing repeated "when" choices in this situation can essentially promote noncompliance by the consumer. However, other types of choices associated with a specific task could be provided such as how or perhaps where to complete the task.

There is also another type of choice that can be beneficial in situations in which an undesired task must be completed—a *"with whom"* choice. A "with whom" choice involves offering a consumer a choice of with whom to do something that needs to be done. This type of choice can be of considerable importance for many adults with severe disabilities but usually is less common in human service agencies relative to the types of choices just described.

People often decide with whom they will do something, such as with whom to go to dinner, with whom to sit during a particular activity, or whom to call on the phone or send a text message. Choosing with whom to do something can significantly enhance one's happiness associated with doing a particular activity. The same effect of choosing with whom to do something exists for adults with autism and other severe disabilities. This is especially the case when individuals can choose to do something with a staff person with whom they have a good relationship.

Many experienced staff are well aware of the beneficial effect of providing a consumer a choice regarding with whom to engage in a particularly disliked activity. Performing an undesired activity with a person whom the consumer chooses and enjoys being around can make the activity much less unpleasant for the person. This type of choice can also reduce problem behavior that the consumer may display when required to engage in an undesired activity.

To illustrate, a person may seriously dislike going to the barbershop for a haircut and react with problem behavior when informed that it is time to go get a haircut. However, if the individual is provided a choice of who will accompany the trip to the barbershop, the person is less likely to display displeasure or problem behavior that is usually associated with getting a haircut. Again, this would be especially the case if the chosen person is someone with whom the individual has a good relationship.

Human service staff should be aware of the effect of providing "with whom" choices on consumer happiness. Staff should also be aware that it is basic human nature for adults with autism and other severe disabilities to like some staff more than others and correspondingly, choose to do things with certain staff more than others. If particular staff are not selected by a consumer when provided a "with whom" choice, they should not be personally offended. Again, it is just natural for adults with severe disabilities to like to do certain things with some staff more than with others, just like staff prefer to do some things with certain people relative to other individuals.

Earlier it was noted that awareness of the five basic types of choices can facilitate staffs' provision of consumer choice opportunities during typical routines in human service agencies. Providing choice opportunities is facilitated because when staff consider each type of choice, it can help them think about specific choice opportunities that they otherwise might not have considered. This is particularly the case when one type of choice is not possible, such as a choice of when to do something, but another type might be possible such as how to do a certain activity.

> **"With whom" choices can be beneficial when instructing a consumer to do something that is necessary but disliked; by choosing to do the task with a person whose presence is enjoyed by the individual, the task can become less unpleasant for the consumer to perform.**

Consideration of the five types of choices is also helpful in situations in which staff believe that consumer choice is not feasible if they are to adequately complete certain work duties. A prototypical example is with job coaches who work with supported workers who have autism or other severe disabilities. There is a somewhat prevalent view that choice is something that is not realistic in work situations because jobs have to be done in a certain way and within set time limits.

There are many aspects of various jobs that do prohibit choice. However, most people still find ways to make choices during their work time, such as how to spend their designated break or what work tasks they will complete prior to completing other tasks. There are likewise various possibilities for offering choice opportunities to supported workers with autism and other severe disabilities if the five basic types of choices are carefully considered. The case illustration on page 122 shows how different types of choices were incorporated into the job routine of a group of supported workers at a publishing company.

In the case illustration, certain job tasks had to be completed within the publishing company during the supported workers' work shift. Hence, there were limitations with the types and number of choice opportunities that could be provided to each supported worker. However, by considering the five different types of choices, the job coaches were able to provide at least one type of choice for each worker.

For example, one supported worker, Ms. Endicott, typically did not have a preference for what work task she performed but usually had a distinct preference each day regarding the job coach who worked with her. Hence, Ms. Endicott was assigned the work task that another supported worker, Mr. Gonzales, did not choose (either placing address labels on advertising fliers or tabs on fliers) to ensure that task was completed while being given a choice of job coaches to assist her. Ms. Endicott was also able to be provided with a choice of where to complete her assigned task.

Sometimes questions arise regarding whether a choice of where to do a task or how to do a task, for example, really enhances a supported workers' happiness at work. A good way to answer such questions is for readers to consider their own work situations and what it would be like if during their work day, they had absolutely no choice regarding what they worked on, when they worked on each task, precisely how they completed each task, etc. Most readers would likely find their work days would be much less enjoyable in the latter situation relative to more typical situations in which they made such choices. The same result occurs regarding reduced happiness when supported workers with disabilities have no choice opportunities while at work.

CASE ILLUSTRATION
Types of Choices Offered in A Supported Work Situation

Background: Three supported workers, who had autism or severe intellectual and physical disabilities, were employed part time at a publishing company. Their job duties consisted of clerical tasks, preparing advertising material with address labels and stamps, and preparing book mailing envelopes. Two job coaches worked with the supported workers.

Types of Choices Offered: The job coach supervisor requested the coaches to begin offering choices to the supported workers. The supervisor reviewed the five basic types of choices with each job coach and described and demonstrated ways to provide choices (all supported workers responded to a vocal choice with two specific options provided or to a two-item choice using samples of work materials). Subsequently, the following types of choices were observed being offered by the job coaches to respective workers.

Supported Worker	Type of Choice Offered
Mr. James	a "how" choice of whether to stamp return addresses on book-mailing envelopes while sitting at a work table or standing at a podium
Mr. Gonzales	a "what" choice of whether to work on placing address labels on advertising fliers or tabs on fliers (to hold folded fliers together)
Ms. Endicott	a "where" choice of whether to work in the group work room or in a private office; a "with whom" choice of whether to work with job coach Liz or job coach May

Special Considerations for Providing Choice-Making Opportunities to Promote Consumer Happiness

A basic premise throughout this chapter is that consumer happiness can be promoted in human service agencies by providing frequent choice opportunities during daily routines. Again, providing choice opportunities is one of the most well-established, evidence-based means of enhancing happiness among adults with autism and other severe disabilities. However, there are also important considerations warranting attention to maximize the likelihood that consumer choice making will result in increased happiness.

Concerns with One-Option Choices

Earlier it was noted that human service staff generally should focus on choice opportunities that provide consumers with at least two options. Providing several options associated with doing something makes it more likely an individual will choose something that is strongly desired relative to when only one option is provided. One exception in this regard is with people whose challenges are so significant that they cannot respond in a meaningful way to choice opportunities involving several options—such as with adults who have profound multiple disabilities for whom a one-item choice is often necessary.

There is another reason for the emphasis on choice opportunities involving more than one option. Sometimes certain staff will not exert the time and effort to provide consumer choice opportunities that involve two or more options. When questioned though, these staff may express that individuals do have a choice opportunity in that they can choose to do or not do something. For example, a staff member may prepare supper for several adults with severe disabilities without any choice opportunities associated with what the individuals will have to eat. Upon being questioned about the lack of any choice with the meal, the staff person might reply that of course the consumers have a choice—they can choose to eat the food or not eat it.

In the situation just described, a truly meaningful choice is not being offered to consumers. There a certain things people must do, such as eating. Purporting that individuals can choose to eat or not is not only a significant misconception about what constitutes an appropriate choice opportunity, it represents a serious lack of sincerity about a consumer's happiness and general welfare.

There are many things adults with severe disabilities in human service agencies should do for their overall well being, just as with people in general. Everybody needs to complete basic self-preservation activities such as bathing and eating. Everybody also usually benefits from having social exchanges with other people, accessing different environments relative to spending the entire day in one room, and experiencing different activities that promote their enjoyment and overall activity engagement. Failure to support consumers in these basic endeavors under the pretext of them choosing not to do such things represents very poor judgement on the part of human service staff.

In short, there are certain activities that are clearly in the best interest of adults with autism and other severe disabilities for which a choice of whether to do the activities generally should not be provided. Such activities should be determined through careful deliberation by an individual's support team (see **Chapter 9** on **Personal Goal Planning** for elaboration). However, these "nonnegotiable" activities do not have to prohibit individual choice making even though they must occur. Other types of choices as described in the previous section can be incorporated within the activities, such as how to do an activity, where or when to do it, or with whom to do the activity.

NECESSARY RESTRICTIONS WITH SOME CHOICES

A second concern that can arise when providing choice opportunities is that some consumers will make bad choices. Agency staff may be concerned that an individual may choose something that could be detrimental to the person's overall well being. To illustrate, if given a choice of what do to during leisure time, a consumer may always opt to repeatedly play the same computer game to the exclusion of all other leisure activities. Engaging in one circumscribed leisure activity can limit a person's opportunities to experience other activities that can promote enjoyment. Another individual may always choose potato fries, for example, when given a choice of what to eat. Consistently consuming only one or a small number of food items can seriously jeopardize a person's nutritional intake and general health.

In other cases, such as with open-ended choice opportunities, consumers may choose something that cannot be honored by staff. For instance, when asked where an individual would like to go for supper, the person may respond by naming a restaurant in a geographic location far away from his/her current residence. Another individual may respond to a choice of what to do on the weekend by choosing to go to a football game when there is no football game being played. In each of these cases, the staff member presenting the choice opportunity would not be able to honor the person's choice in terms of ensuring the individual accesses the chosen option.

Failure to honor choice responses can be detrimental to a consumer's subsequent choice making as described earlier. Additionally, when a person is informed that the chosen option cannot be provided, s/he may express displeasure in the form of problem behavior. Hence, when staff have good reason to believe that an individual may respond to an open-ended choice opportunity in a way that cannot be reasonably honored, then that type of choice opportunity should be restricted with the individual. Generally, "good reason" in this regard means that a person has responded to certain open-ended choice presentations in the past with choice responses that are not feasible in the existing situation.

Restriction of open-ended choice opportunities means omitting the first step of the choice-presentation protocol. The choice presentation should begin by the staff member naming several options that the consumer might desire that can be honored once chosen. In the situations noted above regarding where to go for supper and what to do on the weekend the choice presentation could be initiated by asking, for example, whether the person would like to go to one or another specific restaurant (both of which are close by) or whether the individual would like to go to a movie theater or an ice cream shop (assuming both of which could be easily accessed). In this manner, although the range of choice options is restricted, the individual is still being offered a choice.

> **Staff generally should provide open-ended choice opportunities to consumers only if the staff are reasonably sure that the individuals' likely choice responses can be honored.**

CONCERNS WITH PROVIDING TOO MANY CHOICES

Sometimes a concern exists that providing too many choice opportunities for a consumer can become unpleasant for the individual. This concern is usually based on personal experiences of staff. The staff are aware that at times, they essentially do not want to be bothered by having to make certain choices. Whether due to being very tired or overly stressed, for example, staff may simply prefer that someone else tell them what to do so they avoid having to think about various options and make decisions. In other cases, people may be reluctant to make a choice when doing something with another person. They are not sure what the latter person prefers and do not want to displease the person by choosing something that the individual dislikes.

There are certainly situations in which people do not want to make any choices. Such situations can also occur for adults with autism and other severe disabilities. However, concern over presenting consumers with too many choice opportunities such that making choice responses becomes unpleasant for them is not nearly as much of an issue as it is with most other people. As noted repeatedly, adults with severe disabilities typically have far fewer choice-making opportunities than the general populace. Hence, it is not very likely that consumers will be overburdened or otherwise displeased when presented with choice-making opportunities during daily activities.

Additionally, if a person does not want to respond to a choice presentation, such a desire will usually be apparent by the individual's action. The person will not make a choice response or perhaps attempt to move away from or otherwise avoid the staff person's choice presentation. When staff observe these types of responses to their choice presentations, they can simply discontinue their actions at that time and provide choice opportunities later. In this manner, an individual is still exerting personal control in that s/he is essentially *choosing not to make a choice*. However, staff also have to be aware of the possibility that the person does not understand the choice presentation and then respond with the steps of the choice-presentation protocol as described previously.

SPECIAL CONSIDERATIONS FOR STAFF TO EFFECTIVELY PROVIDE CHOICE OPPORTUNITIES

Many human service agencies acknowledge the importance of providing choices for the people they support and expect staff to routinely provide choice opportunities. However, proclaiming the importance of choice and the desire to provide choice opportunities for consumers of agency services is not sufficient. Agency management must actively support staff in their efforts to provide meaningful choice opportunities for people they support on a routine basis.

One area in which management support is especially important is ensuring staff have adequate time to provide individual choice-making opportunities during daily routines. Providing choice opportunities takes time on the part of staff and particularly for consumers with more significant challenges. The latter people often need two- or even one-item choice presentations to respond with a meaningful choice, which usually requires staff to implement at least several steps of the choice-presentation protocol. It is usually more time efficient for staff to forego choice presentations and do things for people they support.

Even open-ended choice presentations with individuals who have more advanced communication skills require more time for staff relative to completing an activity without a choice presentation. Many adults with severe disabilities require time to respond to the choice presentation, and may require staff assistance following the initial presentation. Although the amount of staff time is usually relatively small in these situations, it still can interfere with staff time to perform various job duties. A prime example is the morning routine when consumers are getting ready to leave their residence to go to work or a day program. Incorporating choices within the morning routine, such as providing options about what to wear, how breakfast will be prepared, or taking a bath or a shower, can extend the amount of time encompassed during the routine.

The essential point is that if agency management espouses staff provision of choice opportunities for people they support, then management must ensure staff have the necessary time with their assigned work routines to provide frequent choice opportunities. Staff should not be put in the unworkable situation of being expected to provide individual choices yet not having sufficient time to do so in light of their other performance expectations. Agency executives and supervisors must carefully review what is expected of staff and ensure sufficient time is allotted to perform priority tasks related to promoting consumer happiness—in this case, providing meaningful choice opportunities.

Another area in which management support is needed if human service staff are to provide frequent choice opportunities to individuals with severe disabilities is *staff training*. Staff must have the skills to provide consumers with choice opportunities to which they can respond in a meaningful manner. In particular, staff need to have the skills to effectively use the choice-presentation protocol highlighted throughout this chapter. In turn, staff cannot be expected to be proficient in using the protocol unless they have had opportunities to be well trained in its use. Ways of effectively training human service staff to provide choice-making opportunities to adults with autism and other severe disabilities, as well as other evidence-based means of promoting happiness, are described in **Chapter 13**.

Management personnel in human service agencies must ensure staff have sufficient time in their work routines to provide frequent choice opportunities for people they support and they are well trained to provide choice opportunities in ways that facilitate meaningful consumer choices.

A Final Note about Providing Choice-Making Opportunities: Multiple Benefits for Adults with Severe Disabilities

The focus of this chapter has been on promoting consumer choice making in human service agencies as a means of increasing their happiness on a daily basis. Providing choice-making opportunities to which individuals can respond with meaningful choices has repeatedly been shown to result in increased happiness among adults with autism and other severe disabilities. However, there are also other benefits for consumers of agency services when they are provided with frequent choice-making opportunities.

One benefit has already been alluded to—choice making can prevent and decrease consumer challenging behavior in a number of situations. This effect of providing choice-making opportunities is particularly the case when problem behavior occurs following an instruction for a consumer to perform an undesired task. Problem behavior often occurs in such situations in an attempt by individuals to avoid or escape engaging in the unwanted task. When choices are provided that are associated with doing an undesired task though, problem behavior is frequently prevented.

Problem behavior is prevented in the situation just noted because choices associated with doing an unwanted task can make the task less unpleasant for individuals to perform. Such choices may pertain to how, where, when, or with whom to do the task. By making the task less unpleasant to perform, a person's desire to avoid or escape doing the task is reduced. Correspondingly, an individual's need to engage in problem behavior is reduced or eliminated.

Another benefit of providing choice-making opportunities relates to increasing consumer engagement in habilitative and other useful activities. When a choice-making opportunity is presented to an individual that allows the person to choose what task to perform, the person is likely to work more diligently on the task relative to the individual being assigned a task with no choice involved. This effect has been repeatedly demonstrated in work situations: adults with severe disabilities usually work on chosen job tasks more diligently than on tasks assigned by agency staff.

In summary, providing choice-making opportunities that result in meaningful choice responses by adults with autism and other severe disabilities has multiple benefits. When consumers make choices during their daily routines, their happiness is often enhanced, they are less likely to display challenging behavior, and they are likely to be more engaged in desired activities. Additionally, with the few potential exceptions noted in the previous section, there are rarely any detriments of providing consumers with opportunities to make choices and have personal control over how they spend their days.

Chapter Summary: Key Points

1. *Providing choice-making opportunities during daily routines is one of the most well-established, evidence-based means of promoting happiness among adults with autism and other severe disabilities in human service agencies.*

2. *A basic protocol for providing consumer choice-making opportunities involves (1) presenting a request for a person to choose between two options, (2) honoring the choice response if one is made, (3) providing more assistance to help the individual un-*

derstand the options provided if a choice response is not made by the person and, (4) repeating the request for the individual to choose between the two options.

3. Choice-making opportunities should be provided to respective individuals in accordance with their unique challenges and skills.

4. The common ways to use the choice-presentation protocol based on individual consumer challenges and skills include providing an open-ended choice, a two-item choice, and a one-item choice.

5. Staff provision of consumer choice-making opportunities can be facilitated by considering five basic types of choices to incorporate into daily routines: what, how, where, when and with whom types of choices.

6. Special concerns when providing choice-making opportunities include potential misuse of one-option choices, restricting the options provided in some situations and in a small number of cases, whether too many choices are being provided.

7. Agency management must ensure support staff have adequate time to incorporate choice-making opportunities within daily routines and are well trained in ways to provide such opportunities that result in meaningful choices by the people they support.

8. In addition to promoting consumer happiness, frequent presentation of choice-making opportunities during daily routines in human service agencies can prevent or reduce challenging behavior and increase consumer engagement with necessary activities.

CHAPTER 8

ACCESSING PREFERENCES

A major determinant of the amount of happiness people experience on a day-to-day basis is how often they access their preferences. Accessing preferences means people have opportunities to do things they prefer. Whether involving opportunities to watch a favorite television show, spend time with a good friend, or read a desired book, for example, accessing personal preferences can significantly enhance an individual's daily happiness.

Accessing preferences is directly related to having choice-making opportunities. When a person makes a choice and that choice is honored as discussed in **Chapter 7**, the individual accesses a preference—the person chooses and then accesses the most preferred option. However, as also discussed in the preceding chapter, there are limits to how many choices an individual has opportunities to make during the day. When choice making is not possible at times, other arrangements often can be made for an individual to access preferred activities.

To illustrate, a person may have been invited to a friend's home for supper later in the week. The friend may not have been able to contact the person on the day of the supper engagement to ask what the person would like for supper. Hence, a choice opportunity is not immediately feasible in this situation. If the friend knows the person's preferred meals though, the friend can prepare a supper meal that the person typically prefers. In this manner even though an immediate choice is not available, the person still accesses a preference in terms of having a desired meal.

For adults with autism and other severe disabilities, choice making is also limited at times because of the schedule-based operations of human service agencies. Although **Chapter 7** described ways to incorporate choices within the daily operations of human service agencies, schedules that require certain activities to occur at specified times are still likely to limit consumer choices to some degree. With appropriate planning however, schedules frequently can be developed to support consumer access to preferences when immediate choice making is not feasible.

This chapter describes how individual access to preferences can be routinely provided in human service agencies to promote happiness among consumers of the agencies' services. The particular focus is on adults with severe disabilities accessing their preferences when immediate choice-making opportunities are not feasible. Just like with promoting choice making, ensuring individuals access their preferences is a well-established, evidence-based means of enhancing happiness among adults with autism and other severe disabilities.

> **Two well-established, evidence-based means of promoting happiness among adults with autism and other severe disabilities is to provide choice-making opportunities *and* to provide access to their preferences when choice making is not immediately feasible.**

Ensuring Consumers Access Their Preferences: A Two-Step Process

Ensuring adults with autism and other severe disabilities access their preferences in human service agencies is basically a two-step process. The first step involves accurately identifying the preferences of each individual person supported by an agency. The second step involves incorporating the preferred items and activities into the daily routines of each person. Each of the two steps also involves various implementation strategies, depending on the skills and challenges of each individual and the particular operations within respective agencies.

STEP 1: IDENTIFY CONSUMER PREFERENCES

Before consumers can be provided with access to their preferences in human service agencies, their individual preferences must be identified. There are two basic ways to identify preferences among adults with autism and other severe disabilities who do not readily describe their likes and dislikes. One way involves *assessing caregiver opinion*. The second way involves conducting *systematic preference assessments*.

Using Opinion to Identify Consumer Preferences. The usual means of identifying preferences among individuals whose disabilities prohibit conventional communication focuses on caregiver opinion. Agency staff and other people familiar with a consumer are queried regarding what the person prefers and does not prefer. Such a process is frequently incorporated within the development of person-centered and related support plans for adults with severe disabilities, with a listing of reported preferences in the plans that are developed.

Although reliance on caregiver opinion is the typical means of identifying likely preferences of adults with autism and other severe disabilities in human service agencies, concerns exist with this approach. The main concern is the same as relying on caregiver opinion to identify happiness indices among consumers of agency services as discussed in **Chapter 3**. Specifically, reliance on caregiver opinion is not a consistently accurate way to identify individual preferences of people who have severe disabilities.

Research has repeatedly demonstrated inaccuracies in reported preferences of people with severe disabilities based solely on caregiver opinion. However, such research has also identified ways to enhance the accuracy of caregiver opinion for determining preferences among adults with autism and other severe disabilities. These ways are the same as with enhancing caregiver accuracy in identifying indices of happiness for individuals.

The first way to enhance the accuracy of caregiver opinion of consumer preferences is to rely on the opinions of caregivers who are very familiar with a respective individual (e.g., caregivers who have worked with a person at least weekly for a minimum of six months). The second way is to obtain agreement between two caregivers in terms of the caregivers independently agreeing about specific preferences of an individual. The third way is to focus on caregiver opinion regarding the strongest preferences of individuals with severe disabilities, or what they prefer the most and least, relative to what they prefer more modestly.

Adhering to the conditions just summarized increases the likelihood that caregiver reports of individual consumer preferences will be accurate. However, even when caregivers are very familiar with a person who has a severe disability, agreement is reached between caregivers regarding reported preferences, and the focus is on the most preferred items and activities of an individual, caregiver reports of preferences will not always be accurate. A more accurate approach to identifying preferences among adults with autism and other severe disabilities is to conduct *systematic preference assessments*.

CAREGIVER OPINION OF PREFERENCES AMONG ADULTS WITH AUTISM AND OTHER SEVERE DISABILITIES IS USUALLY MOST ACCURATE IF:

1. **Caregivers are very familiar with an individual.**

2. **Agreement about a reported preference is obtained between two caregivers.**

3. **The focus is on an individual's strongest preferences relative to more modest preferences.**

Using Systematic Preference Assessments to Identify Consumer Preferences. Systematic preference assessments represent a well-developed, evidence-based technology for accurately identifying the likes and dislikes of adults with autism and other severe disabilities. The technology is based on a very considerable amount of applied research. Such research has resulted in a number of tried and tested means of determining individual preferences for a wide variety of items and activities.

Each type of systematic preference assessment has its relative advantages and disadvantages as well as its degree of applicability based on the skills and challenges of individual consumers. It is beyond the scope of this text to thoroughly describe each type of preference assessment and the respective procedures necessary to conduct each type. However, a basic protocol underlying essentially all evidence-based, systematic preference assessment approaches will be presented.

Additionally, the most common types of systematic preference assessments that are advantageous for adults with autism and other severe disabilities will be summarized. More in-depth information on how to conduct various types of preference assessments is available in the **Systematic Preference Assessment** section of the **Selected Readings** at the end of this text.

Systematic preference assessments consist of providing a person with repeated choice-making opportunities involving a selected number of items or activities. As with providing two-option and one-option choice opportunities described in the preceding chapter, visual referents to the options are presented for individual choice. The referents are usually items with which an individual can choose to engage or that represent activities in which the items are used.

For individuals with more advanced skills, visual referents used when providing repeated choice-making opportunities can involve pictures or printed material. However, because actual items typically are used in preference assessments, the most common assessment processes will be described in terms of involving specific items. The same processes to be presented are essentially the same though when using pictures or printed material as the visual referents.

Following each choice-making presentation within a preference assessment, a recording is made to indicate what item the person chose. After each item has been provided repeatedly within choice-making opportunities, then a determination is made regarding on what percentage of all opportunities a specific item was chosen. Subsequently, the percentage of opportunities a given item was chosen is compared across the choices for all items.

Generally, if an item has been chosen by an individual on 70% or more of all choice-making opportunities involving that item, then the item represents a strong preference or something that is highly preferred. Items that are chosen less than 30% of the opportunities (or with some preference assessment procedures, less than 25%) are nonpreferred by the person. Items chosen between 30% and 70% of the opportunities on average represent preferences that are more moderate, ranging from minimally to mildly preferred items.

Because systematic preference assessments involve providing repeated choice-making opportunities, the particular assessment process used with each person with a disability should be based on the individual's existing choice-making skills as described in the previous chapter. Hence, there are three primary formats for conducting systematic preference assessments that generally correspond to the three basic types of choice-making skills discussed in **Chapter 7**. These formats pertain to offering individuals choice-making opportunities that involve multiple options, two options, and one-option choices.

The *multiple-option preference assessment* (also referred to as a *multi-item preference assessment*) is one of the most useful and practical means of assessing preferences among adults with severe disabilities. Typically three or four items are presented for individual choice in a series of assessment sessions. Initially, the items are placed in front of the person with an instruction for him/her to choose a desired item. If the person does not choose an item, which happens relatively infrequently, then more assistance is provided to help the individual understand the available options (see **Chapter 7** for providing assistance following lack of a choice response to a choice opportunity).

When the person chooses an item, a few minutes are provided for the individual to engage with the item or in the activity represented by the item. Next, that item is removed. The process just described is then repeated with the remaining items that were not chosen on the first choice opportunity. This entire process is repeated until there are only two items left (that were not previously chosen on any choice opportunity), from which the person chooses one of the items and is provided with time to engage with that item.

The entire process of (1) providing several items for choice, (2) allowing individual access to the chosen item, (3) removing the item that was chosen and (4) repeating the process until there are no longer two items to present that have not been chosen previously represents one assessment session. Additional sessions are then conducted at different times during the day or week until at least three sessions have been completed (usually a maximum of five sessions).

Next, the items are ranked based on the percentage of opportunities the person had to choose each item for which the individual actually chose the item. Again, those items chosen on 70% or more of the opportunities are the most highly preferred items relative to all other items presented. An example of a multiple-option preference assessment is provided in the case illustration on page 141.

A notable advantage of the multiple-option preference assessment is that it allows for a ranking of an individual's preference for each item assessed. The person has multiple opportunities to choose each item such that a selection percentage can be obtained for each item presented. This type of preference assessment also often requires less time to conduct relative to other assessment processes.

For some adults with severe disabilities, the multiple-option format for assessing preferences appears too complex. Sometimes the presence of three or four items is overwhelming or confusing for certain consumers. The individuals seem to experience difficulty focusing on each item presented and comparing each item in order to select the most desired one. For these people, a *two-option preference assessment* is likely to be more useful. This type of preference assessment is also sometimes referred to as a *two-item* or a *paired-item* assessment.

The two-option assessment process involves the following steps. First, several items are selected for the assessment. Second, one item is arbitrarily identified by the assessor as the target item. The target item is then presented with one of the other items (also arbitrarily selected) in a two-option choice opportunity as described in **Chapter 7**. Third, when the person chooses an item, the nonchosen item is removed and a few minutes are allowed for the individual to engage with the chosen item.

The fourth step involves presenting the chosen item with one of the items not previously presented with the former item for another two-option choice opportunity. The third step described above is then repeated. Fifth, the entire process is then repeated until the target item referred to in the first step has been offered within a two-option choice opportunity with each of the other items. Next, another item is arbitrarily selected as the target item and the entire process is repeated with that item. This process continues until each item has been presented in a two-option format with each of the other items. At that point, one assessment session has been conducted. At least two more assessment sessions are then conducted.

CASE ILLUSTRATION
CONDUCTING A MULTIPLE-OPTION PREFERENCE ASSESSMENT

Background: Mr. Jenkins, a gentleman with autism who did not speak, was about to assume new duties as part of his supported job at a publishing company. The job routine at the company involved a company supervisor establishing a work schedule each week based on the tasks that needed to be completed. A pre-work assessment was conducted to determine which of three tasks Mr. Jenkins preferred so that when the schedule was established, he could be assigned the task that he preferred the most relative to the other tasks.

Preference assessment: To provide Mr. Jenkins with familiarity of the tasks that would need to be performed, he was initially assisted in completing each task by his job coach. Next, materials representing each task (advertising fliers and tabs representing the job of putting tabs on the fliers when folded, stamps and book mailing envelopes representing the job of putting the stamps on the envelopes, and books and envelopes representing the job of putting a book in each envelope) were laid out on a table. Mr. Jenkins was then instructed to choose the materials for doing one of the tasks. Following his choice (he always made a choice response), he was assisted by his coach in performing the chosen task for three minutes. Next, the materials representing the two remaining tasks were presented for a choice in the same manner. Following three minutes of working on the task that was chosen on the second opportunity, the first assessment session was completed. Two more sessions were conducted on two days for a total of three sessions.

Results: Mr. Jenkins chose the task of putting tabs on fliers on 100% of the opportunities to choose that task, putting stamps on envelopes on 50% of the opportunities to choose that task, and he never chose the task of putting books in mailing envelopes. Hence, putting tabs on fliers represented his most preferred task and putting books in envelopes was his least preferred task. Putting stamps on envelopes represented his moderately preferred task. Subsequently, when the company supervisor prepared the schedule for the week, she could assign Mr. Jenkins his preferred task of putting tabs on advertising fliers whenever possible.

Following completion of all assessment sessions, the items are ranked based on the percentage of times each item was chosen across all times the item was presented in a two-option format for a possible choice. The item (or items) chosen for the highest percentage of opportunities represents the strongest preference and the item(s) chosen for the smallest percentage, or not chosen at all, represent a nonpreferred item. Items chosen some of the time but not as much as the item(s) chosen most frequently yet more often than the least frequently chosen item(s) represent moderate preferences. The case illustration on the following page demonstrates how a two-option preference assessment is conducted.

The primary advantage of the two-option assessment format is that it can be easier for some people with severe disabilities than the multiple-option format as referred to earlier. Additionally, in some situations there may only be two possible options for an individual's forthcoming activity, such that the multiple-option format is irrelevant. A main disadvantage is that the process is usually more time consuming to conduct relative to the multiple-option format. This is especially the case if there are many items to be assessed.

Most adults with autism and other severe disabilities usually respond to a multiple-option or two-option preference assessment. However, for a small percentage of individuals, these formats for assessing their preferences appear too complex. Usually people who have difficulty responding to multiple- and two-option preference assessments in a manner to accurately identify their preferences have profound multiple disabilities.

As discussed in the preceding chapter, adults with profound multiple disabilities have many challenges. They have profound intellectual and physical disabilities that generally prohibit speech and many independent body movements. For these individuals, choice opportunities typically must be presented in a one-option format as also discussed in **Chapter 7.**

CASE ILLUSTRATION
CONDUCTING A TWO-OPTION PREFERENCE ASSESSMENT

Background: Ms. West, a woman with severe intellectual disabilities who was nonvocal, was beginning a supported job in a multi-service agency as part of a work crew. The crew was formed to complete a variety of tasks in the agency. A pre-work assessment was conducted to identify which of the tasks that were expected to be performed was most preferred by Ms. West.

Preference assessment: Initially, a job coach assisted Ms. West in working for a few minutes on each of three tasks to provide her with familiarity with the tasks and work materials. Materials representing two of the three work tasks (paper and a shredder for shredding paper, a water bottle for watering plans, and a container of potting soil to put the soil in plant pots) were then presented for Ms. West to choose one of the items (she consistently pointed to make a choice response). When she chose a task, she was assisted by her job coach in working on the chosen task for three minutes. Next, the task chosen by Ms. West was then paired with the task that was not presented in the initial two-option choice opportunity for Ms. West's next choice and subsequent three-minute work period. This process continued until each of the three tasks had been paired with each other one time in a two-option format, at which point one assessment session was completed. Two more assessment sessions were then conducted on two separate days.

Results: Ms. West chose to water plants on 100% of the times that task was paired with the other two tasks in a two-option choice format. She chose to shred paper on 33% of the times that task was paired with the other tasks, and putting soil in plant pots on 17% of the opportunities to choose that task. Hence, watering plants represented her most preferred task, putting soil in pots her least preferred task, and shredding paper a moderately preferred task. Subsequently, when establishing a work schedule for the entire work crew, efforts could be made to assign Ms. West to work on her preferred task of watering plants.

To review briefly, a one-option choice opportunity involves presenting one item or activity at a time and observing to see if an individual approaches, avoids, or does not respond to what is presented. An approach response indicates a desire for what is presented and an avoidance response indicates the person does not desire what is presented. A lack of approach and avoidance responses indicates neither interest nor disinterest in what is presented, or a lack of understanding that a choice is being presented.

Adults with profound multiple disabilities for whom a one-option choice is the most effective way to provide choice opportunities usually require a *one-option preference assessment* to determine their likes and dislikes. As with the other preference assessment formats, a one-option assessment involves repeated presentations of choices – in this case, one-option choices. One-option preference assessments involving a number of items are more time consuming to conduct relative to the other preference assessment formats. Nonetheless, this type of assessment generally represents the most evidence-based means of determining preferences among this consumer population.

A one-option preference assessment is initiated by determining what items or activities (assessed by using items that are involved in the activities) will be assessed for a person's relative likes and dislikes. The most common application of this type of preference assessment pertains to identifying leisure items with which a consumer would like to engage. Often, the items initially selected for assessment cover a range of sensory experiences. For example, a hand-held vibrator and a small fan might be assessed to identify desired tactile stimulation, different songs might be assessed for preferred auditory stimulation, and various items with different lighting features might be assessed for enjoyable visual stimulation.

The usual preference assessment format involves assessing a dozen or so items, again representing different types of sensations. The number of items to be assessed are usually divided into groups of three, with each item in the group providing a different type of sensation (e.g., a group consisting of a song on an iPod for auditory sensation, a light board for visual sensation, and a soft mitt rubbed on a person's arm for tactile sensation). Each subsequent group of items also involves different types of sensation (e.g., a different song, a switch-activated light mechanism, a hand-held vibrator).

Once the total set of items to be assessed is determined and the items are arranged in groups of three, one group of items is arbitrarily selected for assessment. One item from the group is presented in a one-option choice as described in **Chapter 7** and the individual's response to the item is recorded as approach, avoidance, or neutral. After a few minutes, during which the person is provided access to the item if it was initially approached, a second item is presented in a one-option choice. This process is then repeated for the third item.

When each of the three items in one group has been presented, the next group of three items is presented at a later time. This process continues until each group of three items as been presented for assessment. At this point, one assessment session is completed. At least two more assessment sessions are then conducted at later times (usually a maximum of four more assessment sessions) to complete the presentation of items.

After all items have been repeatedly assessed for a person's approach, avoidance, and neutral responses as just described, then the percentage of times that each presented item was followed by an approach response is determined. The items are then ranked according to their respective percentages of approach responses they evoked. The items with the highest percentage of approach responses represent the most preferred items and those with the lowest percentage represent the least preferred. Items that were followed by avoidance responses represent nonpreferred items. Use of a one-option preference assessment is demonstrated in the case illustration on the following page.

CASE ILLUSTRATION
CONDUCTING A ONE-OPTION PREFERENCE ASSESSMENT

Background: Ms. Valdez, a woman with profound multiple disabilities including profound intellectual and physical challenges, attended an adult education program. It was desired to accurately identify items that Ms. Valdez strongly preferred that could be provided to her during break periods or leisure time.

Preference assessment: Twelve items were selected to be assessed that involved a range of sensory experiences (e.g., a vibrator for tactile stimulation, a light board for visual stimulation, pudding for taste stimulation). The items were divided into four groups of three. The items in one group were first assessed. Initially, each item was presented and Ms. Valdez was prompted to touch, taste, or look at the item to provide her with familiarity with each item. Next, one item was presented and Ms. Valdez's approach, avoidance, or neutral response to the item was recorded. Following brief access to the item if it was approached (or removal of the item if it was not approached), a second item was presented and the process continued, subsequently followed by the same process with the third item. The entire process was then repeated at separate time intervals with the three remaining groups. At that point one assessment session was completed. The entire process was then repeated for four more assessment sessions.

Results: Ms. Valdez approached two items (hand-held leisure item and pudding) on more than 80% of the presentations, which represented her most strongly preferred items. She approached a mechanically operated leisure item, a light board, and a vibrator between 30% and 70% of the presentations, which represented moderate preferences. All other items, approached less than 30% of the presentations or not at all, represented nonpreferred items. Subsequently, Ms. Valdez could be provided with her most strongly preferred items for her leisure pleasure.

In discussing multiple- and two-option preference assessments it was noted that items chosen on 70% or more of the choice opportunities represent very strong preferences of an individual. Conversely, those items chosen on 30% or less of the choice presentations represent nonpreferred items. The same criteria for determining strongly preferred and nonpreferred items pertain to one-option preference assessments. However, there is also a special consideration associated with one-option assessments conducted with adults who have profound multiple disabilities.

The special consideration pertains to an outcome discussed in the preceding chapter that often occurs when providing one-option choices for people with profound multiple disabilities. Specifically, in many cases these individuals will not approach items that are presented, even when provided increased assistance to become familiar with a given item following the initial choice presentation. Consequently, situations arise in which an individual will not approach any item on 70% or more of the presentations.

When the latter outcome occurs, the criterion for identifying a strong preference for an individual will not be met. Several subsequent action steps could be taken in this situation. The first step is to select additional items for the preference assessment and continue to do so until a strong preference for at least one item is identified.

A second action step involves reviewing the approach responses to all items even though no item was approached on 70% or more of the presentations. Items could be selected that were approached on at least some of the presentations. Those items would still be more preferred than items that were not approached at all and could subsequently be used to help an individual access something desired – though not strongly desired.

The action step just summarized allows agency staff to provide consumers with something with which to engage that they prefer more than anything else at a given point in time. In this manner, the individual is likely to experience some happiness when the item is presented, although not as much happiness relative to if a strongly desired item is identified. One caveat with this process is that items presented that were approached some but not consistently should be considered as being preferred only if they were never avoided during the preference assessment. Items that are sometimes approached and sometimes avoided rarely represent strong preferences among adults with profound multiple disabilities.

STEP 2: INCORPORATE ACCESS TO PREFERENCES DURING DAILY ROUTINES

Once an individual's preferences have been identified, the next step for providing access to preferences as a means of promoting happiness is to incorporate such access into the person's daily routine. As discussed in the introductory comments to this chapter, people enjoy their day more when they frequently access things they prefer. When the daily routines of human service agencies are designed to ensure consumers readily access their preferences, they are likely to experience happiness on a day-to-day basis.

Before discussing ways to enhance individual access to preferences, the relationship between accessing preferences and choice making warrants review. The best way to ensure adults with severe disabilities access their preferences is to offer them choice-making opportunities during daily routines. The focus here is on providing access to preferences when providing choice-making opportunities is not immediately feasible. However, it should be emphasized that the ways to promote individual access to preferences to be discussed should be considered *in conjunction with* providing choice-making opportunities; the different ways of promoting access to preferences should not be considered *in lieu of* providing choice-making opportunities.

Consider Access to Preferences when Preparing Activity Schedules. Most human service agencies prepare schedules regarding forthcoming activities of the people they support. Sometimes when preparing activity schedules it is apparent that a choice would not be feasible with a particular activity when that activity is scheduled to occur. In such a situation staff should consider the preferences of the individuals to be involved and attempt to initially select activities to be scheduled in accordance with those preferences.

To illustrate, often in residential settings a monthly schedule is established at the beginning of the month regarding leisure outings that may occur on the weekends for that month. For some of the possible outings, it may not be practical to provide consumers with choices regarding what outing they prefer on the day of the outing because advance reservations may have to be made, transportation has to be secured, etc. However, when initially scheduling outings for the month staff can consider individual preferences and incorporate those preferences in decisions regarding what outings will take place. This process can maximize the likelihood that respective individuals will truly enjoy the outings.

The process just described may appear to be essentially stating something that is obvious. That is, why would leisure outings be selected unless consumers are likely to enjoy the outings? Such reasoning is not always reflected in common practice though.

In some agencies, outings are based more on staff preferences than what the people they support prefer. In other situations outings are planned based on what is easy for staff to do or simply on tradition in terms of planning something that essentially has always occurred. The latter situations represent why consumers in some residential agencies almost always going bowling or to the mall, for example, on weekends—going bowling or to the mall are simply what has always constituted consumer outings in those agencies.

There is also another reason why consumer preferences are not appropriately considered when planning recreational outings and related events that relates to the specific focus of this chapter: agency personnel have not carried out necessary procedures to accurately identify individual preferences associated with the activities. In particular, systematic preference assessments have not been conducted. Consequently, determining what activities would be most enjoyable for consumers is little more than guess work, and guesses frequently are not very accurate.

Consideration of individual preferences should also be incorporated into schedules pertaining to activities that occur more frequently than monthly, such as weekly or daily. For example, a staff member may report to work on the afternoon shift in a group home and be scheduled to prepare supper for the people who live in the home. Because the individuals are not present in the home at that time due to their work or involvement in an adult day program, the staff member would not be able to offer choices regarding what they would like for supper. However, if the staff member was aware of the consumers' previously identified supper preferences, the staff person could prepare the meal in accordance with what they would likely enjoy.

> **Staff preparation of schedules regarding forthcoming consumer activities should incorporate individual preferences for respective activities.**

Consider Preferences When an Undesired Activity is Necessary. Sometimes consumer participation in an activity that is not part of a previously established schedule is necessary even though it is known that the activity is seriously disliked by an individual. To illustrate, an announcement may be made in an adult education program that there will be an all-student activity that afternoon for various purposes. Staff in the adult education program may be aware that a respective individual dislikes being in a room with large numbers of people present, and especially when such an event occurs unexpectedly.

In this situation it may not be possible to allow a person to choose not to attend the activity because it is mandated for all individuals, or because supervision cannot be arranged for the person to be somewhere else during the activity. One means of making this as well as other disliked activities more pleasant for the individual is to pair something the person strongly prefers with the undesired activity (see **Chapters 10** and **11** for elaboration). Hence, when the announcement for the activity occurs, staff could consider the individual's preferences and arrange for access to something highly preferred during the group activity.

For example, the person may have developed a very good relationship with someone in the adult education program (refer to **Chapter 6** on **Establishing Good Relationships**). Staff could arrange for the favorite staff member to accompany the individual to the activity and sit with him/her. Alternatively, results of a previous preference assessment may have indicated that the individual strongly prefers looking at a specific picture book or playing on a hand-held digital device. Arrangements could be made to provide the person with access to the book or device during the activity (assuming that looking at the book or playing with the device would be acceptable behavior during the group activity).

Activities that adults with severe disabilities dislike can be made less unpleasant for them by incorporating their preferences into the activities.

Routinely Review Consumer Access to Preferences. Often activities must occur in human service agencies to provide necessary supports and services that respective consumers do not like. Such activities may include, for example, certain instructional programs, house-hold chores, and various work tasks. To promote individual happiness during daily routines that involve nonpreferred activities, more preferred activities can be interspersed among the disliked activities. The daily schedules and routines within human service agencies should be reviewed on a regular basis to ensure individuals frequently access their preferences even if activities are necessary that they do not enjoy.

One of the best ways to determine if consumers of agency services are routinely accessing preferred items and events is to directly observe for indices of individual happiness. If consumers are frequently displaying happiness indices during daily routines, then they likely have ample opportunities to do things they prefer and enjoy. In contrast, if indices of happiness are not observed very often, or indices of *unhappiness* are apparent on a regular basis, then they probably are not accessing their preferences sufficiently. In the latter case, agency staff should re-evaluate daily routines and make necessary changes to more readily incorporate individual preferences into the routines.

To illustrate, agency staff and particularly supervisors should periodically walk through a setting in which a group of adults with severe disabilities is regularly present (e.g., a classroom, work room, living room). During the walk through, special attention should be directed to observing whether many individuals are smiling or laughing, or displaying any other previously validated indices of happiness. If happiness indices are rarely or never observed across several observations, then it is likely individual access to preferences is seriously limited. This process is especially relevant during leisure times, as those are times when people are most expected to be experiencing enjoyment and happiness.

The highest quality human service agencies are characterized by the people they support frequently displaying happiness indices, along with documented occurrence of other desired outcomes. Incorporating frequent access to individual preferences is one means through which agencies can help accomplish the goal of providing high quality supports and services. As stressed in the opening comments to this text, providing consumers of agency services with a desirable quality of life is a primary mission of human service agencies, and life quality is directly related to individuals experiencing happiness on a day-to-day basis.

> **A good indicator that human service agencies effectively promote consumer access to preferences is frequent observations of indices of happiness among individuals during daily activities.**

SPECIAL NOTE: THE RELATIONSHIP BETWEEN CONSUMER ACCESS TO PREFERENCES AND STEREOTYPIC BEHAVIOR

A number of adults with autism and other severe disabilities, and particularly individuals with autism on the severe end of the spectrum of autism disorders, engage in *stereotypic behavior* or *stereotypy*. Stereotypy is represented by repetitious body movements that serve no apparent purpose. Common examples include body rocking, finger flipping, hair twirling, and hand flapping, to name a few. There is considerable controversy regarding why adults with autism and other severe disabilities engage in this type of seemingly nonpurposeful, repetitive behavior.

Despite controversy regarding why various people display stereotypic behavior, one thing is clear: frequent stereotypic behavior is likely to be harmful to the overall well being of individuals. High frequencies of stereotypy interfere with learning useful skills and participating in important activities of daily living. Stereotypic behavior is also socially stigmatizing for adults with autism and other severe disabilities. Additionally, in extreme cases stereotypic behavior is related to the development of self-injurious behavior.

Stereotypic behavior is noted here because the occurrence of such behavior can present a dilemma for agency staff in regard to promoting individual access to preferences. The dilemma is that for some individuals, stereotypy appears to be a highly preferred activity despite the noted detriments of frequent stereotypic behavior. Given that promoting individual access to preferences is a recognized means of enhancing happiness, questions sometimes arise regarding whether providing uninterrupted time for adults with severe disabilities to engage in stereotypy is a way to enhance their happiness.

There is a well-established, evidence-based approach to resolving the dilemma associated with stereotypic behavior and individual access to preferences. The approach begins with recognizing that when a person engages in frequent stereotypic behavior, there is *something wrong with the person's environment*. Specifically, the environment within a human service agency is not effectively promoting engagement in desirable activities that in essence compete with stereotypy. Whereas frequent observations of happiness indices among consumers of agency services is a characteristic of high quality human service agencies, frequent observations of stereotypic behavior is indicative of problematic agency environments.

If stereotypic behavior is occurring often, then agency staff are not sufficiently supporting individual access to more appropriate, preferred activities. When preferred activities (other than stereotypy) are accurately identified through systematic preference assessments, then individual engagement in those activities can be promoted easier than promoting engagement in activities that have not been documented as preferred (see discussion in **Chapter 7** regarding the beneficial effect of preferred activities for enhancing engagement). In turn, engagement in preferred activities reduces stereotypic behavior because in essence, individuals are doing something else that is preferred.

In short, if preferred activities are accurately identified and then individual access to those activities is promoted, serious concerns over frequent stereotypic behavior are typically resolved. This is another reason for conducting systematic preference assessments with each individual as described in this chapter. Systematic preference assessments are the most well-established, evidence-based means of accurately identifying preferences among adults with autism and other severe disabilities. Providing frequent consumer access to identified preferences not only promotes their happiness, but also enhances their engagement in activities that are much more beneficial for their overall well being relative to engaging in stereotypy.

Accurately identifying individual preferences is also critical in regard to a common intervention strategy for reducing stereotypic behavior. When a person is observed engaging in stereotypy, staff often intervene to interrupt the person's behavior and re-direct the individual to a more beneficial activity. However, unless the latter activity is something that is highly preferred by the person, it is unlikely the individual will engage in that activity relative to resuming the stereotypy. Hence, it is critical that staff be aware of strongly preferred activities of individuals and have those activities readily available to which they can be re-directed if stereotypy does occur.

> **Stereotypic behavior among adults with severe disabilities is not likely to be a problematic issue if they are effectively supported in accessing preferred activities identified through systematic preference assessments.**

Again though, the best way to resolve concerns with stereotypic behavior is to consider it an indication that a consumer's environment is not sufficiently engaging or preferred. The environment should be developed and maintained in a manner that promotes individual access to accurately identified preferences frequently during the day. When human service agencies provide such environments, stereotypy will not have to be interrupted and re-directed very often.

Chapter Summary: Key Points

1. *Just like providing adults who have severe disabilities with choice-making opportunities, promoting their access to preferences is a well-established, evidence-based means of enhancing their happiness in human service agencies.*

2. *Ensuring individuals regularly access their preferences in human service agencies is a two-step process: (1) accurately identifying individual preferences and, (2) incorporating access to preferences within daily routines.*

3. *Preferences of adults with autism and other severe disabilities can be identified through caregiver opinion and systematic preference assessments, with the latter approach generally resulting in more accurate preference identification.*

4. The accuracy of caregiver opinion of individual preferences of the people they support is usually enhanced if: (1) caregivers are very familiar with respective individuals, (2) there is agreement between two familiar caregivers regarding an identified preference, and (3) the focus is on what individuals prefer the most and least relative to more moderate preferences.

5. Systematic preference assessments typically involve: (1) providing repeated choice-making opportunities for different items and activities for an individual, (2) determining on what percentage of opportunities a person chooses each item or activity, and (3) comparing the items and activities based on the relative percentage of opportunities during which each one was chosen. Items and activities chosen with the highest percentage are most preferred and those chosen with the lowest percentage are least preferred or nonpreferred.

6. There are three most common types of preference assessment formats applicable for adults with autism and other severe disabilities depending on a given individual's choice-making skills: (1) a multiple-option preference assessment, (2) a two-option preference assessment and, (3) a one-option assessment.

7. Schedules developed regarding forthcoming consumer activities in human service agencies should incorporate their preferences for respective activities as much as possible.

8. Daily routines in human service agencies that involve necessary but disliked activities by consumers can be made more enjoyable for individuals by interspersing their preferred activities among the disliked activities.

9. A good indicator that consumers of agency services are sufficiently accessing their preferences during daily routines is frequent observations of their indices of happiness.

10. *Concerns over frequent engagement of some adults with severe disabilities in stereotypic behavior usually can be resolved by ensuring they regularly access systematically identified, preferred activities.*

CHAPTER 9

Personal Goal Planning

Throughout preceding chapters the focus has been on ways to promote individual happiness during daily activities. The emphasis has been on what human service staff can do every day to enhance happiness among adults with autism and other severe disabilities as they go about their usual routines. A less frequent but equally important means of promoting happiness that has been noted only briefly to this point pertains to making *major lifestyle changes.*

There are times in the lives of everybody when decisions are made that result in major lifestyle changes. People make decisions, for example, that determine with whom they will live, where they will live, what career options to pursue, and when to change careers or jobs. Such decisions usually have profound implications for the amount of happiness people experience once the corresponding change in their lifestyle occurs. The same effect on individual happiness can result when adults with autism and other severe disabilities experience major lifestyle changes.

There are also major changes people may experience in their lifestyle over which they essentially have no control or decision-making opportunities. These types of lifestyle changes may involve the unexpected loss of a job, sudden inheritance of wealth, or a major health crisis. Because these types of changes usually are not planned for prior to their occurrence, they are not the primary concern here—though their impact on personal happiness can be dramatic. Rather, the focus is on major lifestyle changes that people plan for in a deliberate manner.

The effect of intentional lifestyle changes on individual happiness can take several forms. On a most basic level, one of three outcomes will result. First and most desirably, happiness will increase as a function of the change. Second, the change in lifestyle will have minimal or no effect on one's daily happiness. Third and least desirably, the change will decrease a person's happiness.

Because of the different effects of major lifestyle changes on a person's happiness, people usually give serious consideration before deciding to make these types of changes. Serious planning is likewise critical when considering lifestyle changes affecting people with disabilities supported by human service agencies. This chapter describes how major lifestyle changes for adults with autism and other severe disabilities can be planned in a manner to maximize the likelihood the changes will enhance their future happiness.

The process for making lifestyle changes for consumers in human service agencies is usually incorporated into the development and implementation of individual treatment plans. Essentially every human service agency for adults with severe disabilities develops treatment plans for each individual such as *Individual Support Plans, Individual Program Plans,* or *Individual Habilitation Plans.* The plans are intended to function as a template for providing supports and services to respective individuals, including those that involve significant changes in a person's lifestyle.

> **Major lifestyle changes for adults with autism and other severe disabilities should be planned in a manner that maximizes the likelihood the changes will enhance their future happiness.**

Preparing for Major Lifestyle Changes: Person-Centered Planning

An approach to developing treatment plans that readily lends itself to planning lifestyle changes for promoting future happiness of an adult with autism or other severe disability is *person-centered planning*. Person-centered planning is a value-based approach for thinking about, communicating with, assessing, planning for, and supporting people with disabilities. Most person-centered planning models involve assessment and planning tools along with strategies for designing and implementing the plans. Thus, *person-centered* applies to both the form and content of assessment and planning as well as to the strategies used to implement support plans.

There are a number of ways to conduct person-centered planning in human service agencies. These include Essential Lifestyle Planning, Group Action Planning, Individual Service Design, Lifestyle Planning, MAPS, PATH, Personal Futures Planning, and the PICTURE Method. The **Person-Centered Planning** section of the **Selected Readings** at the end of this text provides references to articles and books that provide detailed information about these and other approaches to person-centered planning.

The various approaches to person-centered planning involve somewhat different procedures. However, a commonality exists across all of the approaches that is particularly relevant in regard to planning major lifestyle changes for adults with autism and other severe disabilities. From the perspective of maximizing the likelihood that such changes will increase their future happiness, the commonality essentially involves achieving two goals.

The first goal is to identify what a person with a severe disability desires in regard to a major lifestyle change. For example, it may be determined that an individual desires to move from a center-based living arrangement to a supported-living apartment or to access a day support program that involves outdoor activities. In other cases it may be determined that an older person desires to retire from work.

The second goal is to identify and implement action steps to enable a person with a severe disability to achieve the designated lifestyle change. The actions steps can be numerous and varied, such as developing and carrying out teaching programs to help an individual acquire skills necessary to live in a less supervised setting. Alternatively, the action steps may be less involved such as deciding a person will stay at home during the day to begin a retirement lifestyle versus going to work each week day.

The primary concern at this point is with the first goal underlying person-centered planning—that of determining what an adult with autism or other severe disability desires in regard to a major lifestyle change. Unless that goal is initially achieved, subsequent aspects of person-centered planning will likely have no effect on enhancing future happiness. Additionally, common problems with successfully carrying out person-centered planning often relate to achieving the initial goal.

There are several problematic issues warranting attention to ensure lifestyle changes identified through person-centered planning will truly result in increased happiness for a person with a severe disability. The issues of concern generally fall in one of two related categories. First, questions exist over the evidence base underlying person-centered planning procedures. Second, there are often inconsistencies in how person-centered planning procedures are carried out relative to the manner in which they are intended to be implemented.

The first issue, that of questions about the evidence base underlying person-centered planning, is of particular concern in regard to accurately identifying preferences of adults with autism and other severe disabilities. Person-centered planning begins with identifying the hopes, dreams, and desires of an individual an agency supports. That is, the process starts by identifying an individual's *preferences*. Of special concern here is determining a specific preference regarding something that requires a major lifestyle change. Unless that preference is accurately identified, then the whole planning process will be seriously undermined.

> **Personal goal planning for a major lifestyle change cannot be successful unless a person's preference for a change is accurately identified.**

Ensuring Person-Centered Planning Accurately Identifies Individual Preferences

When considering a major change in the life of an adult with a severe disability, person-centered planning involves a consensus-building process by a support team regarding what the person desires. The team is comprised of the consumer, the individual's family members, and close friends of the individual. Agency staff who have a close relationship with the person also are usually involved. The involvement of agency staff is particularly necessary for adults who have severe disabilities because in a number of cases, family members of adult consumers of agency services are not actively involved in their lives. Family members may be deceased or over time have lost contact with an individual who no longer lives with them.

Regardless of who constitutes the support team, the most important member of the team is always the person with a disability. In short, the essence of person-centered planning for promoting future happiness is to focus and act on what the *consumer* desires. As indicated in previous chapters though, adults with autism and other severe disabilities often experience considerable difficulty expressing their preferences. Consequently, the process for determining what a consumer desires often relies heavily on the opinions of other team members. Using a variety of strategies depending on the particular model of person-centered planning that is applied, a consensus is formed among the latter team members regarding what the individual desires.

Although the process just noted is common in person-centered planning, there is a serious concern with the degree to which the process *accurately identifies the desires or preferences of the person with a disability* regarding the lifestyle change being considered. Specifically, caregivers and other people who know an adult with autism or other severe disability are not always accurate in their opinions regarding the individual's preferences (see **Chapter 8** for elaboration). In this regard, although evaluative research on person-centered planning is relatively limited, investigations that have been reported indicate the process is not consistently accurate for identifying preferences of adults who have autism and other severe disabilities.

As just emphasized, person-centered planning cannot be successful if a given preference of a consumer regarding a potential lifestyle change is not identified accurately during the initial stages of the process. Hence, when an individual has difficulty expressing a certain desire or preference, special attention must be directed to enhancing the accuracy of the opinions of the other support team members regarding the person's desire. **Chapter 8** noted three conditions that can enhance such accuracy.

To review briefly, the accuracy of caregiver opinion for identifying preferences of adults with autism and other severe disabilities can be enhanced if: (1) the caregivers are very familiar with the individual, (2) agreement is reached among caregivers regarding the identified preference, and (3) the focus is on what the person prefers the most relative to more moderate preferences. When person-centered planning is carried out appropriately, these conditions are usually met. Because person-centered planning teams include friends, agency staff who are close to the consumer, and family members when possible, these people are very familiar with a consumer. Also, the process involves forming a consensus regarding the individual's desires which requires team member agreement. Finally, the process usually focuses on what the person wants the most, or his/her strongest preference.

Even when the conditions just noted are met, however, caregiver identification of the preferences of adults with autism and other severe disabilities is not always accurate (again, see **Chapter 8** for elaboration). Consequently, other steps are necessary to enhance the likelihood that the person-centered process initially identifies what an adult with a severe disability desires regarding a possible lifestyle change. The process begins with the support team's consensus concerning the individual's likely desire, but should not end at that point. The identified preference should be *validated*.

The most apparent validation process is to allow the consumer to choose what change will occur by presenting various options to the person that include the option identified as preferred by the support team. **Chapter 7** described different ways that choice opportunities can be presented to adults with autism and other severe disabilities that result in a meaningful choice by respective individuals. However, the evidence-based ways of providing choice opportunities previously discussed are not always very helpful when considering major lifestyle changes.

Evidence-based ways of providing choices for adults with autism and other severe disabilities discussed in **Chapter 7** are very important but are somewhat circumscribed. Specifically, the ways generally involve choice opportunities that are immediately available in an individual's environment. When considering lifestyle changes, the choices pertain to activities, places, people, etc., that typically are not immediately available in the person's current environment.

To illustrate, consideration may be given to changing weekday activities of an adult who has a severe disability (e.g., participation in a different adult education program). The individual currently may not have formal day activities outside of the home or express discontent with an existing day program through refusal to attend or participate in the current program. It would be difficult to provide the individual a meaningful choice of another day program because s/he would likely lack familiarity with other day program options. Additionally, it would be difficult to provide a visual referent to the day program options as part of the choice opportunity as described in **Chapter 7**. Hence, the person likely would have difficulty understanding the choice that is being provided.

As also indicated previously, sometimes alterations can be made with choice-presentation formats to help a person with a severe disability express a preference for something that is not immediately present. For example, pictures of different day activity options may be provided for a person to choose a desired option by selecting the picture of a specific program location. For individuals who have the skills to effectively respond to such a choice opportunity, this represents one means of validating the support teams' initial identification of a preference regarding a change in a day activity program. Of course for those consumers who can vocally describe their preferences in an accurate manner, they should be asked which potential situations would be most desirable for them.

> **When conducting person-centered planning to consider a lifestyle change for an individual with a severe disability, special attention is warranted to ensure that the change truly represents the *individual's* preference.**

Generally though, the processes just summarized will be beyond the skill level of many adults with autism on the severe end of the spectrum and adults with other severe disabilities. For these individuals, other actions must be taken to ensure that what support team members agree to be an individual's desire truly represents the person's preference. One such means is through *situational preference assessments*.

Situational preference assessments consist of a two-step process. The first step involves providing an individual with access to situations that represent a potential lifestyle change that is being considered. The intent is to allow the person to experience the different situations and gain familiarity with each one.

For example, an individual's support team in a residential center may determine that the person has the skills and possible desire to move to a more independent living arrangement. The team has reached a consensus in this regard but is uncertain whether the individual would be happier living in a group home with three roommates or in a supported apartment with one roommate. A situational preference assessment could be conducted to identify the person's relative preference for each of the alternative living arrangements versus the individual's current residential setting.

In this case, a situational preference assessment would initially involve identification of a group home and a supported apartment arrangement to which the individual could potentially move. Next, the individual would be provided access to each place and spend supervised time with the other potential roommates in each of the identified locations. This process would be repeated until the person has had opportunities to experience the general routines and activities that usually occur in the two locations, as well as the overall physical settings.

The second step in a situational preference assessment is to determine the person's preferences for the identified situations once s/he has gained familiarity with each situation. The basic intent is to determine which of the situations the individual likes the most (and relative to his/her existing situation). That is, the goal is to determine the situation in which the person is *happiest*.

A person's preference for the different situations that are being considered can be evaluated by assessing the degree of happiness and unhappiness indices displayed by the individual in each situation. A comparison is then made to determine the specific situation in which the individual displayed the most indices of happiness and least indices of unhappiness. This is another reason that a critical component in the overall process of promoting happiness among adults with autism and other severe disabilities is initially identifying and validating indices of happiness and unhappiness as discussed in the introductory chapters. The indices represent the basis for determining in which situation representing a potential lifestyle change the person is likely to be the happiest.

To illustrate, in the case just noted, the individual's indices of happiness and unhappiness would be observed while in the group home and supported apartment. Such observations would occur across successive visits to each location to obtain representative samples of the person's happiness. The observations should continue until a consistent pattern of happiness and unhappiness indices is observed within each location. At that point a comparison can be made to determine whether more indices of happiness (and less unhappiness indices) consistently occurred in the group home or the supported apartment. A more detailed example of how a situational preference assessment can be conducted is provided in the case illustration on the following page.

Ensuring Person-Centered Planning Action Steps are Carried Out Appropriately

Once an individual's preference is accurately identified in the initial process of person-centered planning, then attention must be directed to the second issue of concern—that of ensuring the remaining components of the process are conducted appropriately. Actually, this issue also pertains to the initial identification of the person's preference regarding a lifestyle change that is being planned. If the individual's preference has not been accurately identified in the ways previously summarized, then the initial step of person-centered planning has not been carried out appropriately.

Case Illustration
Example of A Situational Preference Assessment

Background: Mr. Jarred, an adult with severe intellectual disabilities who did not speak, spent his weekdays at an adult education program doing table-top activities. There was a consensus among his support team that he preferred more active, outdoor pursuits. Consequently, the team identified a part-time job opportunity on a lawn crew that might represent more preferred day activities. Because it was not clear though what types of lawn-crew tasks Mr. Jarred might desire, a situational preference assessment was conducted.

Assessment: Mr. Jarred was provided brief opportunities across several days to perform different work tasks on the lawn crew with the support of a job coach, including mulching, pushing a wheelbarrow, bagging leaves, and cleaning a porch. Observations of his previously identified indices of happiness and unhappiness were conducted while he performed the different tasks. Observations were also conducted of how much time he actually spent working when assigned each of the tasks.

Results: A comparison of the observations indicated Mr. Jarred displayed the most happiness indices while he was mulching, followed in turn by pushing the wheelbarrow, bagging leaves, and cleaning a porch (he also displayed more happiness indices while doing these work tasks relative to his existing table-top activities). Conversely, he showed relatively less unhappiness indices across the four respective tasks. It was then determined that he liked mulching the most and cleaning the porch the least. Observations of his work behavior corroborated this conclusion in that he spent more of the designated time working on mulching when that task was assigned versus working on cleaning the porch when that was assigned. Subsequently, his yard-crew tasks could be assigned to involve mulching as much as possible and pushing the wheelbarrow the rest of the time such that he could work on tasks that he liked the most (with other personnel being assigned to work on the tasks that were less preferred by Mr. Jarred).

Often what happens with person-centered planning in many agencies is that the necessary steps to accurately identify a respective individual's preference regarding a lifestyle change are not carried out.

Rather, terms are altered on existing treatment plans to reflect person-centered language to give the appearance that the plan is based on what the individual desires. The plan may appear to be person-centered on the surface but again, if it does not accurately represent the individual's preference it is not truly person-centered.

However, even when preferences are appropriately identified, concern needs to be directed to how the remaining aspects of the person-centered process are conducted. The latter aspects center on specific action steps to ensure the individual experiences the preferred lifestyle change. Those steps must be appropriately carried out by the support team members and related personnel.

Sometimes what happens is that once a person's preference has been identified and subsequent action steps have been specified, team members view the person-centered planning process to be basically completed. The person-centered plan has been prepared and it is then placed in the individual's general file. The support team and agency representatives purportedly claim that their supports and services are person-centered in nature and point to the existing plan as proof of their assertion.

The process just illustrated represents a somewhat common view that the development of a person-centered plan is the desired outcome for personal goal planning. Such a view is seriously in error; *person-centered planning is not an end in and of itself but rather, a means to an end.* The desired outcome is for a person with a disability to achieve the lifestyle change and experience increased happiness as a result of the change. For the latter outcome to be realized, the action steps that constitute part of the plan must be appropriately implemented.

For example, if it has been accurately determined that a person desires to work on job tasks that involve frequent social interactions with co-workers relative to job tasks performed in isolation from other people, then a number of action steps would likely be necessary. Such steps might include identifying job tasks that involve working with others and arranging for the person to obtain employment to work on the tasks. Training the individual how to perform the tasks would also be necessary in many cases.

Once the necessary action steps have been identified, then various support team members and related personnel must be assigned the responsibility of carrying out respective steps. Even at this point though, the process is not complete. Follow-up action must be taken to ensure that everybody completes their assigned steps in a proficient and timely manner. Such action requires effective supervision of the performance of the team members and related personnel. **Chapter 13** addresses components of effective supervision. The concern at this point is that fulfillment of the action steps identified in person-centered planning should not be taken for granted; supervision should be provided to ensure the steps are adequately completed.

Person-centered planning for attaining a desired lifestyle change for a person with a disability will not be successful unless action steps identified in the planning process are carried out proficiently and in a timely manner by support personnel.

ADDITIONAL CONCERNS WITH PERSON-CENTERED GOAL PLANNING

Person-centered planning represents the most highly recommended approach for human service agencies to help adults with autism and other severe disabilities experience major lifestyle changes in a manner to promote their future happiness. Many people with severe disabilities have benefitted from the outcomes of person-centered planning and have indeed experienced increased happiness in their lives. However, there are also some special concerns with person-centered planning that warrant attention when considering a possible lifestyle change for a respective individual. The most important of these concerns are summarized in subsequent chapter sections.

Ensuring Person-Centered Planning is Conducted Appropriately

The most important concern with person-centered planning has already been referred to: *the process must be conducted appropriately.* Initially, preferences of an individual regarding a potential lifestyle change must be accurately identified. Subsequently, action steps identified within the planning process must be carried out proficiently and in a timely manner to ensure the person actually experiences the desired change.

Failure to appropriately conduct the two primary components of person-centered planning is the most common problem with this approach to helping an adult with a severe disability achieve a lifestyle change that will promote the person's future happiness. Common examples of how the process is not implemented appropriately have been noted previously. Most commonly, existing treatment plans of individuals are simply re-written to reflect person-centered language (e.g., written as if the plan represents an expressed desire of the person with a disability) without accurately determining what the individual prefers.

Another common example of how person-centered planning is not conducted appropriately pertains to a failure to attend to the plan when providing future supports and services. To illustrate, person-centered planning may result in identifying that an individual desires to move to a more independent living arrangement of a certain nature. However, when the person actually moves to another residence, the move is based on where there was an available opening within one of the agency's homes—regardless of whether the new home represents the individual's desired living arrangement.

There are numerous reasons why individual preferences identified in person-centered plans are not adhered to within an agency's supports and services. Often the reasons relate to logistical considerations associated with how an agency operates, such as limitations with resources (e.g., only a limited number of different living arrangements are offered within an agency). In other cases, the reasons relate to agency personnel simply not considering individual desires relating to forthcoming changes relative to attending to the needs of agency administration.

Regardless of the reasons for failure to conduct person-centered planning appropriately, the outcome is the same: the degree of happiness an adult with a severe disability experiences that is associated with a lifestyle change will be reduced or negated entirely. It is incumbent upon agency management and support team members to exert the time and effort to ensure that lifestyle changes are truly planned and implemented in a person-centered manner. Person-centered planning can be very helpful for promoting happiness among adults with autism and other severe disabilities, but only if it occurs in the manner in which it is intended to occur.

LIMITATIONS WITH PERSON-CENTERED PLANNING

Attempting to Meet the Desires of All Consumers. Even though person-centered planning is generally the most recommended means of assisting adults with autism and other severe disabilities to achieve lifestyle changes that promote their happiness, there are limitations with the process. The primary limitation exists because of the nature of typical human service agencies. Most human service agencies serve *groups* of people with disabilities. When more than one person receives supports and services in one location in an agency (e.g., live in an agency home, attend an agency day support program), the agency cannot be totally person-centered in its operation.

Providing person-centered supports is limited in agencies that serve groups of people with disabilities because sometimes the preferences regarding lifestyle changes of one person conflict with the preferences of another person. For example, an individual may have a strong preference to have another consumer as a roommate in an apartment. However, the latter person does not prefer to live with the former person. In this case, the preferences of both people cannot be totally satisfied in regard to their living situation. One person may be happy with the resulting living arrangement but the other one will not.

Failure to fully satisfy a given preference of an individual because of conflicts with the preferences of one or more other consumers is simply a fact of life in human service agencies. This is also the case with people in general—sometimes a desired lifestyle change of one person cannot be achieved because it would involve another person who does not desire such a change (e.g., a marriage proposal by one individual is rejected by the potential spouse). This limitation of person-centered planning is raised here because it warrants awareness on the part of family members and other people who participate in person-centered planning for consumers of agency services.

Agencies that espouse person-centered planning have an ethical obligation to openly acknowledge the degree to which their supports and services are and are not person-centered. Agencies should readily acknowledge that when considering individual lifestyle changes, consideration also has to be given to the effects of the potential changes on the desires of all people for whom the agencies are responsible. To assert that the agencies are totally person-centered with their supports and services for each individual usually is a misleading claim.

Accessing Some Preferences Is Not Always An Option. Another limitation with person-centered planning is not due to the process itself but with the potential outcome of the process. Specifically, at times a strong preference of an individual may be accurately identified but accessing that preference could be harmful to the person's overall welfare. This type of possible outcome of the person-centered planning process is sometimes referred to as *nonnegotiable* option.

To illustrate, an adult with autism or other severe disability may indicate a very strong desire not to attend a given adult education program on weekdays. Rather, the person strongly prefers to stay at home and repeatedly watch a certain DVD movie all day. In this case the individual's support team may reach a consensus that staying home every day and repeatedly watching one particular movie would be detrimental to the person. The latter activity would likely prohibit the individual from, for example, learning critical life skills, possibly earning an income, developing a social network, and developing other potential preferences.

In this case the individual staying home to repeatedly watch the same movie all day would be considered a nonnegotiable option. The consensus of the other members of the individual's person-centered team would override his/her preference. The team could, however, take other action to enhance the person's daily enjoyment associated with the day placement. For example, changes might be made with the adult education program to incorporate other activities that the person prefers to enhance the individual's interest in attending the program. Alternatively, another day program may be secured that is more to the person's liking.

Because of the intellectual challenges of adults with autism and other severe disabilities, agency support teams often have to make decisions on their behalf that may conflict with their preferences yet are in the best interest of their welfare overall. This is simply part of the nature of providing supports and services for people with severe disabilities. When such decisions appear necessary, it is incumbent upon agency personnel to acknowledge the reason for the decisions as well as the fact that an individual's preferences are not being addressed in the particular case. It is also incumbent upon agency personnel to ensure that the reason for the decision is truly consumer welfare, and not due to other, often misleading reasons as referred to earlier.

Although some decisions affecting the lifestyle of an adult with a severe disability sometimes need to be made that do not support the person's lifestyle preference, these should be the exception and not the rule. Generally, such decisions should only be made when there is a very good likelihood, as well as a team consensus, that certain preferred lifestyle changes would be harmful for an individual. Otherwise, sincere effort should be made to accurately identify the lifestyle preferences of a person with a disability and then take the necessary action steps to help the person access those preferences.

CHAPTER SUMMARY: KEY POINTS

1. *The most highly recommended way to plan major lifestyle changes for adults with autism and other severe disabilities in human service agencies to promote their future happiness is person-centered planning.*

2. *Two key components of person-centered planning for making individual lifestyle changes are identifying the individual's preference for a lifestyle change and taking specified action steps to ensure the person experiences the desired change.*

3. *Special concern is needed to ensure person-centered planning truly identifies what the person with a disability desires in regard to a lifestyle change.*

4. *One good means of validating a team consensus regarding a person's desire for a given lifestyle change is through situational preference assessments.*

5. *Special concern is also needed to ensure action steps developed during the person-centered planning process are implemented in a proficient and timely manner, which requires effective supervision of team member performance.*

6. *Agencies that serve groups of people with disabilities in a given location generally cannot be totally person-centered in regard to their supports and services for each individual; the expressed desires of one individual must be considered in conjunction with the desires of all other people receiving supports within the agency.*

7. *At times, a preference of an individual identified with person-centered planning cannot be adhered to within an agency because accessing the preference would be detrimental to the person's overall welfare; sometimes certain options are non-negotiable.*

CHAPTER 10

PROMOTING HAPPINESS BY REDUCING UNHAPPINESS

The focus throughout previous chapters has been on evidence-based procedures designed to increase happiness among adults with autism and other severe disabilities in human service agencies. A number of ways agency staff can promote happiness among the people they support on a day-to-day basis have been described. Ways to plan and carry out major lifestyle changes to promote happiness on a long-term basis have likewise been discussed. There is also another evidence-based means of promoting happiness that is somewhat less direct than the focus of the procedures presented to this point: happiness can be enhanced by taking specific action to *decrease unhappiness.*

As discussed in **Chapter 2**, a person's experiences related to daily enjoyment fall on a continuum ranging from those involving significant unhappiness to significant happiness. Generally, people enjoy their days most when they have frequent experiences on the happiness end of the continuum and rarely if ever have experiences on the unhappiness end. Hence, the more human service staff can do to prevent and reduce experiences associated with unhappiness, the happier individuals will be on an overall basis. This chapter describes evidence-based ways human service staff can prevent and reduce unhappiness among adults with autism and other severe disabilities during daily routines.

IDENTIFYING SOURCES OF UNHAPPINESS

Before unhappiness can be reduced as a means of promoting happiness overall, *sources* of unhappiness must be identified. It must be accurately determined when an adult with autism or other severe disability tends to experience unhappiness. In some cases, it appears readily apparent when a given individual is unhappy. The person will do what people in general do when unhappy, such as cry or repeatedly grimace or frown. That is, the individual will display common indices of unhappiness as described in **Chapter 3**. In many situations though, it may not be very clear when an adult with autism or other severe disability is experiencing unhappiness; the individual displays unhappiness in ways that are different than how most people act when unhappy (again, see **Chapter 3** for elaboration).

To identify and remedy sources of unhappiness, it must be very clear when a person is experiencing unhappiness. This is another reason that indices of unhappiness must be accurately identified and validated as discussed in **Chapters 3** and **4**. Once valid indicators of a consumer's unhappiness have been determined then systematic monitoring of the occurrence of those indices should be undertaken. The intent is to specifically identify situations in which an individual often displays unhappiness indices. Those situations usually represent sources of unhappiness.

To illustrate, staff may report that a particular individual seems to be unhappy frequently during the day when attending an adult education program. Systematic monitoring subsequently may reveal that the person usually shows indices of unhappiness when instructed to discontinue a preferred activity in order to begin another, less preferred activity. In such a situation, the monitoring would suggest that unhappiness is associated with having to transition from one (preferred) activity to another (nonpreferred) activity. Consequently, action could be taken to determine how to make such transitions less unpleasant for the individual as a means of reducing unhappiness associated with the transitions.

> Before effective action can be taken to reduce unhappiness among adults with autism and other severe disabilities, valid indices of unhappiness must be systematically monitored to determine the situations that result in individuals experiencing unhappiness.

CHANGING SOURCES OF UNHAPPINESS TO PROMOTE HAPPINESS

Once sources of unhappiness are accurately identified for adults with autism and other severe disabilities, then a number of means are available to change the situations such that they are no longer accompanied by unhappiness. How the situations are changed depends in part on the nature of the situations and in particular, the specific features of the situations that result in an individual experiencing unhappiness. However, there are three general approaches to initially consider when situations are identified that result in a consumer's unhappiness. These include (1) eliminating the situations where possible, (2) ensuring a consumer has a good relationship with staff who are involved in the situations and, (3) changing certain features of the situations.

ELIMINATING SOURCES OF UNHAPPINESS

The most straightforward way to overcome unhappiness that a particular situation causes for a person with a severe disability in human service agencies is to eliminate the situation from the person's regular routine. It is relatively common to find certain activities during daily routines in human service agencies that are associated with a given individual's unhappiness and upon close examination, are really not necessary. These types of activities should simply be discontinued as part of ongoing routines. An example of reducing unhappiness in this manner is presented in the case illustration on page 183.

In the type of situation presented in the case illustration, a common approach in human service agencies is to develop a behavior support plan to reduce the problem behavior that accompanies the individual's unhappiness (yelling and wrist biting in the illustration). Even if the plan was successful in reducing the target problem behavior, however, it likely would not resolve the person's unhappiness associated with sitting with nothing to do at his work table. In contrast, removing the situation (by discontinuing periods of time at the table with nothing to do) would eliminate the actual source of the person's unhappiness as well as the problem behavior.

Of course there will be certain situations accompanied by an individual's unhappiness that would not be desirable to eliminate because they are important for the person's overall welfare. For example, it would not be desirable to eliminate vegetables from a consumer's diet because s/he becomes unhappy when served vegetables. Likewise, it would be unwise to discontinue dental appointments because an individual becomes unhappy when visiting the dentist. Nonetheless, it is recommended that when a situation is identified that occasions a consumer's unhappiness, the first step to ask is whether the activity is really necessary. If upon close examination it is determined that the activity is not that important, then serious consideration usually should be given to discontinuing that activity.

THE IMPORTANCE OF GOOD RELATIONSHIPS FOR REDUCING UNHAPPINESS

When a situation that occasions a consumer's unhappiness cannot be removed from ongoing routines in human service agencies then steps should be taken to alter aspects of the situation. The intent is to identify and then change specific features of the situation that the person dislikes and results in unpleasantness for the individual. One particular feature to examine when a situation is identified as being the source of an individual's unhappiness is *who* is involved in the situation with the person.

CASE ILLUSTRATON
EXAMPLE OF REMOVING A SITUATION ACCOMPANIED BY A CONSUMER'S UNHAPPINESS

Background: Mr. Gage, a supported worker who had autism and was nonvocal, worked part time at an office complex. His job coach and other office personnel were concerned that he periodically displayed problem behavior involving yelling and biting his wrist. An observational assessment indicated that this behavior occurred when he was sitting at his work table but there was no work or other activity for him to perform (he was an active person and often displayed indices of unhappiness such as frowning and grimacing when he had no structured activity in which to engage). His work duties involved collating manual pages and putting tabs on advertising fliers to hold the fliers closed as part of an assembly-type task with other supported workers. At times he had to wait for an extended period for other workers to complete their part of the tasks and hand him the pages or fliers—which resulted in him simply sitting and waiting with no work.

Removal of Source of Unhappiness: The job coach negotiated with the company supervisor to prepare some partially completed pages and fliers that could be given to him when he had to wait for other workers to complete their tasks. Subsequently, when he typically would have to wait on the other workers with no work to perform he was given the "back up" materials such that he could continue working while waiting. Once his "wait time" with no activity was eliminated by providing him with the supplementary materials, his problem behavior (and indices of unhappiness) no longer occurred.

The importance of good relationships between an adult with autism or other severe disability and human service staff was stressed in **Chapter 5**. To review briefly, when a consumer of agency services has a good relationship with staff who typically interact with the person during daily routines, the individual is likely to experience at least a degree of happiness associated with the routines. Conversely, if a consumer does not have a good relationship with respective staff—such as, for example, when the individual is not very familiar with the staff—then the person is likely to experience unhappiness when those staff interact with him/her during various situations.

When a situation is identified that is associated with an individual's unhappiness, the situation should be examined to determine if it involves staff with whom the individual has not established a good relationship. If such is the case, then one of two steps can be taken to change the situation to reduce the individual's unhappiness. First, where possible, staff duty assignments should be altered to allow staff who do have a good relationship with the individual to conduct the identified activity. Second, if staff assignments cannot be altered in this manner, then consideration should be given to temporarily discontinuing the activity to allow the involved staff to take steps to develop a good relationship (see **Chapter 5**). Once it is clear the consumer is enjoying interacting with the staff (i.e., a good relationship is developing) then the activity can be resumed.

In short, one means of changing a situation that results in unhappiness for a person with a severe disability is to ensure the situation involves staff with whom the person has a good relationship. If the situation of concern does not involve the individual interacting with staff, or the staff who are involved already have a good relationship with the person, then other changes should be made with the particular situation. Additional ways to change disliked situations that cause unhappiness among adults with autism and other severe disabilities are discussed in the following section.

CHANGING SITUATIONS TO REDUCE CONSUMER UNHAPPINESS

There are a number of evidence-based ways to change features of various situations to make the situations less likely to cause unhappiness among adults with autism and other severe disabilities. Although each way to be described may not always be possible or practical, at least one of the ways is almost always applicable for most situations. Each identified situation should be assessed to determine specifically how it can be changed to reduce unhappiness for a person with a severe disability.

Providing Choices. The importance of providing choices to promote individual happiness during daily activities was discussed in **Chapter 7**. How to provide choices to adults with autism and other severe disabilities in a manner that each individual can respond with a meaningful choice response was also described. Although the focus in the previous discussion was providing choice opportunities to increase happiness, presentation of choices can also reduce or prevent unhappiness.

When a person is provided a choice pertaining to a certain activity or situation, it allows the individual to have some control over what will occur. Such control means the person can change one or more features of the situation. In many cases, the changes the person will make involve altering a feature of the situation that s/he dislikes to something more enjoyable.

When a situation is identified that is accompanied by a consumer's unhappiness, staff should review the situation and determine various ways the person could be offered one or more choices about the situation. **Chapter 7** described different types of choices that can be provided to adults with autism and other severe disabilities. The intent is to determine which types of choice opportunities can be readily incorporated within the particular situation.

One type of choice to consider pertains to the importance of involving staff within a given activity with whom the consumer has a good relationship as just described. That is, when possible the individual could be given a choice of *with whom* to do the activity if a staff member will be involved in the situation. This allows the consumer to choose a desired staff person which in turn will likely make the individual's participation in the activity more enjoyable for him/her.

The other types of choices described in **Chapter 7** should likewise be considered when a situation will occur that has previously been accompanied by a consumer's unhappiness. When considering the different types of choices, such as where, when, and how to do an activity, there is almost always a means of providing a choice for every situation that a person dislikes. Again, by providing a choice pertaining to a disliked situation, the individual can alter features of the situation to make it more desired and subsequently, reduce the unhappiness associated with the situation.

> **Providing people with severe disabilities a choice of with whom to participate in disliked activities often can reduce or eliminate their unhappiness that is associated with the activities.**

Embedding Preferences into Different Situations. As discussed in **Chapter 8**, sometimes it is not possible to provide consumer choice opportunities in certain situations. In those cases individual happiness can be promoted by embedded things the person likes or prefers within activities that constitute the situation. Embedding preferences into activities also represents a means of reducing unhappiness associated with various situations. By embedding preferences into situations that are usually accompanied by an individual's unhappiness, the person's emotional experiences associated with the situations move along the unhappiness/happiness continuum closer to the happiness end of the continuum.

When staff identify a situation that results in an individual's unhappiness they should consider how they can include something the person prefers within the situation. An example of embedding preferences into a situation usually accompanied by a consumer's unhappiness is provided in the case illustration on the following page. The specific situation represented in the case illustration involved a range-of-motion exercise that was prescribed for physical therapy purposes for a woman who had severe intellectual and physical disabilities.

The exercise in the case illustration was necessary to help the woman increase flexibility with her arm movements which was limited due to severe contractures the woman experienced. Although the exercise was necessary for health reasons, it usually resulted in significant indices of unhappiness by the woman, perhaps due to some physical discomfort the exercise caused. Embedding preferences within the exercise routine may not have removed the source of the woman's unhappiness (the possible discomfort) but appeared to alter the overall situation to make it more pleasant as evidenced by the changes in her indices of unhappiness.

CASE ILLUSTRATION
EMBEDDING PREFERENCES INTO A DISLIKED SITUATION TO REDUCE UNHAPPINESS

Background: Ms. Reiss was a 66-year-old women who was nonvocal and had multiple disabilities including profound intellectual disabilities as well as sensory impairments and physical disabilities that prohibited ambulation. She received range-of-motion exercises prescribed by a physical therapist to help maintain flexibility in her arm and hand movements. During the exercises Mr. Reiss frequently displayed indices of unhappiness such as frowning and grimacing.

Embedded Preference Procedure: In an attempt to make the exercises less unpleasant for Ms. Reiss, preferences identified by staff and through systematic preference assessments were made accessible to her before, during, and immediately after each exercise session. The preferred activities included brushing her hair and talking softly to her just before the session, providing a small sip of punch or a bite of pudding at one-minute intervals during the actual exercise routine, and activating an electronic music board immediately after each session. Prior to providing access to the preferences, Ms. Reiss displayed indices of unhappiness during approximately 75% of the time during the exercise routine. In contrast, once access to her preferences was initiated as just described, indices of unhappiness were exhibited during less than 10% of the time.

Reducing Unexpected Situations. A rather common source of unhappiness for a number of adults with severe disabilities in human service agencies is situations that arise unexpectedly. This is particularly the case for adults with autism on the severe end of the spectrum. Many of these individuals show considerable indices of unhappiness when something unexpected happens that disrupts an ongoing activity. For example, some individuals appear quite unhappy when another consumer unexpectedly becomes very agitated, an unannounced emergency weather drill is sounded via an alarm system, or unexpected visitors enter their home.

It is not entirely clear why certain adults with autism and other severe disabilities dislike unexpected situations. It is clear though that such events can cause significant unhappiness among many individuals as demonstrated by their frequent indices of unhappiness. Hence, a means of reducing one source of unhappiness for those people is for staff to minimize the occurrence of unexpected situations.

Of course there will always be some unexpected events in essentially every environment over which staff have no control even though they result in consumer unhappiness. For these events often there is relatively little that staff can do to prevent the accompanying unhappiness with the possible exception of helping respective individuals remove themselves from the environment when the unexpected event begins to occur. However, there are also a number of key types of events in human service agencies that are experienced unexpectedly by individuals over which staff can exert control. Staff should strive to prevent the latter types of unexpected situations from occurring.

One type of unexpected situation, at least from the perspective of consumers, that occurs frequently in many human service agencies that staff can prevent to a large degree is *transitions.* Transitions pertain to when an ongoing activity is discontinued in order to begin another activity. Common examples include when a community recreation activity must be discontinued in order to get ready to depart for home, when it is time to move from one classroom to another, and when it is time to end a leisure activity to get ready for bed.

Because transitions occur in every human service agency, and often result in unhappiness among many adults with severe disabilities, staff should act to make the transitions as predictable as possible. Making transitions predictable reduces their unexpected features and correspondingly the unhappiness they occasion. One means of making transitions predictable is to ensure activity schedules are prepared and presented to individual consumers in a manner that is understandable by the individuals.

Activity schedules should inform consumers when transitions will occur by, for example, giving written schedules to individuals who can read that specify in what order activities will occur or at what time they will take place. Other individuals may benefit from simply being told what the schedule for forthcoming time periods will entail, or by having pictures of what activities will occur in a certain sequence. Still other people may need visual timers that they can observe to predict when an activity will end and another activity will begin.

It is also helpful for many people with severe disabilities if activity schedules are supplemented by giving individuals a signal or cue that an ongoing activity will be ending in a few minutes or other brief time frame. The cue could be as simple as telling a person that the ongoing activity will end in five minutes or so and that another, clearly specified activity will begin at that time. Other individuals may benefit from being taught that a certain visual signal (e.g., a certain picture or diagram) presented by staff means that there are only a few minutes left with the ongoing activity.

In short, staff should strive to make activities in human service agencies as predictable as possible for adults with severe disabilities who display unhappiness when unexpected situations such as transitions arise. By ensuring individuals are effectively informed about forthcoming events and provided with cues or signals when changes are about to happen, the unexpected feature of transitions is reduced or eliminated for the individuals. In turn, the transitions often become much less likely to result in their unhappiness.

Making Difficult Tasks Easier. A common source of unhappiness among most people is completing tasks that are difficult for them to perform. It is basic human nature to prefer doing tasks that are less effortful to complete relative to tasks that are more effortful. The same situation exists for adults with autism and other severe disabilities. Hence, one means of reducing a source of unhappiness for consumers in human service agencies is to make difficult tasks that they are expected to complete easer to perform where possible—assuming that the tasks really need to be completed as discussed earlier in this chapter.

One type of difficult task frequently confronting consumers is participation in teaching programs in which what is being taught is difficult for them to learn. The difficulty they encounter in learning certain types of skills targeted in teaching programs results in considerable unhappiness for them. Ways to reduce unhappiness during teaching activities are addressed in-depth in the following chapter on **Preference-Based Teaching.**

There are also a number of difficult tasks adults who have severe disabilities are expected to complete in human service agencies that do not involve learning new skills. These are tasks that individuals know how to do but are still difficult to perform. Often the difficulty is due to the amount of effort required to perform the tasks appropriately. The effortful nature of completing the tasks makes the tasks undesirable to perform and therefore, occasions unhappiness for them. Finding ways to make the tasks less difficult or effortful to perform can reduce the unhappiness individuals experience when expected to complete the tasks.

To illustrate, cleaning an apartment each week may be a necessary expectation of an adult with a severe disability in a supported living situation but is disliked by the person due to the effort required to adequately clean the apartment. The amount of effort involved in cleaning the apartment at a given time may be reduced by breaking the overall cleaning process into smaller components or steps to be completed on different days of the week. Instead of being expected to clean the entire apartment on Saturday morning, for example, cleaning parts of the apartment may be scheduled for smaller periods of time on several week days toward the end of the week as well as on Saturday morning (e.g., clean the bedroom on Thursday, the living room on Friday, and the kitchen on Saturday).

Often when an effortful task is subdivided into smaller tasks and completed at different time periods the amount of unpleasantness associated with completing the entire task is reduced. The unpleasantness is reduced because the amount of effort to complete each designated part of the task is less than the effort required to complete the entire task all at once. The reduced effort in turn makes completing each part of the task less unpleasant for the individual relative to the unpleasantness associated with completing the entire task. As the unpleasantness is reduced, corresponding reductions in individual unhappiness likewise occur.

Of course the nature of some effortful tasks requires that the tasks be completed in their entirety during a certain time period. This is often the case with certain work duties as part of a supported job. However, the amount of overall effort associated with completing the tasks can be reduced by including frequent breaks within the work routine. For example, a supported worker may begin to tire and show signs of unhappiness after working on an assembly task at a work site for an hour or so. Job coaches and related personnel could negotiate with work supervisors to arrange for the worker to have a brief break scheduled at 45-minute intervals. Breaks would be scheduled in this manner at a point prior to when the worker usually begins to display indices of unhappiness.

The process of reducing unhappiness due to work effort by scheduling frequent breaks must of course consider various expectations associated with completing the task (e.g., the overall time frame with which a task must be completed). Hence, providing frequent breaks may not be feasible in every situation in which the effort involved in completing a task is difficult for an individual and provokes unhappiness. In many other situations though, providing more frequent breaks of a brief duration will not adversely affect task completion and can represent an effective means of reducing individual unhappiness.

> **Unhappiness among adults with severe disabilities associated with performing effortful tasks often can be reduced by breaking the tasks into smaller components to be completed at different times and by including frequent breaks while performing the tasks.**

Special Material Adaptations. Many adults with autism and other severe disabilities have multiple types of challenges, including various sensory and physical disabilities or impairments. Sensory and physical challenges can increase the difficulty and effort necessary to complete certain tasks, which makes the tasks unpleasant to perform. In turn, the unpleasantness increases an individual's unhappiness when attempting to perform the tasks.

In many cases sensory and physical challenges can be overcome or compensated to a degree through special adaptions made with the materials that must be manipulated to perform certain tasks. This is particularly the case with various types of physical disorders that cause difficulty with fine and gross motor movements. Material adaptations to help overcome physical challenges may involve, for example, use of a spoon with an enlarged handle to facilitate eating for someone who has difficulty grasping utensils, specialized seating arrangements for an individual whose physical challenges interfere with maintaining necessary posture to complete a task, and raised toilet seats for someone who has difficulty standing up from a seated position.

Typically the types of material adaptions just exemplified require the involvement of specialty clinicians such as physical and occupational therapists. The adaptations are generally viewed as a means of helping individuals with various physical challenges perform necessary tasks as independently as possible. However, because the adaptations decrease the effort and difficulty involved in performing certain tasks they also can function to reduce unpleasantness associated with individuals completing the tasks.

Material adaptations are also very useful for helping individuals overcome sensory challenges. Everyone is familiar with the use of eyeglasses to help with visual impairments and auditory devices to help with hearing impairments. However, some sensory-related issues and necessary material adaptations are not so apparent. This is especially the case with individuals who have autism on the severe end of the spectrum of autism disorders.

Adults with severe autism often have more difficulty responding to auditory sensations relative to visual stimuli. For reasons that are not totally known, these individuals appear to have difficulty processing certain sounds including what is said to them in particular situations. To illustrate, some individuals have difficulty processing vocal instructions presented to an entire classroom by an instructor who is at the front of the class. Such difficulty makes it hard for the individuals to appropriately respond to the instructions which in turn makes participation in group lecture activities unpleasant.

In these cases, the difficulty can be lessened by providing visual instructions to supplement the spoken instructions. Visual instructions may include use of printed slides shown via an LCD projector, picture cues presented to an individual, or scripted notes provided to a person who can read that highlight key points of the instructions during the group lecture. The visual stimuli are easier for some individuals to comprehend relative to instructions presented vocally and therefore make attending and responding to the instructor easier.

There are numerous other types of material adaptations that can be made to help individuals overcome various physical and sensory challenges. Many readers are undoubtedly aware of many of these beyond what has been illustrated here. Although such adaptations are usually considered as a means of helping someone perform certain tasks more independently as just noted, they are highlighted here because of their importance for reducing unhappiness when performing respective tasks. Again, when a task is made easier to perform through material adaptations, individual unhappiness associated with performing the task is usually reduced.

> **Material adaptations designed to assist individuals with sensory and physical challenges in performing certain tasks not only help promote their independence but also can decrease unhappiness associated with performing the tasks.**

Making "Demand" Situations Less Unpleasant. A somewhat common source of unhappiness for a number of adults with autism and other severe disabilities is when they are given certain demands by agency staff. A demand in this respect means that an individual is instructed by staff to do something that needs to be done. When an instruction is presented by staff, an individual immediately may show indices of unhappiness such as yelling, often accompanied by some type of problem behavior such as aggressing toward the staff member. For example, when a staff member approaches a person in a group home to instruct the individual to clean the table after lunch, the person might yell at the staff member and attempt to push the staff member away.

Unhappiness (and at times problem behavior) in response to staff instructions usually takes one of two general forms. One form is when the unhappiness is restricted to an instruction pertaining to one specific task or event. An example many experienced readers have likely witnessed is when a consumer is instructed at the residence to get on the van to go to the day program. The individual may show multiple indices of unhappiness such as yelling, screaming, or even crying. The person might also show various types of problem behavior such as falling to the sidewalk and refusing to get up to walk to the van.

When individual unhappiness associated with demand situations is restricted to instructions pertaining to one specific task or event, serious attention is warranted on the nature of the task or event. In the case example with the day program, consideration should be given to determining what features of the program are so unpleasant to cause the individual's reluctance to attend. Observations of the person's unhappiness indices should occur while s/he is at the day program setting as referred to earlier to identify what specific features of the program are accompanied by the individual's unhappiness.

Subsequently, changes in the person's participation in the program should be made using any of the strategies discussed throughout this chapter to either eliminate or change the specific features associated with the individual's unhappiness. The intent is to remove or alter the features of the day program that occasion the person's unhappiness, thereby making it less unpleasant for him/her to go to the program. When such actions are successful, the unhappiness and perhaps problem behavior that occur when instructed to get on the van to go to the day program will be significantly reduced or eliminated.

In many human service agencies a common approach to dealing with the situation just illustrated is to implement a behavior support plan. The plan is developed to reduce the problem behavior that often accompanies the consumer's unhappiness. Such an approach was noted previously with the first case illustration pertaining to an individual becoming unhappy and yelling and biting his wrist when expected to sit at a work table without any work to perform. In the illustration here the plan would be designed to reduce the person's refusal to get on the van and specifically the yelling and falling to the ground.

Frequently the intent of behavior support plans in these situations is to disallow the person from using problem behavior to avoid something that is important but apparently disliked (e.g., going to the day program in the current illustration). In this case the plan may involve "waiting out" the individual in terms of a staff member waiting until the individual stops yelling and gets up from the ground and then continue the process of getting on the van. Alternatively, the plan may involve physically escorting the individual to the van.

There are times when behavior support plans are warranted to help an adult with a severe disability overcome challenging behavior associated with instructions to do something. However, when problem behavior typically occurs only when instruction pertains to one specific situation, a more desirable approach is to determine why the situation is so disliked by the person and then alter the situation as just summarized. If the latter approach is not pursued and a behavior support plan is implemented exclusively to target the problem behavior, in essence the primary cause of such behavior is not being addressed. The plan may be somewhat successful in reducing the challenging behavior, but the underlying unhappiness is not resolved because the situation remains disliked by the individual.

Earlier it was noted that consumer unhappiness in response to staff instructions generally takes one of two forms. The first form was just described. The second form involves unhappiness, and often problem behavior, that occurs in response to multiple instructions during the daily routine that pertain to performing a variety of different tasks. Adults with severe disabilities who frequently demonstrate this form are often considered as being noncompliant or to have poor instruction-following skills.

Frequent noncompliant behavior can be a significant problem because it often results in an individual's lack of participation in important activities of daily living, opportunities to learn useful skills, or perhaps failing to perform job duties necessary for earning an income. Many readers have likely observed individuals who frequently refuse to comply with instructions and are aware that if staff persist with attempts to promote compliance, significant problem behavior is likely. This is one reason there are certain individuals in some settings who spend most of their time simply sitting in contrast to appropriately participating in desired activities. Staff have learned if repeated attempts are made to engage the consumers in expected tasks, problem behavior will result. Hence, staff essentially leave them alone as a means of preventing behavior problems.

There are many reasons some adults with autism and other severe disabilities frequently do not comply with staff instructions. One reason is due to a strong dislike of what they are being instructed to do, which is the same type of scenario described previously. In other cases though, individuals do not comply because there has been a history of negative interactions when attempting to comply with staff instructions. The negative interactions may have involved, for example, staff repeatedly telling them to move more quickly, to do something in a better way, etc., which amounts in essence to nagging the consumers. Another reason is that certain individuals simply have not learned the importance of instruction following as part of working and generally interacting with people.

When noncompliance as just described is frequent then a formal treatment plan to increase appropriate instruction following is usually necessary. The plan should first involve an evaluation of events that promote or maintain noncompliance, such as with a functional assessment conducted by a clinician skilled in behavior analysis. The plan should then be developed to address those events. Additionally, strategies usually need to be implemented to effectively teach relevant instruction-following skills. Subsequent chapters on **Preference-Based Teaching** and **Naturalistic Teaching** include descriptions of how such skills can be taught. The latter chapters also focus on how to make teaching of instruction-following and related skills an enjoyable activity for adults with autism and other severe disabilities.

Importance of Routine Monitoring and Evaluation

Earlier the importance of monitoring was noted for identifying situations in human service agencies during which consumers experience unhappiness. However, monitoring indices of unhappiness should not be discontinued once such situations are identified. Monitoring should also occur as action is taken to remove or change the situations.

Ongoing monitoring is necessary to evaluate if actions taken to reduce a consumer's unhappiness are having the desired effect. If results of monitoring indicate that unhappiness indices discontinue or are substantially reduced, then whatever actions have been initiated should be continued. Conversely, if monitoring reveals that there is no significant reduction in an individual's indices of unhappiness then other actions should be undertaken to reduce unhappiness.

In the introductory chapters to this text the overall importance of monitoring for assisting adults with severe disabilities in attaining desired outcomes was stressed. Data resulting from systematic monitoring provide the basis for agencies to evaluate whether desired outcomes are indeed attained—such as ensuring day-to-day enjoyment by reducing unhappiness. Without routine monitoring and the data it provides, there is no formal assurance that agency supports and services have any beneficial impact on consumer outcome attainment.

CHAPTER SUMMARY: KEY POINTS

1. *Overall happiness among adults with autism and other severe disabilities can be enhanced by reducing their unhappiness during routine activities.*

2. *Before individual unhappiness can be effectively reduced, sources of the unhappiness must be identified.*

3. *When a specific situation is determined to result in a consumer's unhappiness, careful consideration should be given to whether the activities constituting the situation are really necessary; if not, the activities should be discontinued as part of the person's regular routine.*

4. *One means of reducing unhappiness of a person with a severe disability that accompanies a certain situation is to ensure staff*

who are involved in the activity or event have a good relationship with the person.

5. Other means of reducing unhappiness of a person with a severe disability that accompanies respective activities include: (a) providing the person choices associated with participating in an activity, (b) embedding the individual's preferences within an activity, (c) reducing the unpredictability of an activity, (d) reducing the difficulty of tasks that the person must perform to participate in an activity, (e) making special material adaptations that assist the individual in participating in an activity more independently and, (f) making instructions or demands directed to the person during an activity less unpleasant.

6. Monitoring indices of unhappiness among adults with severe disabilities should be ongoing to ensure actions taken to reduce unhappiness are truly effective.

SECTION III

PROMOTING HAPPINESS THROUGH INDEPENDENCE

CHAPTER 11

PREFERENCE-BASED TEACHING: PROMOTING HAPPINESS WHILE LEARNING

An underlying premise throughout this book is that happiness among adults with autism and other severe disabilities should be promoted in conjunction with their ongoing skill development and maintenance. Happiness is closely linked to the degree that individuals learn and apply skills to live independently. The more independent skills people possess, the more they can live their lives in ways they desire—ways that promote their happiness.

For adults with autism and other severe disabilities to live as independently as possible, they must receive teaching services to help them learn and use meaningful skills. Providing such services is a critical function of most human service agencies that support this population of people with disabilities. As noted in **Chapter 10**, however, participating in teaching programs is often disliked by many adults with autism and other severe disabilities.

There are a number of reasons why adults with autism and other severe disabilities may dislike participating in a teaching program. The most common reasons usually relate to the difficulty or effort required of the learner to respond to the instructor. There also may be a history of negative instructor-learner interactions associated with past teaching sessions. These and related reasons for dislike of teaching programs have significant implications for both the learner and instructor.

The most apparent effect of a learner's dislike of participating in a teaching session is that it represents a source of unhappiness for the person. Because teaching sessions usually occur multiple times during the day or week, they result in frequent unhappiness for the consumer. The unhappiness also is often accompanied by various types of problem behavior during teaching sessions. Certain learners may strike out at the instructor or destroy teaching materials in an apparent attempt to avoid or get out of the teaching session. Other individuals may simply not respond to the instructional activities. The latter behavior reflects not only the learner's unhappiness, it interferes with the effectiveness of teaching sessions and the learner's skill development.

The implications for instructors when learners dislike participating in teaching sessions are likewise several-fold. In particular, however, the unhappiness and perhaps problem behavior displayed by the learner make teaching sessions more difficult or effortful for the staff instructor. This in turn makes carrying out teaching sessions unpleasant for staff. The unpleasantness results in some instructors hurrying through a teaching program or carrying out only parts of the intended instructional procedures. Consequently, the effectiveness of the teaching session is undermined and learner skill development is compromised. Other staff will simply not carry out teaching sessions when they should be conducted to avoid the unpleasantness that the sessions cause for the staff.

Despite the unhappiness that many adults with autism and other severe disabilities experience during teaching sessions and the corresponding effects on their instructors, participation in teaching programs is critical. Again, teaching is necessary for skill development among people with severe disabilities to enhance their independence and day-to-day happiness. Consequently, human service staff must strive to *teach in ways that learners like*—ways that promote happiness instead of unhappiness. This chapter describes an approach to teaching adults with autism and other severe disabilities that was specifically designed to make participation in teaching sessions enjoyable: *preference-based teaching.*

> **To overcome unhappiness (and problem behavior) that many adults with autism and other severe disabilities experience during teaching sessions, human service staff should take active steps to teach in ways individuals like—ways that promote happiness and not unhappiness.**

Preference-based teaching is an evidence-based approach to making teaching enjoyable while simultaneously ensuring that teaching strategies effectively enhance learner skill development. It was designed specifically for individuals with autism and other severe disabilities who have histories of displaying unhappiness and problem behavior during teaching sessions. The key components of preference-based teaching will be summarized in subsequent sections. More detailed information on this approach to teaching for enhancing learner skill development and enjoyment is available in in the **Selected Readings** section on **Teaching to Promote Consumer Independence and Happiness** (see in particular the book *Preference-Based Teaching: Helping People with Developmental Disabilities Enjoy Learning without Problem Behavior*).

The following discussion on preference-based teaching is focused on *formal teaching sessions*. Formal teaching refers to a staff person (instructor) working one-on-one with an adult with autism or other severe disability (learner) to carry out a written teaching program. The program is usually based on the learner's individualized treatment plan and relates to a particular skill-development goal within the plan and corresponding objectives. Preference-based teaching focuses on formal teaching sessions because this is the type of instructional situation that is most frequently associated with learner unhappiness. More informal types of instructional situations such as naturalistic teaching approaches that can occur briefly as part of routine daily activities are discussed in the next chapter.

A Pre-Requisite for Making Teaching Enjoyable: Good Instructor-Learner Relationships

The importance of developing good relationships between staff in human service agencies and adults with autism and other severe disabilities has been stressed repeatedly. The significance of such relationships is especially important when considering formal teaching sessions. Developing a good relationship between the instructor and learner is a pre-requisite for successful implementation of preference-based teaching to promote learner happiness.

A good instructor-learner relationship is important for all the reasons discussed previously regarding how relationships impact consumer happiness. There are some additional reasons as well that pertain specifically to the nature of formal teaching. In particular, formal teaching sessions typically involve multiple instructions presented to the learner, many of which can be difficult or effortful for the learner to respond to appropriately. As noted in the preceding chapter, receiving instructions or demands and performing difficult or effortful tasks can be unpleasant for many individuals and provoke unhappiness. As also noted in **Chapter 10**, such situations can be made less unpleasant if they involve a staff person with whom the individual has a good relationship and with whom the individual enjoys interacting.

Another reason a good instructor-learner relationship is critical for the success of formal teaching sessions pertains to learner skill acquisition. A key part of the teaching process is for the instructor to motivate the learner to want to learn. This is usually accomplished in large part by the instructor praising learner efforts to respond and especially correct learner behavior in response to specific instructions. The praise is intended to reinforce or strengthen desired learner responding. In essence, the goal is for the learner to want to respond correctly to obtain the instructor's praise or positive attention.

Instructor praise is most likely to function as a reinforcer for learner responding during teaching sessions—again, something the learner will strive to obtain—if the learner truly likes the instructor's attention. The existence of a good relationship between instructor and learner enhances the desirability of the instructor's praise and general attention for the learner. In short, when an instructor has developed a good relationship with a learner not only will teaching sessions be more enjoyable for the learner, the teaching will also be much more successful from a basic learning or skill-development perspective.

The development of a good instructor-learner relationship is a prerequisite for making teaching both enjoyable and effective for adults with autism and other severe disabilities.

THE ABC MODEL OF PREFERENCE-BASED TEACHING

Conducting a formal teaching session with preference-based teaching can be conceptualized as an *antecedent-behavior-consequence* or ABC model. The antecedent (A part of the model) involves what the instructor does immediately prior to the teaching session, the behavior (B) involves the instructor's behavior or what the instructor does during the session, and the consequence (C) involves what the instructor does immediately after the session. The intent is for the instructor to provide learner access to preferences during as many of the ABC components as reasonably possible. The learner preferences should be identified prior to teaching sessions whenever possible through systematic preference assessments, or at least using caregiver opinion in the manner discussed in **Chapter 8**.

The ABC Model that forms the conceptual basis for conducting a preference-based teaching session was exemplified in the case illustration in the preceding chapter. Recall the case concerning the physical therapy exercise that was disliked by the woman who had profound multiple disabilities and resulted in her frequent indices of unhappiness during the exercise routine. Although that situation did not involve teaching new skills to the woman per se, it nevertheless showed how the ABC approach could make an unpleasant activity less unpleasant. The individual was provided access to activities or things she preferred before, during, and after each exercise session which significantly reduced her indices of unhappiness associated with the exercise.

The Antecedent Part of Preference-Based Teaching

The antecedent or A part of preference-based teaching involves the instructor doing something the learner enjoys immediately before a teaching session begins. The intent is to promote the learner's happiness by participating in a preferred event prior to the teaching session. The happiness can then carry over to the actual session. However, there are also some considerations that are relevant even before the A part is implemented. These involve the overall *timing* of when teaching sessions are scheduled to occur.

Timing the Scheduling of Teaching Sessions. Sometimes the degree of unhappiness that an adult who has a severe disability is likely to experience with a disliked activity can be reduced if the individual is provided a signal or cue a few minutes prior to when the activity is initiated (see previous discussion in **Chapter 10** for elaboration). The same holds true for teaching sessions that previously have been accompanied by a learner's unhappiness. The learner should be informed in a manner that s/he readily understands about the forthcoming teaching session. This can be especially helpful for learners with autism who often do not like unexpected changes in their routine.

It can also be helpful when scheduling teaching sessions to consider what reinforcing consequences the instructor will use during teaching to motivate the learner's instructional responses. The primary concern is that the teaching session should not occur immediately after the learner has just contacted the same (reinforcing) consequences that will be used by the instructor during the teaching. For example, if the main reinforcing consequences will be the instructor's praise or positive attention, then the teaching session should not immediately follow an activity in which the learner has been participating with the instructor and receiving a lot of the instructor's attention. Otherwise, the instructor's attention may not be as important or desirable for the learner during the teaching session—the learner already has been receiving attention such that there is often a decreased desire to receive more attention at that point.

Similarly, if a favorite food item is used as a reinforcing consequence during the teaching session it would not be wise to conduct the session immediately following a break time in which the learner had access to the item. If this happens, the learner will likely satiate on the food item and will be less motivated to access it during the teaching session. As a result, the learner will tend to enjoy the teaching session less relative to if s/he really wants the item at that time. The decreased motivation to obtain the food item by appropriately responding to the instructor's teaching procedures will also make the session less effective in regard to the amount of learning or skill acquisition that will occur.

Providing Antecedents Immediately Before Teaching Sessions to Increase Happiness During The Sessions. Again, the A part of the preference-based teaching approach involves doing something the learner enjoys immediately before the teaching session. This usually involves engaging the learner in a brief, highly preferred activity. The goal is to put the learner in a "good mood" to begin the teaching session. A good mood in this respect means that the learner begins to show indices of happiness just before the teaching session starts. Some examples of how instructors have provided preferred events just before a teaching session to enhance the learner's immediate happiness are provided in the illustration on the following page.

There is also an additional benefit of promoting a good mood (i.e., enhancing a learner's happiness) immediately before a teaching session: it can enhance the learner's instruction following during the teaching session. Typically whatever preferred activity is provided as an antecedent to the teaching session involves a learner responding to the staff member's requests to do something. The learner is likely to respond to the requests because they involve something the learner enjoys doing.

For example, the instructor may ask a learner to briefly play a video game with the instructor that the learner enjoys. Playing the game may involve the instructor requesting the learner to turn on the game, press a particular button, etc. Each time the learner responds to a request the instructor can praise the learner's instruction following. Hence, just before the teaching session the learner is following instructions and receiving instructor praise for the desired responses. The repeated instruction following (accompanied by instructor praise) often carries over into the immediately following teaching session in a kind of *behavioral momentum* process. Establishing behavioral momentum in this manner is a good evidence-based strategy for promoting subsequent instruction following among adults with autism and other severe disabilities.

EXAMPLES OF ANTECEDENT ACTIVITIES USED IN PREFERENCE-BASED TEACHING TO PROMOTE LEARNER HAPPINESS IMMEDIATELY BEFORE A TEACHING SESSION

Teaching Situation	Antecedent Activity
Teaching a learner to wash her hands at the sink	Doing "high fives" at the sink right before starting the teaching session
Teaching a learner to select color-coordinated clothing	Describing how nicely the the learner looks when he is dressed up
Teaching a learner how to use a picture communication wallet to show what she wants to order at a fast-food restaurant	Pointing to pictures of food items in the restaurant while asking the learner what she really likes to eat

To effectively carry out the A part of preference-based teaching as a means of making a disliked teaching session more enjoyable for a learner, two aspects of the process warrant attention. First, the preferred antecedent activity must be brief in nature, usually encompassing only a few minutes at most. Otherwise the learner can become tired with the activity such that existing enjoyment may wane before the teaching session is initiated.

Second, the preferred activity must lead directly into the teaching session with no discernable break or time lapse. If a clear break occurs between the antecedent activity and the teaching session then essentially what happens is the teaching session that has historically been disliked by the learner follows termination of a more preferred activity. As noted in previous chapters, discontinuing a preferred activity to immediately begin a less preferred one can evoke unhappiness and problem behavior. To avoid this situation, the preferred antecedent activity should lead almost inconspicuously into the teaching session such that over time, the former activity basically becomes to be viewed by the learner as a part of the actual teaching session.

Happiness during teaching sessions can be enhanced if instructors provide a brief, preferred activity for a learner immediately before a teaching session that leads inconspicuously into the teaching process.

THE BEHAVIOR PART OF PREFERENCE-BASED TEACHING

The behavior or B part of preference-based teaching involves the instructor providing the learner with brief access to preferred items or activities while the teaching session is ongoing. In this case the behavior part pertains to what the instructor *does* (i.e., the instructor's behavior) during the session to promote the learner's happiness. By incorporating something the learner likes within the teaching session, the overall enjoyment the learner experiences with the session is increased.

What the instructor does in this regard should be based on previous assessments of what the learner prefers. This is another reason that systematic preference assessments should be routinely conducted with adults with autism and other severe disabilities in human service agencies (**Chapter 8**). Having conducted such assessments equips instructors with knowledge about what to do during each teaching session that the learner truly enjoys and is likely to promote the learner's happiness. However, before providing preferred events during teaching sessions, it is important to know *when* preferences should be incorporated within the sessions.

When to Provide Preferences During Teaching Sessions. Teaching sessions usually occur in one of two ways. The first way involves multiple instructional trials on a particular skill that is being taught. For example, a teaching session for an adult with profound disabilities may focus on helping the learner learn to press an adaptive switch to activate a CD player so the learner can listen to music when so desired. Typically the session involves repeated instructions (trials) for the learner to press the switch, followed by instructor assistance through prompting if the learner needs help in pressing the switch. Each activation of the switch is followed by the instructor's praise and brief opportunities for the learner to listen to the music.

When multiple instructional trials occur in a teaching session, the instructor periodically can provide something the learner likes briefly after a few trials. With the example of the learner with profound disabilities, this may consist of the instructor briefly massaging the learner's hands after every three or four trials if the learner enjoys having his/her hands massaged. Immediately following each brief massage, the instructor resumes providing more instructional trials. When this occurs across several teaching sessions, the learner comes to associate each session with enjoyment that comes with having his/her hands massaged.

The second way teaching sessions usually occur involves teaching a learner to complete each behavioral step in sequence that constitutes an overall skill. The skill is *task analyzed* into its constituent steps to facilitate the individual's learning of how to perform the overall skill by completing each step one at a time in sequence. To illustrate, a teaching session may be scheduled to teach an adult with autism how to operate a washing machine so the individual will learn how to wash his/her clothes. Operating a washing machine can be broken down with a task analysis into a series of steps such as taking dirty clothes to the laundry room, sorting white from colored items, putting the clothes in the washing machine, etc.

When a teaching session involves using a task analysis to teach a skill to a learner, the instructor can provide a brief, preferred event after the learner completes every few steps in the sequence. With the learner with autism and the teaching session on using a washing machine the event may involve, for example, providing the learner with an opportunity to take a sip of a preferred beverage—just like many adults take a drink of coffee or other desired beverage periodically while performing a chore. The simple act of briefly doing something preferred while completing a task can make the overall process (i.e., the teaching session) more desirable and enhance happiness associated with doing the task.

The discussion to this point has focused on the instructor's behavior as the B part of the ABC preference-based teaching approach. However, the learner's behavior is also an important consideration and especially in regard to deciding when to provide preferred items or activities during a teaching session. In particular, the instructor should consider how the learner has behaved in previous teaching sessions. Special attention should be given to *when* in previous sessions the learner has tended to show indices of unhappiness or even problem behavior.

More specifically, the instructor should note how many instructional trials or steps in a task analysis are completed before the learner has shown unhappiness. The goal is to provide the learner with access to a preference *at or before* the point at which unhappiness has usually occurred. For example, if a learner usually seems fine through three or four trials of a 10-trial teaching session but then appears unhappy around the fifth trial, the preferred event should occur after three or four trials. Similarly, if a learner typically begins to appear unhappy after completing seven steps of a 15-step task, the event should be provided after five or six steps have been completed. In this manner, unhappiness that usually occurs often can be prevented by enhancing the learner's happiness with the preferred event before unhappiness occurs.

Deciding Preferences to Provide During Teaching Sessions. Deciding what items or activities to build within teaching sessions should be based on what has been previously determined to be liked by a learner. Usually the best determination in this respect is based on what systematic preference assessments have revealed about an individual's likes as emphasized previously. However, there are also some general types of activities that are often preferred by many adults with autism and other severe disabilities while teaching sessions are ongoing.

One type of activity that is often liked is brief breaks during a teaching session. One of the most common reasons learners dislike teaching sessions is the effort required of them to repeatedly respond to instructions to do something. The more instructional trials or task-analyzed steps constituting a teaching session, the greater the effort required of the learner to respond. In turn, the more likely it is that such effort will cause unhappiness for the learner. Such effort and the accompanying unhappiness can be prevented or reduced by providing brief breaks during teaching sessions.

Brief breaks allow a learner to relax a little bit before exerting more physical or mental effort to continue responding to instructions. The instructor should be astute in observing when the learner's effort is likely becoming too burdensome and inform the learner that s/he can take a brief break for a minute or so. The instructor also should subsequently inform the learner that the teaching session will begin again in the next few minutes. The latter procedure can make the transition back to responding to instructions predictable for the learner and reduce unpleasantness often associated with unpredictably changing from one activity to another.

Another activity that is frequently preferred by learners with autism and other severe disabilities during teaching sessions pertains to another reason teaching sessions can promote unhappiness: they can be difficult for the learner. Exerting the physical or mental effort to do something that one is not very skilled or fluent in doing can be hard for learners. An instructor can reduce the immediate difficulty a learner experiences with a given instructional task by occasionally instructing the learner to do something that s/he knows how to do and can perform easily.

The process just noted is referred to as *interspersal*. Easy instructional tasks are interspersed among more difficult tasks during a teaching session. Interspersal is a well-established, evidence-based means of making a teaching session periodically easier for a learner and correspondingly, less unpleasant overall.

To illustrate, a session may involve teaching a learner how to identify common signs in community settings such as pedestrian crosswalk indicators, exit signs in buildings, and restroom signs. A learner may have difficulty identifying certain signs that are presented multiple times in a session such as the signs distinguishing a restroom for a man versus a woman. When an instructor observes that a learner is having consistent difficulty identifying specific signs when presented across repeated instructions, the instructor can occasionally intersperse other signs that are easier for the learner to identify.

The interspersal process has several advantages for making a teaching session less unpleasant for a learner. First, it can function as a type of break as illustrated above. In this case, the break does not involve a stop in the session, but a break from having to try to respond to difficult instructions in lieu of responding to an instruction that is easy for the learner.

Second, when learners are presented with difficult instructions such as, for example, those to identify signs for the men's and women's restrooms in the previous example, they often respond incorrectly. Incorrect responses need to be corrected by the instructor and are not followed by the instructor's praise (that usually follows correct responses). The correction procedure by nature involves informing the learner that s/he did not respond in the desired manner, which can be an unpleasant experience for the learner.

Additionally, the learner is receiving less positive attention from the instructor due to the reduced praise statements, which also adds to the unpleasantness. By interspersing an easier instruction, such as by requesting the learner to identify an exit sign which the learner can do easily, a correction procedure does not have to be provided and additional praise can be presented by the instructor. The overall result is that the learner's unhappiness is at least temporarily reduced, which in turn increases the amount of happiness overall.

Another type of preferred activity that can be easily built into teaching sessions is for the instructor to periodically pause between instructions and briefly interact with the learner in a way the learner enjoys. This may involve something like doing a few "high fives" with the learner or a couple of brief "fist bumps". Of course, the instructor must know how the learner likes to be interacted with, such as by doing "high fives" or "fist bumps." If the instructor has taken the time to develop a good relationship with the learner as previously emphasized, knowledge of how to interact with the learner in a way the learner enjoys usually will be quite easy.

> Common preferred activities to provide briefly during teaching sessions include short breaks, presentation of instructions that are easy for the learner to respond to, and interacting with the learner in a way the learner usually enjoys.

THE CONSEQUENCE PART OF PREFERENCE-BASED TEACHING

The consequence or C part of preference-based teaching consists of the instructor providing something that is highly preferred by the learner at the completion of the teaching session. A consequence provided in this manner is different than how preferred consequences are typically used during a teaching session as referred to previously. During teaching sessions desired consequences usually are provided by an instructor to motivate a learner to want to respond correctly to instructions by reinforcing correct learner responses.

Of concern here is to provide something strongly desired by the learner after all instruction is completed. The highly preferred consequence should be presented in addition to the preferred items or activities provided after correct learner responses. How a consequence can be provided in the latter manner, as well as the other (A and B) parts of preference-based teaching is demonstrated in the case illustration on the following page.

When something happens immediately after a teaching session that a learner really likes, it can have a big effect on the learner's happiness associated with future teaching sessions. The learner becomes aware that as soon as s/he completes a session, enjoyable things will happen. The session is essentially paired with enjoyment, which tends to evoke happiness that basically functions to override or reduce the previous unhappiness that a session typically evoked. Additionally, a learner can begin to look forward to forthcoming teaching sessions because in essence, the learner knows that the sessions lead to something very enjoyable.

CASE ILLUSTRATION
EXAMPLES OF PREFERENCES PROVIDED IN PREFERENCE-BASED TEACHING

Background: Ms. Pender, who was 48 years old and lived in a group home, had profound multiple disabilities including spastic quadriplegia. She had a pleasant disposition and enjoyed interactions from support staff. One of her teaching goals was learning to use a hairbrush (she had sufficient mobility to hold and use the brush). However, her home staff reported Ms. Pender appeared to dislike the program as indicated by frequent indices of unhappiness while the program was being conducted. She often frowned and turned away from her staff instructor. It was decided to alter her program with preference-based teaching using previously identified, preferred items and activities.

Preferences provided before each teaching session (A part of preference-based teaching): Just before each teaching session the instructor turned on soft music, talked softly to Ms. Pender, and provided a lighted make-up mirror for her to look at.

Preferences provided during each teaching session (B part): The instructor turned on the soft music and brushed her hair for a few seconds while talking to her.

Preferences provided after each teaching session (C part): The instructor brushed her hair in a styling fashion and provided Ms. Pender a choice of barrettes to put in her hair.

Results: Prior to implementation of the preference-based teaching approach, Ms. Pender displayed unhappiness indices during 15% of the time the teaching program was being implemented. After the approach was initiated she never showed any unhappiness indices. Her independence in using the hairbrush also increased in that she began completing the program steps with just vocal assistance from the instructor whereas previously she always required physical assistance.

As with the other parts of preference-based teaching, what the instructor provides as a consequence after a teaching session should be based on what has previously been shown to be preferred by a learner. It is also important that what is provided is something that has been shown to be among the learner's strongest preferences in contrast to more moderate preferences of the learner (**Chapter 8**). This may involve, for example, the instructor playing a favorite computer game with the learner or a well-liked outdoor activity—whatever it may be that is strongly preferred by each individual learner.

THE IMPORTANT ROLE OF LEARNER CHOICE IN PROMOTING HAPPINESS DURING TEACHING

Providing learners with access to their preferences within the ABC components of preference-based teaching as just described usually makes teaching sessions much more enjoyable for adults with autism and other severe disabilities. In turn, their unhappiness associated with participating in teaching sessions is decreased and their happiness is increased. However, determining specifically how to build preferences into the teaching process can require some preparation on the part of instructors. One way to facilitate the preparation is to ensure learners have choices associated teaching sessions.

The benefits of providing choice opportunities for adults with autism and other severe disabilities were described in **Chapter 7**. All of the benefits can occur with teaching sessions if the sessions involve some choices on the part of learners. Most importantly, providing choices as part of a teaching session allows a learner to access something that is immediately preferred at that specific point in time (i.e., by choosing the most preferred option provided). Providing learner choice opportunities also gives learners increased control over aspects of the teaching process, which is often desired by many individuals.

Providing choices as part of teaching sessions is most practical during the A and C parts of the preference-based teaching approach—that is, immediately before and after a teaching session. Providing choices while teaching is actually ongoing (the B part) is usually less practical. It can be difficult to build choice opportunities within teaching strategies that involve presenting instructions to learners, assisting correct learner responses through prompting, etc., because the choices can interfere with the instructor activities as well as correct learner responses. Nonetheless, there are still many ways to provide choices during the A and C components.

When considering how to provide learner choices immediately before a teaching session it is helpful to consider different types of choices as described in **Chapter 7**. Usually the types of choices that are most applicable to provide to learners immediately before beginning a teaching session are the "what", "how", "where", and "with whom" choices. Examples of how these types of choices have been presented with the A part of preference-based teaching are provided in the following illustration.

Providing "when" choices, such as when a learner would like to participate in a teaching session, can present difficulties in many cases for reasons noted in **Chapter 7**. Specifically in regard to teaching sessions, some learners will likely always choose to participate in a teaching session later rather than sooner. This can cause practical problems when a teaching session can no longer be delayed during a given period of time. Hence, it is generally recommended to use caution if considering "when" types of choices while planning a teaching session.

There are also numerous ways to incorporate choices within the C part of preference-based teaching. One of the most helpful ways is to provide a learner with a choice of what is preferred to do as soon as the teaching session is completed. This type of "what" choice can involve simply asking the learner what s/he would like to do once the teaching session is completed, provided the learner has the skills to respond to a choice presented vocally in this manner.

Asking a learner what is desired to do after a teaching session can also be done before the teaching session is initiated. A learner can be asked at the beginning of the session what s/he would like to do right after the session. Sometimes providing this type of choice can enhance the learner's happiness to a degree before beginning the teaching process. In essence, the learner becomes aware that once the teaching is started, s/he will soon be doing something highly desired. Such awareness can also enhance the learner's willingness to respond appropriately to the instructions provided by the instructor; the learner will want to proceed through the teaching process quickly to access the preferred activity that will be forthcoming.

EXAMPLES OF CHOICES PROVIDED BEFORE A TEACHING SESSION TO ENHANCE LEARNER HAPPINESS

Teaching Situation	Antecedent Choice
Teaching a learner to put stamps on envelopes and put letters in envelopes at work	Choice of which work task to do in a given session: put stamps on envelopes or put letters in envelopes (*what* type of choice)
Teaching a learner to print her name	Choice of printing with a pencil with an animal eraser or a flower eraser on the top of the the pencil (*how* choice)
Teaching a learner to collate manual pages at work	Choice of working at a work room table or in a separate office (*where* choice)
Teaching a learner to make microwave popcorn	Choice of working with staff member "Sue" or staff member "Alice" to make the popcorn (*with whom* choice)

Across all of the choices provided, both before and after a teaching session, it is critical that the choices be presented in a manner appropriate to the learner's skill level for making meaningful choice responses. These may include an open-ended choice, a variety of two-item choices, or even a one-item choice for learners who have the most significant challenges. Each of these types of choices should be presented using the basic protocol for providing consumer choice-making opportunities described in **Chapter 7**.

Certain types of choices can be provided to a learner immediately before and after a teaching session to enhance the learner's happiness that is associated with the session.

SOME SPECIAL CONCERNS WITH PREFERENCE-BASED TEACHING

As indicated earlier, preference-based teaching is an evidence-based means of enhancing enjoyment for adults with autism and other severe disabilities who have histories of showing unhappiness indices and problem behavior during teaching sessions. Research has demonstrated the effectiveness of the overall preference-based teaching approach for increasing indices of happiness as well as with individual strategies used within the overall approach (e.g., providing choice opportunities). However, there are also several concerns with this approach to teaching that warrant attention in certain cases.

One concern pertains to whether incorporating learner access to preferences during teaching sessions will increase the amount of time to conduct the sessions. The concern in this regard exists because in essence, instructors must include procedures within teaching sessions in addition to the basic instructional strategies typically used when teaching. Specifically, instructors must provide preferred items and activities and allow learners time to access their preferences. Choice-making procedures may also be used as described in the previous section.

Applications of preference-based teaching have indicated this to be a valid concern but usually not a significant one. In many cases, teaching sessions using preference-based approaches do not increase the duration of teaching sessions. One explanation for the lack of expanded teaching time is the increased motivation of the learner to access the highly preferred item or activity that immediately follows each session as discussed earlier. The increased motivation can influence the learner to try harder and more quickly to respond appropriately to instructions, which makes the session move more efficiently. Reduced problem behavior that often accompanies preference-based teaching can also expedite the teaching process.

In other cases, preference-based teaching does extend the length of teaching sessions but only by a few minutes. Consequently, the increased time to conduct each session can be relatively insignificant. However, even if increases in time to conduct teaching sessions may be more significant, the overall benefits of enhancing learner happiness during teaching should be weighed against the increased time commitment. If increased happiness among adults with autism and other severe disabilities is valued, as well as decreased unhappiness and challenging behavior, then the extra time to conduct teaching sessions in a preference-based manner would seem worthwhile.

A second issue is more technical in nature and relates to basic learning principles. Concern exists that providing access to preferences as part of teaching may inadvertently reinforce or strengthen problem behavior that occurs during a teaching session. There are two parts to this concern. The first is that if a learner displays problem behavior during a teaching session and the session is immediately followed by something highly desired (the C part of preference-based teaching), the learner may engage in problem behavior in future sessions because it is followed by something the learner really likes. The second part of the concern is similar to the first but pertains to providing preferences during the teaching (the B part): the learner may display problem behavior because it appears to result in the learner accessing something desired.

Research to date suggests that problem behavior does not increase when preference-based teaching procedures are applied—though additional research is needed to be more conclusive in this regard. To guard against inadvertently increasing problem behavior, two features of preference-based teaching associated with the two special concerns just noted warrant close attention when conducting teaching sessions.

First, the preferred item or activity provided immediately after a teaching session should follow the appropriate termination of the session. Appropriate termination means finishing the session when the learner responds correctly to the last instructional request presented. This is a basic requirement of any good teaching session, but is especially important for the concern here. By concluding a teaching session when the learner responds correctly to the last instructional request, the preferred consequence provided at the end of the session by definition follows *appropriate* learner behavior, not problem behavior. Hence, the latter behavior is not likely to be inadvertently reinforced.

The second feature that warrants attention is the provision of preferred items and activities during the teaching session. The instructor should be careful not to provide these right after any problem behavior. Access to preferences is intended to take place prior to when problem behavior has typically occurred in previous teaching sessions. The intent is to *prevent* such behavior by briefly doing something the learner enjoys before unhappiness has usually occurred and has led to problem behavior (that represents a learner's attempt to escape from or avoid ongoing instruction). If the instructor provides brief access to something the learner prefers in this way, unhappiness usually does not increase and problem behavior does not occur.

Chapter Summary: Key Points

1. *Because teaching services are critical for promoting independence among adults with autism and other severe disabilities but are often disliked by many individuals, human service staff must take active steps to teach in ways that learners enjoy— ways that promote happiness and not unhappiness.*

2. *Preference-based teaching is an evidence-based approach to making teaching sessions enjoyable for adults with autism and*

other severe disabilities while maintaining teaching effectiveness for enhancing learner skill development.

3. *A pre-requisite for making teaching enjoyable for adults with autism and other severe disabilities is developing good instructor-learner relationships.*

4. *Preference-based teaching involves an antecedent-behavior-consequence or ABC model. The A part involves providing learner access to preferences immediately before a teaching session, the B part involves the instructor's behavior during the teaching session in terms of embedding preferences within instructional strategies, and the C part involves providing access to highly preferred activities or items immediately after the session.*

5. *When scheduling teaching sessions, the timing of the sessions should be considered so that preferences provided in association with the sessions are likely to be highly desired by learners.*

6. *Antecedent activities provided immediately before a teaching session should lead inconspicuously into the teaching process.*

7. *Common preferred activities to provide briefly during teaching sessions include short breaks, presentation of instructions that are easy for the learner to respond to (interspersal), and interacting with the learner in a way the learner usually enjoys.*

8. *Items and activities provided immediately after a teaching session should represent the strongest preferences of learners.*

9. *Providing choices in association with teaching sessions is a well-established, evidence-based means of enhancing learner enjoyment with the sessions.*

10. *Special concern is warranted regarding how preferences are provided during and after teaching sessions to avoid inadvertently reinforcing or strengthening possible problem behavior among learners.*

CHAPTER 12

TEACHING NATURALISTICALLY TO INCREASE INDEPENDENCE AND PROMOTE HAPPINESS

By now the importance of teaching and otherwise supporting independence as a way to promote happiness among adults with autism and other severe disabilities should be evident. The more independent skills individuals learn and use, the more they will live their lives in ways they want—ways that enhance their daily happiness. Learning and using functional skills also allows adults with autism and other severe disabilities to be less dependent on others to meet their daily needs, which gives them increased control over their lives. People usually enjoy their lives more when they have personal control over how they live on a day-to-day basis.

The preceding chapter focused on how formal teaching programs can be implemented to increase learner happiness during teaching sessions. Carrying out formal teaching programs within specifically designated teaching sessions is critical for adults with autism and other severe disabilities to learn necessary life skills. It is the most widely recognized way of providing teaching services in human service agencies. However, though necessary and important, the impact of formal teaching programs is limited in most human service agencies.

Limitations with the effects of teaching programs exist because there are only so many formal teaching sessions that can be conducted on a daily basis in human service agencies. Formal teaching sessions usually involve one staff person (instructor) working with one consumer (learner) for instructional purposes. Because there are almost always more consumers than staff in an agency, there are practical limits as to how many formal teaching sessions can be conducted with each individual who has a severe disability. Support staff in human service agencies have numerous duties to fulfill every day, each of which competes with available time for carrying out formal teaching programs.

Due to time constraints for conducting formal teaching sessions, human service staff must look for other ways to help people they support learn and use meaningful skills. Specifically, they must find ways to teach *naturalistically*. Naturalistic teaching consists of providing brief instruction within typically occurring activities when formal teaching sessions are not being conducted.

Naturalistic teaching may relate to goals drawn from person-centered plans of individuals but usually does not involve implementation of written teaching plans with specific learning objectives. Naturalistic teaching also does not involve scheduled sessions as occurs with formal teaching. Rather, the teaching is based on agency staff recognizing and taking advantage of naturally occurring opportunities to teach during the routine course of the day.

Naturalistic teaching is referred to in a number of ways. Some of the most common are *embedded teaching, incidental teaching,* and *in-vivo teaching.* Embedded teaching derives its name from the process of *embedding* instruction within an ongoing activity that occurs for some other purpose, such as a self-help routine, a social interaction, or a community recreational event. *Incidental* teaching generally refers to instruction that is basically incidental to the purpose of the activity in which the instruction is provided. *In-vivo* teaching is so named because it refers to teaching within the actual life situation in which a particular skill is needed at the moment.

Despite the various names for naturalistic teaching approaches they all share a common goal of providing instruction on an informal basis during naturally occurring activities. This chapter describes naturalistic teaching as a means of supplementing formal teaching programs and sessions to maximize skill development among consumers in human service agencies. Although the focus is on naturalistic teaching to increase independence, the important relationship between independence and happiness should be kept in mind: increased independence in daily living results in increased happiness among adults with autism and other severe disabilities.

> **To help adults with autism and other severe disabilities learn new skills to develop to their maximum potential, staff should teach *naturalistically* by embedding brief instruction within ongoing activities in human service agencies.**

WHEN NATURALISTIC TEACHING IS MOST APPLICABLE

Naturalistic teaching is most useful in two general situations. The first is when support staff are about to do something for a person with a disability that needs to be done. Instead of performing the task for the person though, staff can use the situation to teach the individual to perform the task him/herself at the exact moment the task needs to be completed.

Staff in human service agencies frequently do things for adults with autism and other severe disabilities in contrast to teaching them to do the tasks themselves. Often staff do things for people they support out of a sincere desire to be helpful. In other cases, staff do things for individuals with disabilities because they can do it more quickly than teaching them to perform the tasks. Still in other cases it is simply easier for staff to do certain things for consumers relative to exerting the effort to teach them.

When human service staff consistently do necessary tasks for adults with autism and other severe disabilities there are major impacts on consumer welfare—many of which are undesirable. In particular, they are promoting *dependence* among consumers of agency services in contrast to independence. As emphasized repeatedly, lack of independence among adults with autism and other severe disabilities impedes happiness on a day-to-day basis.

Continued dependence on others for completing necessary life tasks also results in a *learned helplessness* phenomenon: individuals learn to let others do things for them and lose the motivation to do things for themselves. If agency staff continuously teach people they support naturalistically to do things for themselves when something needs to be done, however, dependence is reduced and learned helplessness is prevented.

The second situation in which naturalistic teaching is most useful pertains to the skill that is desired to be taught to a person with a severe disability. Naturalistic teaching is designed to teach relatively simple skills that involve one or a few specific behaviors that require brief amounts of time to perform. For example, when a staff member is on an elevator with an individual and starts to push the button for the desired floor, instead of pushing the button the staff member could use the immediate opportunity to teach the individual to push the button. Operating an elevator in this manner involves only a brief amount of time and a few skills (i.e., identifying the correct button and then pushing it).

More complex skills usually are not amenable for naturalistic teaching. Complex skills are those that involve a number of specific behaviors or take relatively substantial amounts of time to complete—generally more than a few minutes or so. To illustrate, naturalistic teaching conducted in an impromptu manner would not usually be recommended for teaching a person how to cook a steak on an outdoor grill. Cooking a steak on a grill requires a number of steps or behaviors and cannot be accomplished in just a few minutes.

Teaching adults with autism and other severe disabilities skills that involve many behaviors and require more than a few minutes to perform usually should be taught with a more formal approach as described in **Chapter 11**. However, this does not mean that formal teaching should not occur in the specific situations in which skills are needed, such as when cooking a steak for a weekend meal. As much pre-planned, formal teaching as possible should occur in the situation in which certain skills are needed. The focus here though is on those unplanned moments in which a teaching opportunity arises. Again, this pertains to when a staff person starts to do something for a consumer that the individual could be taught to do on-the-spot without any formal planning.

Naturalistic teaching is usually not recommended for teaching complex or time-consuming tasks for several reasons. One reason is that natural opportunities to teach generally occur without any prior notice; they just arise when a staff person starts to do something for a consumer. As such, the formal planning necessary to teach complex skills (e.g., constructing a task analysis of behaviors that need to be performed) is not possible. A second reason is that on-the-spot teaching by definition occurs within an already ongoing activity. If the teaching requires a person to perform a lot of behaviors or a substantial amount of time, the teaching will interfere with the ongoing activity.

Another reason naturalistic teaching is usually not recommended with complex skills is because of unwanted attention it can place on an adult with autism or other severe disability in certain situations. Naturalistic teaching is especially useful in typical community settings in which other people are present such as restaurants, ball parks, and malls. Many situations can arise in these settings in which something needs to be done that an individual has not had the opportunity to learn to perform. If what needs to be done requires a lot of specific behaviors or skills, teaching will involve a number of instructor actions with the person. These include, for example, presenting repeated instructions and providing assistance with prompting for different skill steps.

Repeatedly instructing, prompting, etc., an adult who has a severe disability in a public place often results in attention directed to the person from other people. The increased attention occurs because it is not common to observe an adult being interacted with in this way, and unusual activity naturally draws attention from others. Frequently the attention directed to the individual with a disability is negative in nature. The negative attention may be in the form of continued staring at the person, pointing at him/her while talking about the situation to companions, and at times, even asking what is wrong with the individual. All of these actions can be unpleasant for adults with autism and other severe disabilities, just as they are for most people.

> **Naturalistic teaching is most applicable when: (1) staff are about to do something for a consumer—instead of doing the task they teach the individual at that moment to do it and, (2) the skill to be taught is simple and involves only a few behaviors to perform and a brief period of time to complete.**

A NATURALISTIC TEACHING PROTOCOL

There is a basic teaching protocol that is usually applicable across all approaches to naturalistic teaching. The protocol is based on well-established principles of learning developed through research and application in applied behavior analysis (ABA). It was designed specifically for support staff in human service agencies to maximize learning opportunities for individuals with autism and other severe disabilities as they go about their daily routines and activities.

THE THREE STEPS OF NATURALISTIC TEACHING

The basic protocol of naturalistic teaching consists of three steps: (1) instruct, (2) prompt if necessary and, (3) reinforce. The second step—providing assistance with prompting—is not always necessary as described below. However, the first and third steps of instructing and reinforcing should always be included.

Instruct. When a staff member is about to do something for a consumer as part of an ongoing activity, the first thing the staff person should do within naturalistic teaching is refrain from completing the task and *instruct* the individual to do it. This involves simply telling the person to do what needs to be done, usually by just saying what needs to be done or perhaps with manual signing for individuals who communicate with signs. As just noted, the best situations in which to begin the naturalistic teaching process with an instruction is when the task the staff member is about to do involves only a few behaviors to complete and a brief amount of time.

Prompt. In a number of cases, when a staff member instructs a consumer to do something that the staff person was about to do, the individual immediately responds in the desired manner by doing what was requested. At this point the staff member should reinforce the individual's actions (see below). However, in many other cases the consumer will not respond to the instruction. When this happens the staff member should provide some assistance by *prompting* the individual to do what was instructed.

Providing assistance through prompting was referred to in the preceding chapter. An effective prompting process involves providing increased assistance to a person to make it more likely the individual will appropriately complete the instructed task. The instructor (staff person) should begin with the least amount of help that s/he thinks the learner (person with a disability) requires to correctly complete the task. If the increased assistance is insufficient in promoting the learner's desired response then the instructor should provide even more assistance. This process should continue until the learner correctly performs the instructed task.

In some cases a learner may respond to the instructor's request but do something other than what is desired to complete the task. That is, the learner will make an error. When this happens, the learner's actions should be immediately interrupted. The instructor should then implement the prompting process by repeating the instruction and providing increased assistance sufficient to result in the learner's successful completion of the task.

Reinforce. The third step of the naturalistic teaching protocol consists of *reinforcing* the learner's correct completion of the instructed task. As discussed with formal teaching (**Chapter 11**), reinforcement involves following the learner's behavior with something preferred by the learner that will increase the learner's behavior. In this case, the intent is to reinforce the learner's instruction-following behavior associated with correctly completing the task requested by the instructor.

The reinforcement step of naturalistic teaching almost always consists of the instructor praising the learner's correct behavior in some manner. Of course, the instructor's praise or positive attention must be something the learner will strive to obtain if it is to effectively reinforce the desired behavior of the learner. This represents one more reason that staff in human service agencies must develop good relationships with consumers with whom they work and interact. If a good relationship between an instructor and learner has been established, the instructor's positive attention will likely be something the learner desires and will strive to obtain as discussed in **Chapter 11**.

In the discussion on formal teaching in the preceding chapter it was emphasized that sometimes preferred items and activities other than praise are necessary to motivate a learner to respond appropriately to instructions. However, in naturalistic teaching the latter reinforcing consequences are rarely used. Special items and activities are usually not possible to use as reinforcers during naturalistic teaching. Because naturalistic teaching is not pre-planned and occurs impromptu when an occasion arises, special items and activities are usually not available to provide as reinforcers for the learner's behavior.

Even if available in some cases, items and activities are usually not desirable to use within a naturalistic teaching context to reinforce learner responding. In essence, the items and activities typically are not part of the naturally ongoing activity and bringing them in as part of the teaching process can interfere with the activity. More importantly, however, use of items and activities that are not part of an ongoing activity—and especially when the teaching occurs in a community situation—can bring unwanted attention to the learner as described previously. In contrast, a brief praise statement or other expression of approval can be provided in a manner that is not unusual in community settings and does not draw unwanted attention from others.

> **Three basic steps of naturalistic teaching are: (1) instruct a learner to do something, (2) provide assistance if necessary to help the learner do the instructed task with prompting and, (3) reinforce the learner's completion of the task.**

HELPING STAFF TO USE NATURALISTIC TEACHING: SWAT

One reason many human service staff do not teach naturalistically during the course of the day is they simply do not think about opportunities to teach. Conscientious staff are busy trying to get everything done that they are charged with doing and become preoccupied with completing their numerous duties. One way to help staff remember to refrain from doing things for adults with severe disabilities and take advantage of opportunities to teach individuals to do things for themselves is to familiarize staff with the *SWAT* process. SWAT is basically a mnemonic strategy in the form of an acronym.

SWAT stands for say (S), wait (W), act out (A), and touch to guide (T). It was designed through applied research to help staff (again, representing the instructors) remember to initiate naturalistic teaching at the moment they begin to do a simple but necessary task for a consumer (learner). SWAT can help staff remember to instruct the learner and provide assistance as needed through a least-to-most assistive prompting strategy.

The "say" or S part of SWAT means to say or tell a learner to do something that immediately needs to be done (the instruction step of the naturalistic teaching protocol). To illustrate, when preparing to open a bottle of soda for a learner, instead of opening the bottle the instructor could say something like "You can open the bottle for yourself; you open it". Next, the instructor should wait (W) to see if the learner begins to twist the cap off the bottle. If the learner does not begin to do so, the instructor could then "act out" (A) what is desired for the learner to do by gesturing to twist the bottle cap. If the learner still does not initiate twisting the cap, the instructor could then provide slight physical assistance (touch to guide or T) to help the learner twist open the bottle cap.

The A and T parts of SWAT, or act out and touch to guide, represent a common means of implementing a less-to-more assistive prompt sequence when teaching adults with autism and other severe disabilities. The acting out represents a type of *modeling* in which a learner is shown how to do something. The touch to guide represents a way to provide partial physical guidance to help a learner, which generally provides more assistance than modeling. As much physical assistance can be provided within the touch-to-guide step as necessary to ensure the learner completes the desired task.

The W part of SWAT is included simply to help instructors remember to give a learner time to respond to an initial instruction to do something. One of the most common mistakes human service staff make when teaching people with severe disabilities is failure to give time for individuals to respond to an instruction. People with intellectual disabilities and autism often need more time than most people to process or understand something that is said to them. Hence, there is frequently a delay after an instruction is presented before individuals will respond to the instruction.

Failure of instructors to provide time for learners to respond to an instruction is particularly common at moments that naturalistic teaching can be conducted. Naturalistic teaching occurs during an ongoing activity and staff are often focusing on getting the activity done in an expeditious manner. By recalling the W part of SWAT and adhering to that step can increase the likelihood that staff will allow individuals time to respond to an instruction. This can prevent staff from providing increased assistance through prompting prematurely when more assistance is not really needed.

It should be noted that a key part of the basic teaching protocol is not included in the SWAT acronym—that of reinforcing the learner's appropriate response to the initial instruction or subsequent prompt. As with all good teaching as described in the preceding chapter, correct learner responses should be reinforced by the instructor. With the naturalistic teaching protocol, and with SWAT, this usually means praising or otherwise providing positive attention for the learner's completion of the correct response. The reinforcing aspect of teaching is not included in SWAT simply to keep the acronym brief and easy to remember. Additionally, most human service staff have received training in how to reinforce desired learner behavior and tend to provide reinforcement more readily than other aspects of teaching.

> **SWAT is a way to help staff remember to teach naturalistically during daily activities and stands for Say (S), Wait and Watch (W), Act Out (A) and Touch to Guide (T).**

An example of how SWAT has been used in a naturalistic teaching application in a community setting is provided in the following illustration. Additional information on SWAT and related naturalistic teaching approaches is provided in the **Selected Readings**.

CASE ILLUSTRATION
EXAMPLE OF NATURALISTIC TEACHING IN A COMMUNITY SETTING

Background. Mr. Henne was a gentleman with autism on the severe end of the spectrum. Although he did not speak (he communicated with familiar people through idiosyncratic gestures and a few manual signs), he usually responded to requests and instructions that were spoken and signed to him by his support staff. Every week or two he went to a grocery store with a support staff, Mr. Lowe, to obtain groceries for his home. Mr. Henne and Mr. Lowe had known each other for many years and appeared to have a very good relationship as indicated, for example, by Mr. Henne frequently smiling when Mr. Lowe interacted with him and approaching Mr. Lowe when he entered the room. During one of the shopping trips Mr. Lowe's supervisor went along and noticed that Mr. Lowe performed most activities at the store for Mr. Henne such as pushing the shopping cart and selecting items from store shelves to put in the cart. Mr. Henne merely followed behind Mr. Lowe as Mr. Lowe performed essentially all the shopping tasks.

Naturalistic Teaching. The supervisor explained to Mr. Lowe that he could help Mr. Henne do more things for himself by using naturalistic teaching during the shopping trips. The supervisor explained the SWAT approach, showed Mr. Lowe how to use it during a meeting, and then had Mr. Lowe practice it in a role-play situation. The supervisor then asked Mr. Lowe to begin applying SWAT in the grocery store.

Outcome. The supervisor continued going to the grocery store and observed Mr. Lowe using the SWAT steps during the next shopping trip. By the third shopping trip after the meeting Mr. Henne was observed to be pushing the cart by himself and selecting items from the store shelves when Mr. Lowe pointed out which items to select from the grocery list. At this point Mr. Henne was shopping in a manner similar to other adults in the grocery store.

KEY SITUATIONS FOR NATURALISTIC TEACHING

Two general situations in which naturalistic teaching is most applicable were emphasized previously. The first situation is when support staff are about to do something for a consumer. Instead of doing the task for the individual, a staff member can teach the person to do it for him/herself. The second is when the task that a staff member is about to do involves only a few behaviors and a brief amount of time to complete. However, there are also some more special situations that are especially advantageous to teach in a naturalistic manner.

Naturalistic Teaching in Community Settings and Activities

One good time for naturalistic teaching has already been noted: activities within typical community settings. Adults with autism and other severe disabilities have the right to participate in the same activities that other people do outside their homes. Multiple benefits occur when adults with severe disabilities participate in community activities. These include, just to name a few, opportunities to develop new preferences, interact with others, develop new acquaintances, and learn many functional skills. The benefits are much more significant if individuals are supported in actively participating in community activities in contrast to simply *being in* a community setting without having the skills and support to actively participate.

Community activities almost always involve doing new or varied things. As adults with autism and other severe disabilities encounter new situations, applications of naturalistic teaching can be highly useful for helping them learn to function independently within those situations. Whether it is the simple act of filling a cup with ice at a soda machine in a convenience store, stepping on an escalator at the mall for the first time, or putting a token in a coin collection machine on a bus, for example, the act represents a basic skill that can be taught to people with severe disabilities naturalistically at the point in time when the skill is needed.

Human service staff should be continuously vigilant about recognizing moments in which they are about to do something for a consumer in a community situation and use that moment as a naturalistic teaching opportunity. Teaching with the SWAT approach or similar approaches (again, see **Selected Readings** for references to other naturalistic teaching applications) can be readily incorporated into the ongoing activity in a brief manner without interrupting the natural flow of things. Each application of naturalistic teaching in this impromptu manner can help adults with autism and other severe disabilities become more independent and active members in their local communities.

Teaching When Consumers are Naturally Motivated to Learn

One of the best times for naturalistic teaching is when an individual wants staff help to do something. A common example relates to the situation just noted in which a staff member teaches an individual to open a bottle of soda. Sometimes a consumer will approach a staff member and hold a soda bottle in front of the staff member. At that moment it is clear the individual wants the staff member to open the bottle. Instead of opening the bottle, however, the staff member could use naturalistic teaching to teach the person to open the bottle. With good teaching in this manner, in the future the consumer would not be dependent on finding a staff member to open the bottle when a soda is desired.

When it is apparent that a consumer wants a staff member's help to do something, a good opportunity to teach usually exists because the individual is naturally motivated at that point. The person wants to accomplish something to attain a desired outcome (e.g., getting a bottle of soda opened to consume the beverage in the previous example). Consequently, the individual is likely to try diligently to respond to the staff member's instruction to do the task. Responding to the staff member's instruction (and prompting if necessary) will be followed by a naturally reinforcing consequence—whatever desired outcome initially motivated the individual to seek the staff member's assistance.

TEACHING TYPICAL INSTRUCTION FOLLOWING

In **Chapter 10** it was noted that some adults with autism and other severe disabilities display what are considered poor instruction-following skills. These individuals frequently do not comply with requests and instructions from staff and others to do something. In the most serious cases, attempts by staff to follow up on initial instructions to do something are accompanied by consumer problem behavior. The problem behavior represents efforts by individuals to avoid having to do what is instructed. Naturalistic teaching can be a pleasant and effective means to help teach such individuals typical instruction-following skills.

Before describing how naturalistic teaching can be used to teach instruction-following skills, it should be emphasized that the focus is on *typical* instruction following. That is, adults with autism and other severe disabilities can benefit from learning how to respond to instructions that most adults typically respond to in an appropriate manner. This means appropriately responding to such instructions as "Please pass me the salt", "Would you turn on the light please", "Put on your seat belt", and numerous other typical instructions that most adults usually comply with on a routine basis. The goal is to help adults with severe disabilities participate in common interactions with other people in socially acceptable ways like most adults.

It is important to note that the goal *is not to make adults with autism and other severe disabilities compliant to everything staff instruct them to do.* In some agencies there is a philosophy among staff that they are in charge and consumers should always do what they say. When individuals do not consistently comply with staff instructions, they are considered noncompliant. They may even have a behavior support plan because the noncompliance is considered a behavior problem. Such a view is problematic from several perspectives. Most notably, no adult always does what someone instructs him or her to do, and adults with autism and other severe disabilities likewise should not be expected to always do what is instructed by others.

When human service staff expect total compliance by people they support they are in essence attempting to be in control of the consumers' lives. As stressed in this chapter and others, individual happiness is enhanced in proportion with how much control a person has over his/her daily life—not how much control the staff have. Hence, sound judgment is needed by staff when considering the degree of instruction following that should be expected among people they support. Such judgment should be based on what is typically expected of most adults in regard to following instructions of others, as well as on what are considered highly important instructions to follow in accordance with individual person-centered plans (**Chapter 9**).

Additionally, frequent lack of instruction following or what is considered noncompliance should not be viewed as a behavior problem among adults with autism and other severe disabilities. Rather, it represents a failure of staff to teach typical instruction-following skills. Such skills are necessary to help people with severe disabilities participate in important activities as identified in their person-centered plans as well as to help them successfully participate in social situations with other adults.

Some types of typical instruction-following skills can be addressed in formal teaching programs as described in **Chapter 11**. Naturalistic teaching can also be applied to help adults with autism and other severe disabilities learn socially appropriate instruction-following skills. Naturalistic teaching of instruction following can also be done in a manner that is usually quite pleasant for most adults with severe disabilities.

Lack of instruction following, or noncompliance, among adults with autism and other severe disabilities should not be considered a problem behavior; it represents a failure of caregivers to teach typical instruction-following skills.

As with naturalistic teaching in general, teaching instruction following naturalistically means embedding the teaching within typically occurring activities of consumers. The basic naturalistic teaching protocol and variations of the protocol such as SWAT are used during ongoing activities specifically to teach instruction following. However, in contrast to teaching how to do something on the spot that an individual does not know how to do as occurs with other applications of naturalistic teaching, the intent is to teach a general *skill set* of instruction following. This is also referred to as a *response class* in which the desired response is doing what is instructed at that moment.

Building an instruction-following skill set involves a consumer having opportunities to respond to an instruction, responding appropriately, and having the instruction-following behavior reinforced. The more times instruction following is reinforced across different instructions, the more likely it becomes that the individual will appropriately respond to future instructions. Hence, naturalistic teaching of instruction following means embedding instructions within ongoing activities that are very likely to be appropriately responded to by consumers so that their responses can be reinforced.

To make it likely that a person will appropriately respond to a given instruction, the instruction should be one that the individual can easily respond to (i.e., the person has already learned how to perform the instructed behavior). The person should also have a history of responding appropriately to the instruction in the past. On a practical basis, this means that the individual should be instructed to do something s/he can do quickly and easily and whenever possible, enjoys doing. For example, if a person knows how to do "high fives" with someone and seems to enjoy giving "high fives", then requesting the individual to give a "high five" would be good for naturalistic teaching of instruction following. Once the person gives a staff member a "high five" following the staff member's instruction (e.g., "Give me a high five"), then the "high five" instruction-following behavior can be reinforced by the staff member.

Instructions to do something that a person usually does allow for the individual to receive a lot of reinforcement for following instructions. Again, the more often a person's behavior is reinforced—in this case, instruction-following behavior—the more likely the behavior will occur in the future. Additionally, by providing instruction-following opportunities and reinforcement across a variety of different instructions (all of which a consumer is likely to respond to as just emphasized), the person begins to develop a skill set of instruction following that will carry over to many more instructions.

In short, to teach instruction-following skills with naturalistic teaching, human service staff should try to embed instructions that are easy to follow within a variety of day-to-day situations. Using instructions that a consumer has a history of responding to makes it likely the person will comply with each embedded instruction and receive reinforcement for such compliance. In those cases where a consumer might not immediately respond to the embedded instruction then the naturalistic teaching protocol can be implemented to help the individual respond with prompting. However, if certain instructions require follow-up prompting, then usually they should be withdrawn from the naturalistic, instruction-following teaching process in favor of instructions that are more likely followed by the individual's compliance.

> **Naturalistic teaching is especially advantageous for helping adults with severe disabilities learn useful skills within community settings and activities, when they are naturally motivated to learn, and to enhance their general instruction-following skills.**

PROMOTING STAFF APPLICATION OF NATURALISTIC TEACHING

Just as with all the other evidence-based approaches to promoting happiness among adults with autism and other severe disabilities, human service staff need active support to carry out naturalistic teaching effectively. In particular, staff need to be well trained and actively supervised to ensure people they support are consistently provided with naturalistic teaching services. The final chapter in this book summarizes the essence of effective staff training and supervision.

In considering the information in **Chapter 13** on supervisory support for staff performance that increases consumer happiness, special attention is warranted to ensure such support focuses on naturalistic teaching by staff. Initially, staff need to be well trained in how to teach naturalistically. This is an area in which staff training has traditionally been lacking in many human service agencies.

Many agencies recognize the importance of training staff how to teach people with severe disabilities. Generally, however, that training focuses on carrying out formal teaching programs in designated teaching sessions as discussed in the previous chapter. Such training is critical for helping staff promote consumer independence and happiness by teaching them meaningful life skills. It is not sufficient though to equip staff with the specific skills to teach naturalistically during daily activities.

Behavior analytic research has shown that staff also need training specific to naturalistic teaching. Such training should include how to apply teaching procedures used in formal teaching sessions (e.g., prompting, reinforcing) briefly within ongoing activities. The training should also include how to recognize and take advantage of naturally occurring opportunities to teach.

Additionally, once staff have been effectively trained in how to teach naturalistically, their day-to-day use of naturalistic teaching must be actively supervised. Research has demonstrated repeatedly that without ongoing supervision, staff performance is almost always of a lessor quality than what it could and should be on routine basis.

Again, the next chapter summarizes what that supervision should entail.

A Final Note on Naturalistic Teaching and Happiness

Earlier it was noted that naturalistic teaching represents a pleasant way to teach. That is, the teaching process is often enjoyed by adults with autism and other severe disabilities. Being the recipient of a naturalistic teaching application is pleasant for people for several reasons. The first reason pertains to one of the specific situations in which naturalistic teaching is very applicable—when it is apparent that a person with a severe disability wants staff help to do something. By teaching the individual to do what is desired instead of staff doing it for the person, the individual learns that s/he can now do what was desired without having to wait or otherwise depend on staff. Such a realization is usually quite pleasing for adults with autism and other severe disabilities just as it is for all of us.

Many experienced staff have observed the satisfaction experienced by individuals with autism and other severe disabilities when they accomplish something for themselves for the first time. The satisfaction is evident when a consumer who has just been taught to do something in the moment it needs to be done looks at the staff person (instructor) and smiles. It is evident that the individual is happy with him/herself, which in turn can be most satisfying for the instructing staff person.

Most of us tend to be pleased when we are able to do something for the first time that previously we needed someone else to do for us. This may be, for example, when we are able to successfully program the remote control for a new television instead of having to call technical assistance from the company that sold us the television. Similarly, many people are quite pleased when they change a tire on their car for the first time and did not have to call and wait for roadside assistance. We generally feel good about such accomplishments for a variety of reasons, and the same holds true for adults with autism and other severe disabilities.

A second reason that naturalistic teaching is usually pleasant for the individual being taught is due to one of the more general situations in which it is applied. Specifically, because it is used to teach new skills that involve only a few behaviors to perform and a short period of time, responding to the instructor is not very effortful for the learner. Performing things that are less effortful are generally preferred by people relative to performing more effortful things. Hence, some of the reluctance people have with trying to learn complex skills that require a lot of effort does not occur with usual applications of naturalistic teaching. Learning the skills is usually quick and easy, which tends to make the process rather pleasant.

CHAPTER SUMMARY: KEY POINTS

1. *Naturalistic teaching involves providing brief instruction within typically occurring activities at the moment a particular skill is needed.*

2. *Naturalistic teaching is most applicable when a staff member is about to perform a simple, brief task for a person with a severe disability; instead of performing the task for the person, the staff member teaches the individual how to perform the task at that moment.*

3. *One approach to naturalistic teaching that can be used in many ongoing situations is SWAT: Say, Wait, Act out, Touch to guide. The staff member says (S) or instructs what needs to be done, waits (W) to see if the person does it and if not, acts out (A) what needs to be done by gesturing or modeling and if the person still does not do it, provides slight physical assistance (touches to guide or T).*

4. *Naturalistic teaching or SWAT is well suited for teaching adults with autism and other severe disabilities in community situa-*

tions, when a person indicates a desire for help in getting something done, and for teaching typical instruction-following skills.

5. *For naturalistic teaching to occur on a routine basis to promote independence among adults with autism and other severe disabilities, support staff must be effectively trained in how to conduct naturalistic teaching and actively supported by their supervisors in teaching during routinely occurring activities.*

CHAPTER 13

WORKING WITH STAFF TO PROMOTE CONSUMER HAPPINESS

Preceding chapters have presented the most evidence-based strategies staff can use to promote happiness among adults with autism and other severe disabilities in human service agencies. When considered in total, the strategies provide human service staff with many ways to help people they support experience happiness on a day-to-day basis. However, for the strategies to actually have the intended effect of enhancing individual happiness, staff must use the strategies in the way they are supposed to be used.

For human service staff to effectively use evidence-based strategies to promote consumer happiness, the staff must be aware of the strategies and skilled in their application. Most people who obtain human service jobs though have no formal preparation for working with adults with autism and other severe disabilities—and particularly people hired into direct support positions. Consequently, they must be specifically *trained* how to perform their job duties, including how to use strategies to promote happiness among individuals who have severe disabilities.

Ensuring staff are well trained is critical for staff to be able to promote individual happiness as they go about their daily work. However, although training is necessary in this regard, it is rarely sufficient; staff also must be effectively *supervised* once trained. It is well established through research and every day experience that supervision is necessary to ensure human service staff perform their work diligently and proficiently. Of particular concern here, staff performance must be supervised to ensure strategies to promote happiness among the people they support are routinely used by staff *and* used appropriately.

This chapter provides an overview of what constitutes effective training and supervision of staff performance in human service agencies. The approach to working with staff that will be described is based on over four decades of behavior analytic research. Such research provides a strong evidence base for the staff training and supervision approach to be presented.

Notice that the purpose of the chapter is to provide an *overview* of evidence-based staff training and supervision. All aspects of effectively working with staff in human service agencies cannot be adequately described in one chapter. Hence, only key features of an evidence-based approach to training and supervision will be presented. The section in the **Selected Readings** on **Working with Staff** provides references to other sources that describe this area in much more detail. Additionally, references to specific sources that are especially pertinent to key points in this chapter will be provided where relevant.

For staff to effectively apply evidence-based strategies to promote happiness among adults with autism and other severe disabilities in human service agencies, the staff must be properly trained and supervised in using the strategies.

IMPORTANCE OF WORKING WITH STAFF TO PROMOTE WORK QUALITY *AND* WORK ENJOYMENT

Supervisory responsibilities in human service agencies are usually considered with respect to ensuring staff perform their duties diligently and proficiently. In short, supervisors are expected to work actively to support quality staff performance and when necessary, take action to improve performance that is not of sufficient quality. However, there is another key aspect of supervision that is especially relevant for ensuring staff effectively promote happiness among the people they support: supervising in a manner that enhances staff enjoyment with their work.

There are a number of reasons why supervisors should strive to help staff enjoy their jobs. In particular, enhancing work enjoyment can lead to increased productivity on the job. Increased work enjoyment can also reduce staff absenteeism and turnover, which in turn affects productivity. Most importantly for the concern here though, how much staff enjoy their work in human service agencies directly affects enjoyment among consumers of their supports and services.

The relationship between staff work enjoyment and consumer happiness is well illustrated by considering what happens when staff do not enjoy their jobs. When staff are disgruntled with their daily work they tend to complain to each other or otherwise engage in negative interactions. The disgruntlement and negativity carries over to their interactions with consumers. Basically, being displeased with the day-to-day job puts staff in a bad mood. Being in a bad mood sets the occasion for staff to be rather negative or unpleasant as they go about their daily duties, including duties directly involving consumers of agency services.

Lack of staff work enjoyment also affects their work motivation. When staff dislike their job they often tend to do the least amount of work necessary. They simply do only what is required to avoid the wrath of their supervisors and get through the work day as easily as possible. This lack of work motivation reduces the amount of work they complete, including what they do to promote happiness among the people they support.

In contrast, when staff truly enjoy their work they are much more likely to be in a good or generally upbeat mood. Being in a good mood usually means staff go about their work in a much more pleasant manner, including how they interact with the people they support.

Staff are also more likely to exert extra effort in completing their job duties instead of just getting through the work day with the least amount of effort possible. Exerting more effort can lead to doing more things specifically to help the people with disabilities they support enjoy their day and experience happiness.

The following discussion is presented with specific concerns for not only promoting quality job performance but also staff enjoyment with their work. Many of the **Selected Readings** on working with staff also include a focus on work enjoyment as part of recommended supervisory practices. Additionally, a curriculum for training supervisors in this approach to supervision, *The Supervisor Training Curriculum: Evidence-Based Ways to Promote Work Quality and Enjoyment Among Support Staff*, is referenced in the **Selected Readings.**

> **The most effective supervision involves promoting diligent and proficient staff performance *and* staff enjoyment with their work.**

AN EVIDENCE-BASED PROTOCOL FOR SUPERVISING STAFF WORK PERFORMANCE

Working with staff to effectively promote work quality and enjoyment involves a systematic supervisory process. The key steps of the process are summarized in the following evidence-based supervision protocol. Each of the steps will be discussed in subsequent sections. More detailed information on this systematic approach to supervising staff in human service agencies is provided in *The Supervisor's Guidebook: Evidence-Based Strategies for Promoting Work Quality and Enjoyment Among Human Service Staff* referenced in the **Selected Readings**.

EVIDENCE-BASED SUPERVISION PROTOCOL

Step 1: Identify desired consumer outcomes.

Step 2: Specify what staff must do to assist consumers in attaining identified outcomes.

Step 3: Train staff in performance duties specified in Step 2.

Step 4: Monitor staff performance.

Step 5: Support proficient staff performance.

Step 6: Correct nonproficient staff performance.

Step 7: Continuously evaluate staff performance and consumer outcome attainment.

SUPERVISORY STEP 1: IDENTIFY DESIRED CONSUMER OUTCOMES

The evidence-based supervisory process begins with identifying outcomes that are desired for consumers of agency services to attain. For purposes of promoting happiness, the desired outcomes focus on frequent indices of consumer happiness and infrequent indices of unhappiness. **Chapters 3** and **4** described how such indices can be clearly identified and validated.

Sometimes other outcomes also are desired to be attained that relate to happiness of consumers of agency services. For example, selected outcomes may include increased choice making **(Chapter 7)** or enhanced independence through skill development **(Chapters 11 and 12)**. However, when the main concern is to promote individual happiness, the latter types of outcomes should always be accompanied by outcomes relating directly to indices of happiness and unhappiness as points of emphasis with the supervisory protocol.

Supervisory Step 2: Specify What Staff Must Do to Assist Consumers in Attaining Identified Outcomes

Once desired consumer outcomes have been identified, then what staff should do on the job to help individuals attain the outcomes should be carefully specified. In particular, those performance expectations necessary for staff to promote individual happiness should be specified as precise work behavior in which staff are expected to engage. In some cases, it may also be necessary to specify when, where, and with whom staff should engage in the targeted work behavior.

How staff performance expectations related to consumer happiness can be specified as observable work behavior has been described in previous chapters. Some of these are relatively straightforward, such as how to interact with people who have severe disabilities as discussed in **Chapter 6** (e.g., how to interact in positive versus negative ways, providing each individual in a group with attention on a regular basis). Others are more complex, such as establishing good relationships with consumers **(Chapter 5)**, identifying individual preferences **(Chapter 8)**, and embedding preferences within disliked but necessary activities to make the activities more enjoyable **(Chapter 10)**.

It is a supervisor's job to make sure performance expectations related to promoting consumer happiness are very well specified and clear for staff. Human service staff cannot be expected to perform work duties proficiently if they are not clear what they must do to fulfill those duties. Specifying important staff duties as precise things to do—or work behavior in which to engage—is also necessary for carrying out the remaining steps of the evidence-based approach to supervision. Again, information provided in previous chapters can serve as a guide for how to delineate strategies for promoting happiness as specific staff actions.

SUPERVISORY STEP 3: TRAIN STAFF IN PERFORMANCE DUTIES SPECIFIED IN STEP 2

The importance of training human service staff in the skills to perform their jobs proficiently has already been noted. It has been emphasized that because staff usually begin their human service roles with no formal preparation for working with adults who have autism and other severe disabilities, they must be trained once they obtain their jobs. What has not been emphasized, although of equal importance, is that experienced staff in human service agencies also require training at least on a periodic basis.

Even the most experienced human service staff frequently have not been trained in specific ways to promote happiness among adults with autism and other severe disabilities. It is simply assumed they will go about their job duties in ways that consumers enjoy. However, just as consumer happiness should not be taken for granted in human service agencies, staff skills for effectively promoting such happiness should not be taken for granted. Staff usually need formal training in evidence-based strategies to enhance happiness among adults who have severe disabilities.

Human service agencies typically acknowledge the importance of training their staff in necessary job skills and offer a variety of training programs. A problem exists though in how agencies usually go about staff training. Investigations have shown repeatedly that typical staff training programs in the human services are often ineffective for equipping staff with the work skills required to perform their jobs proficiently. Fortunately, there is a well-established technology that agencies can use to train work skills to staff in a highly effective manner. The basic components of this evidence-based, staff training protocol are provided in the illustration on the following page.

The staff training protocol (sometimes referred to as *behavioral skills training* with staff) is both *performance-* and *competency-based.* The performance aspects pertain to what the staff trainers should do or perform as well as what the staff trainees must perform. The competency aspect involves ensuring that staff trainees demonstrate competence in performing the skills that are the focus of the training before completing the training process. How the staff training approach is performance- and competency-based is exemplified in the following description of the component steps of the training protocol. The description pertains to training a group of staff in a formal training session but is also relevant when training an individual staff person in a more informal manner.

PERFORMANCE- AND COMPETENCY-BASED STAFF TRAINING PROTOCOL

Step 1: Describe the target skill to be trained.

Step 2: Provide a written description of the target skill to be trained.

Step 3: Demonstrate the target skill.

Step 4: Have staff trainees practice performing the target skill and provide feedback.

Step 5: Repeat steps 1, 3, and 4 until staff demonstrate competence in performing the target skill.

Training Step 1: Describe The Skill To Be Trained. A training session should begin by the trainer describing the target skill that the staff trainees are expected to learn how to perform. The description should be very detailed in terms of specifying the exact behavior staff need to engage in to perform the target skill (refer back to Step 2 of the evidence-based supervision protocol). The presentation of the skill to be trained should also be accompanied by a rationale for why the skill is important for the trainees to learn how to perform.

For example, when training staff how to provide choice opportunities for adults with severe disabilities in a manner appropriate to each individual's skill level (**Chapter 7**), the benefits of people having choice-making opportunities should be presented. This could involve explaining that when consumers make choices during daily activities, they gain personal control over their day, they are more likely to actively participate in the activities, their happiness with the activities can be enhanced and, in some cases problem behavior can be prevented or reduced. Staff trainees can be much more accepting of being required to participate in a training session if they understand why they are expected to learn to perform the new skill as part of their work routine.

Training Step 2: Provide A Written Description of The Target Skill. Following the trainer's description of the target skill to be trained, a written summary of the skill should be provided to trainees. Just like the vocal description, the written version should be very specific in terms of describing the exact behavior the trainees will need to engage in to perform the skill. One of the best ways to provide the written version is through a *performance checklist*. A performance checklist is much like a task analysis of a skill that is taught to individuals with intellectual and other developmental disabilities. In this case though the written document describes the staff behaviors and the sequence in which the behaviors should be completed to perform the target skill.

It is critical that the written summary be provided to each participating staff trainee. The written summary also should be prepared in a manner commensurate with the trainees' reading skills and be as concise as possible. The written description can be kept by each trainee after completion of the training session and serve as a reminder for conscientious staff regarding how to perform their new work skill.

Training Step 3: Demonstrate The Target Skill. After trainees have listened to and read the description of the target skill, the trainer should demonstrate how to perform the skill for the trainees. This often involves a role-play exercise by the trainer. If the skill being trained involves interaction with a consumer in some way, the trainer can solicit the help of a staff trainee to play the role of the consumer.

In the latter situation the trainer should give the assisting trainee clear instructions about what to do during the role play.

The trainer should be careful to perform the target skill in the exact manner the skill has been described vocally and on the written information given to staff. An underlying assumption of this training step is that the trainer is proficient in performing the skill that is being trained to staff. To make sure this assumption is accurate, the trainer may need to practice performing the target skill prior to the training session to ensure the demonstration occurs appropriately.

At this point in the training process the trainees have been provided with several formats for learning how to perform the target skill. They have listened to a description of the skill, read the description, and seen the skill being performed. Presenting the skill in several formats enhances the likelihood respective trainees will grasp how to perform the skill based on each trainee's preferred learning style. That is, some staff learn best by listening whereas others learn best by reading. Most of the time, however, staff learn best by seeing relative to listening or reading. Consequently, the trainer's demonstration of the skill is critical. It also represents the first part of the performance-based aspect of this evidence-based means of training work skills to staff—the trainer *performs* the skill.

Training Step 4: Have Staff Trainees Practice Performing The Target Skill and Provide Feedback. The next step in the training process involves the trainees practicing the target skill and receiving feedback from the staff trainer. Trainee practice performing the target skill represents the second part of the performance-based aspect of the training protocol. The practice can involve a role-play situation as with the trainer's initial demonstration. The role play should be preceded by the trainer instructing the trainees what they will need to do during the role play. Again if the target skill involves direct interaction with a consumer, the trainer or another trainee can play the role of the consumer while one trainee practices performing the target skill.

As each staff trainee practices performing the target skill the trainer should provide feedback regarding the trainee's performance. The feedback should specify each behavior constituting the skill the trainee performed correctly and if applicable, the behavior(s) the trainee did not perform correctly. In the latter case, the trainer should also inform the trainee what needs to be done to correct the behavior the next time. The trainer can use the written description of the skill previously given to the trainees to guide observation of the correct or incorrect performance of each aspect of the skill by trainees.

Training Step 5: Repeat Steps 1, 3, and 4 Until Staff Demonstrate Competence in Performing The Target Skill. The final step in a training session involves ensuring each trainee demonstrates proficiency in performing the target skill. This represents the *competency* part of performance- and competency-based training. Specifically, the trainer should repeat Steps 1 (describe the skill), 3 (demonstrate the skill), and 4 (have staff practice with feedback) until each trainee performs the skill correctly.

On-The-Job Training. The description to this point of the staff training protocol pertains to what is generally considered *classroom training* with staff. The training is conducted in a location (i.e., the classroom) with a group of trainees when they are not involved in their usual work activities with consumers. As just indicated, the classroom training is completed when each trainee has demonstrated competence in performing the target skill in a role-play situation. However, the overall staff training process is not yet completed.

Classroom training with staff must be followed by *on-the-job training.* On-the-job training involves the staff trainer observing each trainee applying the skill targeted in the classroom training while performing routine work duties in the regular job site. The observation should be accompanied by feedback from the trainer and if need be, repeated practice with feedback until the trainee is observed to perform the target skill correctly during the usual work routine.

Sometimes trainees have difficulty carrying over what they have learned to do in a classroom to their regular work situation. In other cases unpredicted events occur when a staff trainee attempts to perform the newly learned skill in the regular work site and the trainee is not sure how to proceed. For these reasons, the on-the-job component of staff training is critical and should always be conducted by the staff trainer. It is only when the trainer observes a trainee perform the target skill correctly during routine work conditions that the overall training process can be considered successfully completed.

As just described, the on-the-job part of staff training must be conducted individually with each staff trainee in contrast to the classroom training that involves a group of trainees. In those cases when just one staff person needs to be trained in a particular work skill, usually the entire training process can be conducted in an on-the-job manner. The trainer follows all steps of the training protocol while working with the staff person in the latter's usual work area.

Special arrangements may also need to be made when training one staff person on the job to make sure the training does not interfere with the trainee's completion of expected job duties while the training takes place. If such arrangements cannot be made, such as when the target skill to be trained is complex or requires a substantial amount of time to initially practice and master, the trainer should arrange for a separate meeting time with the trainee. At that time the trainer essentially conducts the classroom style training with the individual trainee and then follows up on the job to complete the process.

Training of human service staff should be considered successful only when each trainee is observed to perform the target skills competently during the routine work situation.

SUPERVISORY STEP 4: MONITOR STAFF PERFORMANCE

Once desired consumer outcomes and staff performance necessary to assist individuals in attaining the outcomes have been identified, and staff have been trained in the identified performance area, the next step is to monitor staff performance. Routinely monitoring staff performance is a critical part of effective supervision. Monitoring is necessary for supervisors to know the degree to which staff are performing their assigned duties proficiently.

Monitoring is also necessary to effectively implement the subsequent steps of the supervision protocol. Monitoring provides information for a supervisor to support staff performance observed to be of appropriate quality and to correct staff performance that is not of sufficient quality. Monitoring likewise allows for informed evaluation of what the supervisor is doing to support or correct staff performance.

The importance of an evidence-based approach to supervision has been discussed to this point in regard to using supervisory strategies that have been shown through sound research to affect staff work performance. However, supervisors also need evidence that what they are doing on the job is having the desired effect on staff work behavior. Monitoring provides this type of evidence or what is considered in essence a *local evidence base*. Monitoring of staff performance can be conducted on both a formal and informal basis. Both types of monitoring should be an ongoing part of a supervisor's job.

Formal Monitoring of Staff Performance. Formal monitoring involves observing staff work behavior using an established observation form on a set time schedule and recording information about the proficiency of the observed behavior. Often the form used when monitoring can be a version of the written specification of a performance area that was provided to staff during their training. For example, to monitor how how well staff provide two-item choices to adults with severe disabilities, a form based on the choice presentation protocol

(Chapter 7) could be used after staff have been trained to provide choices using the protocol (see illustration on next page).

Formal monitoring with a form based on the choice presentation protocol would give a supervisor specific information about the proficiency with which staff provide two-item choice opportunities for specific consumers. The same general process can be used with any job duty in which staff have been trained and are expected to perform to promote happiness among the people they support. The monitoring can be conducted by the staff supervisor as well as by appropriate designees such as supervisor assistants or representatives from an agency's quality assurance department. When monitoring is conducted by agency personnel other than the staff supervisor, they should then provide the results of the monitoring to the supervisor on a regular basis. However, when nonsupervisory personnel formally monitor staff performance the staff supervisor should also conduct at least some of the monitoring him/herself (see subsequent discussion on supporting staff performance).

Although formal monitoring of staff performance is an integral part of evidence-based supervision, there is a problem associated with this supervisory responsibility. Specifically, many staff do not like to have their performance formally monitored as they go about their work duties. When staff are aware, for example, that the supervisor has just entered their work area for the explicit purpose of monitoring their work performance their reaction is usually not very positive. Many readers probably can recall when their supervisor entered their work area and began formally monitoring their performance. The most likely reaction involved apprehension or concern.

Consequently, formal supervisory monitoring is one aspect of staffs' jobs that often impedes their work enjoyment. Special actions are therefore warranted by supervisors to formally monitor staff work behavior in a manner that is as acceptable to staff as reasonably possible. Research as well as the views of experienced supervisors and human service staff have indicated several things supervisors can do to reduce the unpleasantness of formal monitoring for staff.

FORM FOR MONITORING STAFF PROFICIENCY IN PROVIDING A TWO-ITEM CHOICE

Date of observation: _____

Time of observation: _____

Observer: _____

Observed staff person: _____

Instructions: *for each of the following steps mark "yes" if the staff person completed it, "no" if s/he did not complete it, or "NA" for nonapplicable if the step did not need to be completed.*

Step 1: Shows the person two items and asks the person to choose one item.	Yes No	
Step 2: If the person chooses one of the items, provides the item to the person.	Yes No	NA
Step 3: If the person does not choose an item, assists the person in sampling each item.	Yes No	NA
Step 4: Repeats Steps 1 and 2.	Yes No	NA

Note: To provide the choice opportunity satisfactorily, there can be no "No" recordings.

For example, supervisors can make sure staff know beforehand what aspect of their performance is being monitored. An advantageous way to inform staff about what their supervisor will be monitoring is during the staff training process. As noted earlier, formal monitoring forms should be based on the specific work behaviors that constitute a particular job skill such as a performance checklist. Staff should have received the checklist or similar written summary during their training. At that point staff should be informed that when a supervisor observes their performance of the skill on the job, the focus of the monitoring will be the specific behavior provided on the summary.

With the process just described, staff should know what they are supposed to do with a certain performance area in terms of specific work behavior and that the supervisor will be observing that behavior. Staff may not be aware precisely when a supervisor will come to observe their performance but still know what the supervisor will be monitoring with a particular job duty. In this manner, staff apprehension or concern that often accompanies supervisory monitoring when staff do not know what the supervisor is observing can be reduced substantially.

Another thing supervisors can do to reduce the negative effect of formal monitoring on staffs' work enjoyment is to provide feedback to staff quickly after the monitoring. Supervisory feedback is discussed more in-depth later. The point of concern here is that providing information to staff about the results of the monitoring through feedback can reduce anxiety or concern staff have about how their performance was evaluated. In turn, the reduction in anxiety or concern reduces the overall unpleasantness of the monitoring.

> **Because formally monitoring staff work performance is a supervisory responsibility that is often disliked by staff, supervisors must take specific actions to conduct the monitoring in ways acceptable to staff.**

There are other things supervisors can do when formally monitoring staff work behavior to make the monitoring more acceptable to staff. It is beyond the scope here to discuss all the intricacies of acceptable monitoring of staff performance. Interested readers are referred to the **Selected Readings** for more detailed information and particularly the reference to *Motivating Human Service Staff: Supervisory Strategies for Maximizing Work Effort and Work Enjoyment.*

Informal Monitoring of Staff Performance. Informal monitoring involves a supervisor briefly observing staff performance when the supervisor is present in the staff work area for other supervisory purposes. In contrast to formal monitoring, informal monitoring of staff performance does not involve an established form or a set time schedule. A supervisor simply observes staff performance informally while going about other supervisory duties.

For supervisors to monitor effectively on an informal basis they must know exactly what staff are expected to be doing when they are present in staffs' work site. This is one of the reasons that staff performance expectations must be clearly specified as observable work behavior. To illustrate, if a supervisor enters a group home during leisure time, the supervisor would know how staff should be interacting with consumers based on performance expectations for group interactions (**Chapter 6**). More specifically, the supervisor would know to observe if staff are providing frequent positive attention (versus no attention or more negative attention) and distributing their attention among all individuals in the group.

Informal monitoring is advantageous because it can occur frequently during the typical work day. Again, a supervisor simply observes staff performance briefly whenever the supervisor is present in staffs' work site while attending to other supervisory duties. In contrast, a disadvantage of informal monitoring is that generally it is less objective than formal monitoring.

Informal monitoring does not involve systematic observations according to an established form and does not include written records of staff work proficiency. The information obtained through informal monitoring therefore is usually not as reliable or thorough as that resulting from formal monitoring. Hence, informal monitoring generally should be considered a supplement to formal monitoring for supervisory purposes and not the only means of obtaining information on staff work proficiency.

Monitoring Consumer Outcome Attainment. In addition to staff performance, supervisors should monitor consumer outcome attainment on a regular basis. In particular, monitoring how often individuals display indices of happiness and unhappiness should be an ongoing supervisory responsibility. The importance of routinely monitoring happiness and unhappiness indices, as well as how to conduct the monitoring, was discussed in the introductory chapters. The point here is that supervising staff to promote consumer happiness in an effective, evidence-based manner requires information on the degree to which individuals routinely experience happiness. Monitoring happiness and unhappiness indices provides that essential information.

SUPERVISORY STEP 5: SUPPORT PROFICIENT STAFF PERFORMANCE

Supervisory actions discussed to this point essentially set the stage for staff to perform their job duties proficiently. When staff performance expectations have been specified as observable work behavior in which they are expected to engage, staff have been successfully trained to perform the identified work duties, and their work is regularly monitored, a number of staff will go about their job duties in a quality manner. However, these supervisory actions by no means guarantee that staff will work proficiently on a consistent basis.

Ensuring staff work proficiently day in and day out requires supervisors to actively respond to what staff are doing in the work place. In particular, supervisors must respond to observations of proficient work performance in a manner that supports such performance. Supporting quality staff performance means taking action to help staff continue performing their duties proficiently. It also means helping staff feel good about their work efforts and accomplishments. In short, supervisors must actively strive to *ensure staff feel good about doing a good job.*

There are many ways supervisors can actively support good work performance among their staff. However, all of the ways involve to at least some degree providing *positive feedback* about staffs' work activities. Positive feedback involves informing staff about the quality of their work with an explicit expression of approval or appreciation.

Providing positive feedback represents a well-established, evidence-based means of supporting quality work performance among human service staff. The most practical and readily available ways to provide positive feedback are quite informal in nature. A supervisor simply commends staff work performance periodically during the work day whenever the supervisor observes work activity of a desired level of proficiency. Supervisors who consistently promote quality performance (and staff work enjoyment) are almost always known for routinely providing positive feedback to staff as they go about their daily duties.

Informally presenting positive feedback can also occur in ways other than telling staff about the good aspects of their work performance during the routine day. These include, for example, sending informal notes to staff or short e-mails for the sole purpose of commending some aspect of their performance that the supervisor has observed. However, the latter means of providing positive feedback generally take somewhat more time on the part of the supervisor and therefore should usually be viewed as a supplement to commending staff performance in a face-to-face manner.

> **The most evidence-based, readily available, and cost-efficient means of supporting quality staff performance and staff work enjoyment is positive feedback presented informally by a supervisor.**

There are likewise more formal ways to support proficient work performance with feedback. Probably the most recognized is the annual performance evaluation that supervisors conduct with their staff. Annual performance evaluations are usually necessary in human service agencies for a variety of reasons. Though necessary, however, the way performance evaluations are typically conducted rarely has much of an effect on daily staff performance. Positive feedback provided within formal evaluations usually is too infrequent, and often too general, to truly support staff in performing quality work day in and day out.

For performance evaluations and other types of formal feedback (e.g., when a supervisor has a scheduled meeting with a staff person to review the individual's work performance) to effectively support staff performance, they must be much more frequent than yearly. Due in large part to the infrequency of formal feedback, it is typically a less effective way of supporting quality staff performance than routine presentations of informal feedback as discussed above. Therefore, formally presented feedback should be used in conjunction with much more frequently presented feedback of an informal nature.

SUPERVISORY STEP 6: CORRECT NONPROFICIENT PERFORMANCE

Taking action to support quality staff performance is not the only way supervisors must respond to how staff perform their work duties. At times, supervisors must respond when staff are not performing their work in an appropriate manner. Specifically, supervisors must act to correct nonproficient performance. This is another part of supervisory duties that is typically not very well received or acceptable among staff. Nonetheless, nobody works perfectly all the time and supervisory corrective action will be needed.

In most cases nonproficient work performance of staff can be corrected by supervisors responding to the performance with feedback. As with positive feedback to support quality staff work, supervisory corrective feedback is the most evidence-based means of improving nonproficient performance. A well-established means of providing feedback to improve staff work behavior is provided in the following illustration. This way of providing corrective feedback can also reduce the unpleasantness that staff often experience when their performance has to be corrected by a supervisor.

EVIDENCE-BASED PROTOCOL FOR PROVIDING FEEDBACK TO STAFF

Step 1: Begin feedback with a positive statement.

Step 2: Specify what staff performed correctly.

Step 3: Specify what staff performed incorrectly if applicable.

Step 4: Specify what staff need to do to correct the work behavior identified in Step 3.

Step 5: Solicit questions from staff about the information provided.

Step 6: Inform staff about subsequent supervisory actions regarding the target work behavior.

Step 7: End feedback with a positive statement.

The feedback protocol represented in the illustration is generally most applicable when providing feedback to staff in a formal nature. Generally this means when a supervisor is meeting individually with a staff person with the primary purpose of improving some aspect of the person's work activities. The main components of the feedback protocol for improving the individual's work are specifying what the staff person did incorrectly (Step 3) and then specifying what the person needs to do to improve the performance (Step 4).

The other steps in the feedback protocol have been included to help make the overall feedback more acceptable to staff. Steps 1 and 7, which involve beginning and ending the feedback session in a generally positive manner, can help the overall process be more acceptable to staff (e.g., versus just telling the staff member what was done wrong). Step 2, in which positive feedback is provided regarding some other aspect of performance that was observed to be appropriately carried out, adds another element that can increase the acceptability of the overall process—as well as support the individual's good work behavior.

Providing the staff person an opportunity to clarify what the supervisor said about the performance (Step 5) likewise can make the feedback more acceptable through a type of participative management process. Finally, letting the staff person know what will happen next from a supervisory perspective (Step 6) is usually a nice thing to do for staff (e.g., informing the staff person that the supervisor will observe and work with the individual in the next week or so to help with the improvement process). This stands in contrast to the usually unpleasant process of leaving the staff member uncertain about future supervisory actions.

Various steps of the formal feedback protocol can also be carried out by a supervisor more informally. This usually occurs when a supervisor observes staff performance that is not completed appropriately when the supervisor is in staffs' work area and desires to immediately correct the performance. To correct the work behavior in this situation the supervisor informs staff what was not performed appropriately and what needs to be done to improve the performance. However, it is almost always beneficial to include positive feedback about some aspect of proficient performance that was observed. This can make the informal feedback more pleasant for staff while still addressing what needs to be immediately corrected.

Although the formal feedback protocol has been shown repeatedly through research and application to improve nonproficient staff performance, and in a way that usually minimizes the negativity for staff, it is not always applicable. Every supervisor in the human services likely experiences situations in which a given staff person does something that is highly inappropriate or totally unacceptable in the work place. This may involve, for example, consumer abuse, sleeping on the job, or stealing agency or consumer property. When this type of performance issue is apparent, the necessary supervisor action should entail formal disciplinary action and often termination of the staff person's employment. More detailed information on appropriate use of disciplinary action for highly inappropriate staff behavior is provided in *The Supervisor's Guidebook* in the **Selected Readings** referred to earlier.

SUPERVISORY STEP 7: CONTINUOUSLY EVALUATE STAFF PERFORMANCE AND CONSUMER OUTCOME ATTAINMENT

The final step of the evidence-based supervision protocol is to evaluate staff performance and consumer outcome attainment. Information resulting from monitoring should be regularly reviewed to determine if staff are performing specified duties in the appropriate manner and consumers are attaining desired outcomes. For purposes here, the focus should be on whether staff are doing what needs to be done such that frequent indices of happiness are observed among consumers of agency services as well as infrequent indices of unhappiness.

If evaluation of the results of monitoring indicates that staff are indeed performing specified duties proficiently and consumers are routinely showing indices of happiness, then supervisors should continue their ongoing actions for supporting staff performance. In contrast, if monitoring does not reveal desired staff performance and satisfactory consumer happiness, then supervisors should take other action. The latter action should focus on changing staff work behavior to better promote consumer happiness.

Supervisor action to improve staff performance typically involves increased provision of feedback as described previously. Other steps of the supervision protocol may also need to be re-implemented depending on the evaluation of information obtained through monitoring. For example, performance expectations may need to be more precisely specified or certain staff may need re-training in the skills to fulfill various expectations. Supervisors should continue to take whatever actions seem necessary until the monitoring shows that the performance area of concern has improved sufficiently to result in satisfactory indices of consumer happiness.

Although evaluation is listed as the final step of the supervision protocol, it is really not a "final" step per se. Rather, evaluation of staff performance and consumer outcome attainment must be an ongoing process. Once formal monitoring has been initiated, evaluation should then occur routinely. This is the only way that supervisors can obtain the necessary information to be truly assured that their staff are doing what needs to be done to promote happiness among the people with disabilities they support.

> **Supervisors must routinely monitor staff performance and consumer outcome attainment to truly know if staff perform their duties sufficiently to promote consumer happiness.**

SPECIAL SUPERVISORY ACTIONS FOR PROMOTING STAFF WORK ENJOYMENT

Throughout this chapter an emphasis has been on supervising staff performance in human service agencies in a manner that promotes not only work quality but also work enjoyment. The reasons why supervisors should specifically strive to help staff enjoy their work were also summarized. Of particular relevance for promoting consumer happiness is that when staff regularly enjoy their work, they are more likely to carry out their duties in ways that are also enjoyable for the people they support.

This chapter has likewise described how supervisory actions to promote quality staff performance that are often poorly received by staff can be conducted in ways that are more acceptable for staff. There are also special actions supervisors can take to promote staff enjoyment beyond what has been discussed with the supervision protocol. Subsequent sections describe some of the most effective supervisory actions for promoting staff work enjoyment.

The following strategies are provided only as examples. Specific means by which supervisors attempt to enhance staff work enjoyment should be based in large part on what supervisors are comfortable with and what seem to be most well received by staff. The primary point is that taking specific action to promote staff enjoyment with their work—whatever that action might be—should be an ongoing part of supervisory duties in conjunction with using evidence-based procedures to ensure work quality.

THE POWER OF POSITIVE FEEDBACK

Just as positive feedback is the most readily available means of supporting quality work among staff, it is also one of the most practical ways to help staff enjoy their work. Most people like it when their supervisor expresses sincere appreciation or commendation for something they have done on the job. Receiving positive feedback also helps staff feel good about their work accomplishments. In turn, feeling good about something on the job helps staff enjoy their jobs.

For supervisors to provide positive feedback to staff frequently, the feedback must often be impromptu in nature as described previously. Again, feedback should be provided based on whenever supervisors happen to notice a staff person doing something commendable. To illustrate, upon entering an adult day program a supervisor may see a staff member interacting socially with a consumer during break that involves the consumer smiling or showing other indices of happiness. The supervisor can then comment to the staff person about how nice the interaction appeared in that the individual seemed to be really enjoying it. This type of unplanned or impromptu feedback can have a powerful effect on the staff person's immediate work enjoyment.

Positive feedback and related expressions of commendation or appreciation can also be more formal on occasion. For example, a supervisor may schedule a brief meeting with a staff person. At the beginning of the meeting the supervisor informs the staff person that the sole reason for the meeting is to let the staff person know how impressed or appreciative the supervisor is with something the staff person has done. Similarly, during a regularly scheduled meeting with a group of staff for a work-related purpose, the supervisor may ask one staff person to stay a few minutes after the meeting. At that point the supervisor meets with the staff person solely to commend some aspect of the staff person's observed performance.

> **Supervisors should make a point of providing feedback to staff as often as possible whenever they happen to observe commendable staff performance during the routine work day.**

SPECIAL RECOGNITION PROCEDURES

Another way to promote staff enjoyment with their work at least on a periodic basis is with *special recognition procedures.* Many human service agencies have special recognition events, such as when providing someone with an "Employee of the Year" award or similar commendation. When someone is recognized in this manner, the person usually feels quite good about the recognition. Again, a staff person feeling good about something associated with the job can increase the staff person's enjoyment with the job at that point in time.

Although special recognition procedures can help staff enjoyment with their jobs at times, a common misconception regarding such actions warrants highlighting. Specifically, many human service agencies hold annual or other regularly scheduled recognition events with the assumption that the special recognition significantly promotes daily work proficiency among agency staff. There is little hard evidence to support such an assumption.

Like annual performance evaluations discussed earlier, special recognition such as giving an "Employee of the Year" award occurs too infrequently to have much effect on a staff person's daily performance. This type of special recognition also affects only a very small portion of an agency's staff pool at any point in time. Hence, although periodic special recognition procedures may help promote staff enjoyment at times, they should not be relied on as a supervisory strategy to ensure day-to-day work proficiency.

MAKING DISLIKED WORK ACTIVITIES MORE ENJOYABLE FOR STAFF

As with almost any job, there are certain duties staff in human service agencies must perform that they dislike. One way supervisors can promote staff work enjoyment is to take action to reduce various disliked aspects of the job. In essence, the fewer disliked duties staff are required to perform on a regular basis the more their work enjoyment is enhanced overall.

There is a systematic approach supervisors can take to make a specific, disliked duty of staff more desirable to perform—or at least less undesirable to complete. The approach involves the following steps (see the reference to *Changing Less Preferred Duties to More Preferred: A Potential Strategy for Improving Work Enjoyment* in the **Selected Readings** for more detail). First, a supervisor should query staff to determine the most disliked job duty relative to all other routine duties of staff. Although there are usually some differences across staff regarding their job-duty preferences, there is often at least one duty that many if not most staff tend to dislike.

The second step is for the supervisor to question staff regarding the specific features or aspects of the designated job duty that make it so unpleasant to perform. The third step is for the supervisor and staff to discuss ideas regarding how performing the duty could be altered to reduce the unpleasantness. This process usually involves trying to identify how, where, when, or with what materials performing the duty could possibly be changed. Finally, the supervisor should try to make as many of the identified changes with the duty as realistically possible.

The above process can have a significant effect on reducing staff dislike of having to perform certain work duties in human service agencies. Even when the process is not very successful, however (e.g., because some duties cannot be altered significantly and still be completed appropriately), going through the process can still enhance staff work enjoyment. The latter effect occurs because staff can be most appreciative of a supervisor who takes the time to try to make their work life better. Such appreciation can enhance staff work enjoyment and especially their enjoyment in working for a particular supervisor.

Practicing Common Social Courtesy When Working With Staff

One of the most important determinants of day-to-day work enjoyment is the quality of interactions staff have with other people on the job. When staff typically have pleasant interactions with others in the work place, their daily enjoyment is usually much greater relative to when they have unpleasant interactions. The degree to which staff interactions with their supervisors are pleasant or unpleasant has a particularly important effect on staffs' daily work enjoyment.

Surveys of experienced staff have repeatedly indicated the importance of the quality of interactions they have with supervisors on their work enjoyment. To illustrate, when questioned about what supervisors can best do to maximize their work enjoyment, the most frequently reported response by staff was their supervisors simply interacting with them in socially courteous ways (see reference to *The Best and Worst Ways to Motivate Staff in Community Agencies* in the **Selected Readings**). Examples of courteous interactions included supervisors merely greeting staff socially upon entering the work area, speaking to staff when passing in a hallway or other work space, and taking the time to listen and respond when staff speak to the supervisors.

Emphasizing the importance of supervisors practicing common social courtesy in their interactions with staff might seem to be stating the obvious; common courtesy is generally an expectation for any social or interactive encounter. Such importance is highlighted, however, because the same surveys just noted have indicated that many supervisors frequently do not interact with their staff in this manner. Specifically, in response to a question about what supervisors do that most often impedes staff work enjoyment, the most common response reported by staff was supervisors interacting in unpleasant or discourteous ways. Reported examples included supervisors ignoring staff greetings, not responding or responding curtly to staff questions, and generally refraining from interactions with staff except to criticize or correct staff actions.

The most successful supervisors generally go about working with their staff in a manner that helps staff do a good job and is viewed as respectful and generally pleasant by staff. Helping staff do a good job requires consistent application of evidence-based supervisory strategies as exemplified by the steps of the supervision protocol. Treating staff respectfully and pleasantly means in large part practicing common social courtesy in routine interactions with staff. It is incumbent upon executive personnel in human service agencies to ensure supervisors are well trained in, and routinely practice, evidence-based supervision and do so in a socially courteous manner.

Chapter Summary: Key Points

1. *Effective supervision in human service agencies involves promoting diligent and proficient staff performance as well as staff enjoyment with their work.*

2. *An evidence-based approach to supervision involves a systematic process consisting of seven basic steps: (1) identifying desired consumer outcomes, (2) specifying what staff must do to assist consumers in attaining the desired outcomes, (3) training staff in performance duties specified in Step 2, (4) monitor-*

ing staff performance, (5) supporting proficient staff performance, (6) correcting nonproficient staff performance and, (7) continuously evaluating staff performance and consumer outcome attainment.

3. Training staff to perform necessary job duties should be a performance- and competency-based process involving the following steps: (1) describing the target skill to be trained, (2) providing a written description of the target skill, (3) demonstrating the target skill, (4) having staff trainees practice performing the target skill and providing feedback, and (5) repeating Steps 1, 3, and 4 until staff demonstrate competence in performing the skill.

4. Supervisors must routinely monitor staff performance and strive to do so in a manner acceptable to staff.

5. The most evidence-based, readily available, and cost-efficient way to support quality staff performance as well as staff work enjoyment is by supervisors routinely providing positive feedback.

6. Providing feedback is also the most readily available means of correcting nonproficient staff performance and should be performed using an evidence-based format that is not only effective but also usually well received by staff.

7. Evaluation of staff performance and consumer outcome attainment must be an ongoing duty of supervisors and form the basis for their future actions with staff.

8. Supervisors should take action specifically to promote staff work enjoyment in addition to using evidence-based strategies to promote quality work based on what they are comfortable with doing and what appears most acceptable to staff.

SECTION IV

APPENDIX AND SELECTED READINGS

Appendix

Special Circumstances Affecting the Validation of Happiness and Unhappiness Indices

A basic protocol for validating indices of happiness and unhappiness was described in **Chapter 4**. Applying the protocol usually results in validation of behavioral indicators of private emotional experiences associated with happiness and unhappiness among adults with autism and other severe disabilities. However, as also noted in **Chapter 4**, at times special circumstances arise that can affect the process such that alterations with the validation procedures are necessary. This section describes the most common types of these circumstances and how implementation of the protocol should be altered to result in successful validation of specific indices.

Difficulty Obtaining Caregiver Agreement Regarding Opinions of Happiness Indices

When assessing caregiver opinion, sometimes results of the assessment fail to reveal agreement between two caregivers regarding what a consumer does when happy. There are several courses of action when agreement is not reached. The first course of action is to assess the opinion of additional caregivers who are familiar with the individual. This action could continue until agreement is eventually reached with two caregivers. If family members of the consumer have not been involved in the initial process, then they should be questioned.

If agreement is still not reached after many caregivers have been questioned as well as family members, then a second course of action is available. Specifically, several different indices reported by various caregivers could be selected even though there was no agreement between two caregivers on any given indicator. The same validation steps described in **Chapter 4** can then be initiated with several of the indicators reported by individual caregivers. In a number of these cases, results of the observation step of the validation process will reveal initial support for the validity of at least one of the indicators. Subsequently, the final choice validation step can be completed.

If the first two strategies do not result in sufficient information to identify or validate indices of happiness, then the next course of action is to systematically assess different preferences of the adult with a severe disability. As noted in **Chapter 3**, systematic preference assessments can result in identification of what a person does when happy and unhappy. As also discussed previously though, conducting systematic preference assessments requires more time relative to assessing caregiver opinion regarding happiness indices. Certain technical skills are also required to conduct preference assessments. Hence, this course of action is possible only if an agency has access to someone with relevant training and skills in performing systematic preference assessments (see **Chapter 8** for information on conducting preference assessments).

DIFFICULTY OBTAINING CAREGIVER AGREEMENT REGARDING OPINIONS OF UNHAPPINESS INDICES

Difficulty obtaining caregiver agreement regarding what an adult who has a severe disability does when unhappy tends to occur more frequently than with reaching agreement about happiness indices. Actually, when caregivers do not agree about indicators of unhappiness, or have difficulty identifying any unhappiness indices, such a situation can reflect favorably on an agency's services. Sometimes indices of unhappiness cannot be identified because caregivers never observe the individual to be apparently unhappy. Hence, it is likely the agency is effectively preventing unhappiness. It is still useful though to take additional action to identify unhappiness indices in case they occur in the future.

The first recommended course of action when caregiver agreement is not reached regarding what a consumer does when unhappy is the same as that with difficulty identifying indices of happiness: question additional caregivers and especially family members if they have not been questioned previously. The second action is also the same as with identifying happiness indices. Specifically, indices that were reported by individual staff (despite a lack of agreement among staff regarding each reported indicator) can be used in the subsequent validation steps.

Difficulty in identifying unhappiness indices could also be resolved through systematic preference assessments. In this case, the intent is to identify activities or items that are strongly nonpreferred. When an individual is presented with something highly nonpreferred, by definition the individual does not like the ongoing situation and likely experiences unhappiness. Consequently, what the individual does when presented with something very disliked can reveal indices of unhappiness. However, it is important to include items and activities in the preference assessment that are potentially nonpreferred that *already exist* in a consumer's environment. It would be undesirable to create new items or activities for purposes of determining something that results in unhappiness of an individual.

If indices of unhappiness are not identified through the actions just noted, a more refined identification process is necessary. The latter process involves observing a consumer when a preferred activity is discontinued or a preferred item is withdrawn. The preferred activity or item may be something identified with a preference assessment or something that is consistently accompanied by indices of happiness.

When something that is preferred must be immediately discontinued (e.g., preferred computer time must be terminated to begin another necessary activity, consumption of a favorite snack must be discontinued to avoid overeating, a preferred staff person has to stop interacting with an individual to perform another work task), the immediate pleasure a person is experiencing is terminated. Correspondingly, the individual is likely to immediately experience varying degrees of unhappiness. This is especially the case when the preferred situation is discontinued due to staff action in contrast to the consumer voluntarily choosing to discontinue the ongoing activity.

Unhappiness in the scenario just described is also most likely to occur if the activity that immediately follows the ongoing preferred situation is nonpreferred by a person with a severe disability (e.g., beginning to work on a difficult academic task, being instructed to participate in an unfamiliar activity, having to perform a household chore). The individual's behavior can be observed at the moment the preferred situation is terminated and the nonpreferred activity is initiated. Such behavior often represents likely indices of unhappiness.

To use the process just described to identify potential indices of unhappiness, the existing routine of an adult with a severe disability must be scrutinized. The focus of the scrutiny should be to determine at what times the individual is usually engaged with something highly preferred that has to be discontinued as part of the ongoing schedule (and those times when the next scheduled activity is likely to be something that is much less preferred by the person). The identified times represent when the individual should be observed for likely displays of unhappiness.

DIFFICULTY OBTAINING CAREGIVER AGREEMENT REGARDING SITUATIONS IN WHICH AN INDIVIDUAL IS HAPPY

In most cases there is little difficulty obtaining caregiver agreement regarding situations in which a respective adult with autism or other severe disability appears happy. However, such difficulty does occur in a small number of cases. When there is difficulty initially identifying happiness situations, or agreement between caregivers is not readily obtained, the general action steps are basically the same as when there is difficulty identifying *indices* of happiness.

The first action step is to question additional caregivers regarding situations in which a consumer is happy, and particularly family members if they have not already been questioned. If results of that step do not result in at least one situation for which two caregivers report an individual is happy, then the second step is to select situations reported by individual caregivers. Several of those situations should be targeted for the validation steps, despite lack of agreement between caregivers for any of the individually identified situations.

The third course of action is to conduct systematic preference assessments with an individual of concern. The intent is to identify activities or items that the consumer strongly prefers. Subsequently, the happiness situation consists of the time period when the individual is accessing the most strongly preferred activity or item. As discussed earlier, engaging in something highly preferred usually represents a situation that is liked by an individual and therefore, accompanied by happiness.

There is also a fourth course of action that is relevant when difficulty exists in identifying situations in which an adult with autism or other severe disability is typically happy. That action involves questioning several staff about what they think would make a consumer happy that does not regularly take place. For example, although several staff may not be able to identify a situation that occurs weekly in which an individual is clearly happy, they may agree on something that usually occurs only every few months or so (e.g., going on a picnic). Where possible, those activities could be arranged to occur more frequently on a short-term basis for the purpose of observing whether they are accompanied by indices of happiness.

Difficulty Obtaining Caregiver Agreement Regarding Situations in Which an Individual is Unhappy

Difficulty obtaining caregiver agreement regarding situations in which a person with a severe disability is unhappy is more common than with identifying situations in which a consumer is happy. The difficulty is due to the same reasons that problems arise in initially identifying what a person does when unhappy (i.e., identifying *indices* of unhappiness). In particular, there may be no regularly occurring events within an agency that are accompanied by a consumer's unhappiness.

Nonetheless, it is still important to identify situations in which a consumer is unhappy. Such situations should be identified so indices of unhappiness can be determined and validated such that unhappiness can be effectively decreased if observed in the future. The recommended actions when caregivers do not agree regarding unhappiness situations also are the same as with problems identifying unhappiness *indices*. Again, those actions involve questioning additional caregivers, assessing several situations reported by individual staff even though different staff have not agreed on a specific situation, and conducting preference assessments. In the latter case, subsequent presentations of an identified, nonpreferred activity can represent the unhappiness situation for observation and validation purposes.

There is also a unique circumstance that impedes identification of situations in which an adult who has a severe disability is unhappy, at least in regard to validating unhappiness indices. At times caregivers agree on a situation in which an individual is unhappy but the situation occurs infrequently such as once a month or less (e.g., a dental appointment). The infrequency of the situation impedes the validation process because observations of the person's participation in the situation must encompass several months to observe the individual's behavior in the situation. The lengthy observation period extends the validation process and delays subsequent use of procedures to decrease unhappiness.

If unhappiness situations occur infrequently and the other action steps have not resulted in validation of any unhappiness indices, there is still one other course of action. A situation can be selected in which a consumer has consistently displayed indices of happiness or for which the person has shown a strong preference. When that activity has to be discontinued, the immediate result is a situation that is usually at least relatively disliked by an individual as discussed earlier. Hence, the latter situation can be considered to represent an unhappiness situation for purposes of continuing the validation process.

Minimal Occurrence of Happiness Indices during Observations of Reported Happiness Situations

One difficulty that can interfere with carrying out the process for validating reported indices of happiness is when very low frequencies of happiness indices are observed during happiness situations. When happiness indices are observed infrequently questions arise regarding whether a particular situation is truly accompanied by a consumer's happiness. Generally though, a low frequency of observed happiness indices is not a serious issue, as long as *some* indices are observed. Actually, it is quite common to observe infrequent happiness indices during a reported happiness situation. For example, when observing happiness indices with an interval system as described previously, often such indices will occur in ten percent or less of the observed intervals.

Low frequencies of happiness indices are observed for several reasons. One common reason is that the observed situation is accompanied by only a moderate degree of a person's happiness. Hence, it would not be expected that the individual would display a high frequency of happiness indices. Another reason is that as illustrated in **Chapter 4**, people do not always show happiness overtly even though they are very happy. Nevertheless, in situations with low levels of happiness indices the validation process can continue by offering a choice of those situations versus situations in which there were no or less indices of happiness. If a person chooses a situation previously observed to have more happiness indices over a situation with less happiness indices, even if the level of such indices was quite low in the former situation, the indices are usually a valid representation of the individual's happiness.

A circumstance that is related to that involving a low frequency of observed happiness indices is when there are *no* indices of happiness observed in reported happiness situations. This scenario is uncommon but may occur from time to time. When it does occur, there are several recommended courses of action. One course of action is to extend the observations of respective happiness situations to more than the usually recommended three to five observation periods. Extending the number of observations of reported happiness situations often results in a person displaying at least some indices of happiness during the additional observation periods.

A second course of action is to revisit the reported indices of happiness as well as the situations in which a person with a severe disability is reported to be happy. Sometimes the reported happiness indices are not valid, even if identified by two caregivers. Other reported indices may then be selected for observation that were identified by individual caregivers even though each respective indicator represents different behavior of the consumer. Similarly, sometimes the situations that staff agree represent when a consumer is usually happy are not accurate such that other situations reported by individual staff could be targeted for observation.

If the two courses of action just noted prove unsuccessful, the validation process is affected but not to the point of total abandonment. It can be useful to continue the overall validation process even without having observed happiness indices during reported happiness situations, as long as some *unhappiness* indices are observed during an *unhappiness* situation. More specifically, if unhappiness indices are observed in a situation in which caregivers have reported that a consumer is usually unhappy, then a choice can be offered between that situation versus the reported happiness situation (even though no happiness indices were observed in the latter situation).

In offering the type of choice just described, it is also important that the level of unhappiness indices observed in the unhappiness situation be greater than the level of unhappiness indices observed (if any) during the happiness situation. If a person consistently chooses to access a situation in which there were less unhappiness indices previously observed relative to a situation in which there were more unhappiness indices, then validation is still obtained for the *indices of unhappiness*; the person is choosing to avoid a situation in which the individual has displayed (more) indicators of unhappiness.

Although the desired outcome of the overall validation process is to validate both indices of happiness and unhappiness, it is still useful if the process only results in validation of indices of unhappiness in the manner just described. Once valid indicators of unhappiness are identified, then steps can be taken to reduce the amount of unhappiness an individual experiences. As discussed in **Chapter 3**, one means of increasing happiness of an individual overall is by reducing how often the person experiences unhappiness during the daily routine.

MINIMAL OCCURRENCE OF UNHAPPINESS INDICES DURING OBSERVATIONS OF REPORTED UNHAPPINESS SITUATIONS

It is more common for difficulties to exist with the validation process due to lack of observed unhappiness indices during reported unhappiness situations than with a lack of observed happiness indices. One explanation for the lack of observed unhappiness indices is the same as that noted previously with difficulties in identifying unhappiness indices and situations. That is, there simply may be minimal situations during an agency's daily routine in which a consumer is truly unhappy.

Given the scenario just noted, it is important to continue to attempt to identify and then validate a consumer's indices of unhappiness. As indicated previously, such attempts are necessary to determine if the individual begins to display indices of unhappiness at a later time. Generally, the validation process can continue per usual when unhappiness indices are observed at low levels—again provided that at least some unhappiness indicators are observed.

If absolutely no unhappiness indices are observed during reported unhappiness situations, then the recommended courses of action are essentially the same as when no *happiness* indices are observed in happiness situations. Again, these include extending the number of times the unhappiness situations are observed and revisiting the previously identified unhappiness indices and situations. If these actions do not result in validation of unhappiness indices, then it is generally recommended to discontinue the process and periodically attempt to validate such indices after several months have passed.

When no indices of unhappiness can be validated, the overall process of increasing an individual's happiness can still take place provided that the individual's *indices of happiness* have been validated. However, the process of validating happiness indices is altered somewhat. The alteration occurs when comparing happiness situations that are accompanied by indices of happiness with other situations. Instead of comparing observed indices of happiness between a happiness situation and an unhappiness situation, the comparison involves the happiness situation with a *neutral situation.*

A neutral situation pertains to any ongoing activity in which a person with a severe disability routinely participates that caregivers agree are not something in which the individual is generally happy or unhappy. These situations typically represent most of what is usually ongoing in a human service agency—they are just routinely occurring events. Hence, neutral situations are easy for caregivers to identify.

Using neutral situations to validate happiness indices involves the following process. Indices of happiness are initially identified by caregivers along with situations in which a consumer is usually happy. The latter happiness situations are then observed to initially validate that happiness indices are displayed by the person during the situations. Subsequently, the individual is offered a choice of a happiness situation (accompanied by happiness indices during the observations) versus any neutral situation. If the person consistently chooses a happiness situation over a neutral situation, then the happiness indices usually are a valid representation of the person's private experience of happiness.

Selected Readings

Identifying Indices of Happiness among Adults with Autism and Other Severe Disabilities

Dillon, C. M., & Carr, J. E. (2007). Assessing indices of happiness and unhappiness in individuals with developmental disabilities: A review. *Behavioral Interventions, 22,* 229-244.

Favell, J. E., Realon, R. E., & Sutton, K. A. (1996). Measuring and increasing the happiness of people with profound mental retardation and physical handicaps. *Behavioral Interventions, 11,* 47-58.

Green, C. W., & Reid, D. H. (1996). Defining, validating, and increasing indices of happiness among people with profound multiple disabilities. *Journal of Applied Behavior Analysis, 29,* 67-78.

Green, C. W., & Reid, D. H. (1999). A behavioral approach to identifying sources of happiness and unhappiness among individuals with profound multiple disabilities. *Behavior Modification, 23,* 280-293.

Parsons, M. B., Reid, D. H., Bentley, E., Inman, A., & Lattimore, L. P. (2012). Identifying indices of happiness and unhappiness among adults with autism: Potential targets for behavioral assessment and intervention. *Behavior Analysis in Practice, 5,* 15-25.

Providing Choices for Adults with Autism and Other Severe Disabilities

Parsons, M. B., Harper, V. N., Jensen, J. M., & Reid, D. H. (1997). Integrating choice into the leisure routines of older adults with severe disabilities. *Journal of The Association for Persons With Severe Handicaps, 22,* 170-175.

Parsons, M. B., McCarn, J. E., & Reid, D. H. (1993). Evaluating and increasing meal-related choices throughout a service setting for people with severe disabilities. *Journal of The Association for Persons with Severe Handicaps, 18,* 253-260.

Payne, D., & Wu, P. (2011). Review of the choice and preference assessment literature for individuals with severe to profound disabilities. *Education and Training in Autism and Developmental Disabilities, 46,* 576-595.

Reid, D. H., Green, C. W., & Parsons, M. B. (2003). An outcome management program for extending advances in choice research into choice opportunities for supported workers with severe multiple disabilities. *Journal of Applied Behavior Analysis, 36,* 575-578.

Shogren, K. A., Faggella-Luby, M. N., Bae, S. J., & Wehmeyer, M. L. (2004). The effect of choice-making as an intervention for problem behavior: A meta-analysis. *Journal of Positive Behavior Interventions, 6,* 228-237.

Systematic Preference Assessments

Carr, J. E., Nicolson, A. C., & Higbee, T. S. (2000). Evaluation of a brief multiple-stimulus preference assessment in a naturalistic context. *Journal of Applied Behavior Analysis, 33,* 353-357.

Graff, R. B., & Karsten, A. M. (2012). Assessing preferences of individuals with developmental disabilities: A survey of current practices. *Behavior Analysis in Practice, 5,* 37-48.

Graff, R. B., & Karsten, A. M. (2012). Evaluation of a self-instruction package for conducting stimulus preference assessments. *Journal of Applied Behavior Analysis, 45,* 69-82.

Hagopian, L. P., Long, E. S., & Rush, K. S. (2004). Preference assessment procedures for individuals with developmental disabilities. *Behavior Modification, 28,* 668-677.

Karsten, A. M., Carr, J. E., & Lepper, T. L. (2011). Description of a practitioner model for identifying preferred stimuli with individuals with autism spectrum disorders. *Behavior Modification, 35,* 347-369.

Lohrmann-O'Rourke, S., Browder, D. M., & Brown, F. (2000). Guidelines for conducting socially valid systematic preference assessments. *Journal of The Association for Persons with Severe Handicaps, 25,* 42-53.

Parsons, M. B., Reid, D. H., & Green, C. W. (2001). Situational assessment of task preferences among adults with multiple severe disabilities in supported work. *Journal of The Association for Persons With Severe Handicaps, 26,* 50-55.

Reid, D. H., Parsons, M. B., Lattimore, L. P., Green, C. W., & Brackett, L. (2007). Identifying work preferences among supported workers with severe disabilities: Efficiency and accuracy of a preference-assessment protocol. *Behavioral Interventions, 22,* 279-296.

PLANNING MAJOR LIFESTYLE CHANGES: PERSON-CENTERED PLANNING

Claes, C., Hove, G. V., Vandevelde, S., van Loon, J., & Schalock, R. L. (2010). Person-centered planning: Analysis of research and effectiveness. *Intellectual and Developmental Disabilities, 48,* 432-453.

Everson, J. M., & Reid, D. H. (1999). *Person-centered planning and outcome management: Maximizing organizational effectiveness in supporting quality lifestyles among people with disabilities.* Morganton, NC: Habilitative Management Consultants.

Green, C. W., Middleton, S. G., & Reid, D. H. (2000). Embedded evaluation of preferences sampled from person-centered plans for people with profound multiple disabilities. *Journal of Applied Behavior Analysis, 33,* 639-642.

Holburn, S. (2002). How science can evaluate and enhance person-centered planning. *Research & Practice for Persons with Severe Disabilities, 27,* 250-260.

Holburn, S., Gordon, A., & Vietze, P. (2007). *Person-centered planning made easy: The PICTURE method.* Baltimore: Brookes Publishing.

Holburn, S., & Vietze, P. M. (2002). *Person-centered planning: Research, practice, and future directions.* Baltimore: Brookes Publishing.

Reid, D. H., Everson, J., & Green, C. W. (1999). Systematic evaluation of preferences identified through person-centered planning for people with profound multiple disabilities. *Journal of Applied Behavior Analysis, 32,* 476-477.

Teaching to Promote Consumer Independence (And Happiness)

Cuvo, A. J., & Davis, P. K. (2000). Behavioral acquisition by persons with developmental disabilities. In J. Austin & J. E. Carr (Eds.), *Handbook of applied behavior analysis* (pp. 39-60). Reno, NV: Context Press.

Green, C. W., Parsons, M. B., & Reid, D. H. (1993). Integrating instructional procedures into traditional congregate care situations for people with severe disabilities. *Behavioral Residential Treatment, 8,* 243-262.

Green, C. W., Reid, D. H., Rollyson, J. H., & Passante, S. C. (2005). An enriched teaching program for reducing resistance and indices of unhappiness among individuals with profound multiple disabilities. *Journal of Applied Behavior Analysis, 38,* 221-233.

Parsons, M. B., Reid, D. H., & Lattimore, L. P. (2009). Increasing independence of adults with autism in community activities: A brief, embedded teaching strategy. *Behavior Analysis in Practice, 2,* 40-48.

Reid, D. H., & Green, C. W. (2005). *Preference-based teaching: Helping people with developmental disabilities enjoy learning without problem behavior.* Morganton, NC: Habilitative Management Consultants.

Reid, D. H., & Green, C. W. (2006). Preference-based teaching: Helping students with severe disabilities enjoy learning without problem behavior. *Teaching Exceptional Children Plus, 2.*

WORKING WITH STAFF TO PROMOTE QUALITY PERFORMANCE AND WORK ENJOYMENT

Daniels, A. C. (1994). *Bringing out the best in people: How to apply the astonishing power of positive reinforcement.* New York: McGraw-Hill.

Green, C. W., Reid, D. H., Passante, S., & Canipe, V. (2008). Changing less-preferred duties to more-preferred: A potential strategy for improving supervisor work enjoyment. *Journal of Organizational Behavior Management, 28,* 90-109.

Parsons, M. B., & Reid, D. H. (1995). Training residential supervisors to provide feedback for maintaining staff teaching skills with people who have severe disabilities. *Journal of Applied Behavior Analysis, 28,* 317-322.

Parsons, M. B., Reid, D. H., & Crow, R. E. (2003). The best and worst ways to motivate staff in community agencies: A brief survey of supervisors. *Mental Retardation, 41,* 96-102.

Parsons, M. B., Rollyson, J. H., & Reid, D. H. (2013). Teaching practitioners to conduct behavioral skills training: A pyramidal approach for training multiple human service staff. *Behavior Analysis in Practice, 6,* 4-16.

Parsons, M. B., Rollyson, J. H., & Reid, D. H. (2012). Evidence-based staff training: A guide for practitioners. *Behavior Analysis in Practice, 5,* 2-11.

Reid, D. H., & Parsons, M. B. (2002). *Motivating human service staff: Supervisory strategies for maximizing work effort and work enjoyment. 2nd Edition.* Morganton, NC: Habilitative Management Consultants, Inc.

Reid, D. H., Parsons, M. B., & Green, C. W. (2012). *The supervisor's guidebook: Evidence-based strategies for promoting work qual-*

ity and enjoyment among human service staff. Morganton, NC: Habilitative Management Consultants, Inc.

Reid, D. H., Parsons, M. B., & Green, C. W. (2011). *The supervisor training curriculum: Evidence-based ways to promote work quality and enjoyment among support staff.* Washington, DC: American Association on Intellectual and Developmental Disabilities.

ADDITIONAL RESEARCH LITERATURE ON PROMOTING HAPPINESS

Carr, E. G., McLaughlin, D. M., Giacobbe-Grieco, T., & Smith, C. E. (2003). Using mood ratings and mood induction in assessment and intervention for severe problem behavior. *American Journal on Mental Retardation, 108,* 32-55.

Davis, P. K., Young, A., Cherry, H., Dahman, D., & Rehfeldt, R. A. (2004). Increasing the happiness of individuals with profound multiple disabilities: Replication and extension. *Journal of Applied Behavior Analysis, 37,* 531-534.

Green, C. W., Gardner, S. M., & Reid, D. H. (1997). Increasing indices of happiness among people with profound multiple disabilities: A program replication and component analysis. *Journal of Applied Behavior Analysis, 30,* 217-228.

Green, C. W., & Reid, D. H. (1999). Reducing indices of unhappiness among individuals with profound multiple disabilities during therapeutic exercise routines. *Journal of Applied Behavior Analysis, 32,* 137-148.

Ivancic, M. T., Barrett, G. T., Simonow, A., & Kimberly, A. (1997). A replication to increase happiness indices among some people with profound multiple disabilities. *Research in Developmental Disabilities, 18,* 79-89.

Lancioni, G. E., O'Reilly, M. F., Singh, N. N., Oliva, F. C., Campodonico, F., & Groeneweg, J. (2003). Stimulation and microswitch-based programs on indices of happiness of people with profound multiple disabilities. *Behavioral Interventions, 18,* 53-61.

Lancioni, G. E., O'Reilly, M. F., Singh, N. N., Oliva, D., & Groeneweg, J. (2002). Impact of stimulation versus microswitch-based programs on indices of happiness of people with profound multiple disabilities. *Research in Developmental Disabilities, 23,* 149-160.

Reid, D. H., & Green, C. W. (2006). Life enjoyment, happiness, and antecedent behavior support. In J. K. Luiselli (Ed.), *Antecedent assessment & intervention: Supporting children & adults with developmental disabilities in community settings* (pp. 249-268). Baltimore: Paul H. Brookes Publishing.

Reid, D. H., Green, C. W., & Parsons, M. B. (1998). A comparison of supported work versus center-based program services on selected outcomes for individuals with multiple severe disabilities. *Journal of The Association for Persons with Severe Handicaps, 23,* 69-76.

Smith, A. J., Bihm, E. M., Tavkar, P., & Sturmey, P. (2005). Approach-avoidance and happiness indicators in natural environments: A preliminary analysis of the Stimulus Preference Coding System. *Research in Developmental Disabilities, 26,* 297-313.

INDEX

absenteeism (staff) 62, 64, 251
adult education programs 8, 71, 174-175
antecedents 207, 208-211, 221
applied behavior analysis 232, 245, 250
assessment 54, 73, 94
    of caregiver opinion 27-35, 41-42, 135-136, 164
    of happiness and unhappiness indices 25-37
    of happiness and unhappiness situations 41-44
    of preferences (see preference assessments)
behavior support plans 94, 182, 195-197
behavioral momentum 210
behavioral objectives 25
caregiver opinion
    for identifying happiness indices 27-35, 39
    for identifying happiness situations 41-44
    for identifying consumer preferences 135-136
case illustrations 68, 71, 122, 141, 143, 146, 169, 183, 187, 218, 238
challenging behavior 46, 60, 61, 64, 69, 87, 92, 119, 125, 129, 194-197, 222, 223, 241, 257
choice 11, 19, 52-54, 99-131, 133, 134, 138, 148, 185-186, 204, 219-222, 253, 256-257, 261-263
communication challenges 3, 7, 16, 18, 65, 72, 96, 103, 106, 127
community activities 231, 235, 239-240, 244
consequences 207, 208, 217-219, 223
day programs 47, 60, 66, 100, 161, 165
demand situations 194-197, 206
disciplinary action (with staff) 271
embedded teaching 228
emotions 7, 16, 17, 19, 20, 22, 26
engagement (in activities) 129, 154
environments 153-155
evidence-based
    definition 5
    importance of 5, 6, 261
executive personnel 128
families 31, 59, 61, 66, 82, 163, 174
feedback 21, 89, 256, 258-259, 264, 267-271, 273-274
functional skills 106
goals 25, 159, 205, 228
group homes 48, 60, 66, 82, 109, 150, 167, 168, 265
incidental teaching 228
independence (see also teaching) 4, 4-12, 99, 167, 203-205, 229-232, 253
instructions 44, 193, 194-197, 208, 212-216, 231-233, 236, 240

instruction following 241-244
interspersal 215-216
interval recording 46-49
in-vivo teaching 228
job coaches 120, 121
learned helplessness 230
leisure 48, 92, 117, 124, 149
lifestyle changes 102, 159-177, 179
management personnel 127, 173
material adaptations 192-194
modeling 236
monitoring
    of consumer outcome attainment 4, 21, 266, 271-272
    of happiness and unhappiness indices 4, 15, 20-21, 45-49, 180, 195, 197-198
    of staff performance 261-266, 271-272
motivation (staff) 251-252
noncompliance 194-197, 241-242
observation procedures (see monitoring)
outcomes 4, 25, 152, 253, 266, 271-272
participative management 270
performance checklists 257
person-centered planning 73, 102, 124, 135, 159-177
personal control 10, 99, 114, 185, 227, 242, 257
physical challenges 110-116, 192-194
praise 85, 97, 206, 210, 212, 216, 234, 235, 237
preferences 19, 53, 133-157, 162, 186-187, 208-218, 224, 258
preference assessments 35-37, 135-148, 163-168, 212, 214
private events 16, 39
problem behavior (see challenging behavior)
profound multiple disabilities 110-116, 142, 144
prompting 212, 231, 232-234, 235, 236, 240, 244, 245
quality of life 3, 4, 8, 11, 19, 29, 59
reinforcement 206, 208, 223, 224, 232, 233, 234-235, 237, 240, 243, 244, 245
relationships 59-79, 81, 83, 151, 181-184, 206-207, 234, 254
research 5, 9, 27, 30, 31, 66, 103, 245, 250
residential agencies 8, 92, 100, 149
response class 243
rights 3
role playing 257-259
routines (in human service agencies) 28, 81, 100, 127, 182
sensory challenges 192-194
schedules 100, 148-150, 151, 189, 208
sincerity (in relationships and interactions) 77-78, 85
skill development 9-11, 162, 203-226, 227-248, 253
social attention 81-98
    different types 83-90, 197, 254, 265
    in group situations 90-93, 254, 265
social courtesy 276-277
special recognition (for staff) 274-275
stereotypic behavior 153-155
supervision 171, 245, 249-278
supervisors 8, 21, 64-65, 249-278
supported work 19, 121-122, 191

SWAT 235-238
task analysis 213, 214, 257
teaching 4-12, 115, 162, 190
    formal 81, 205-226, 227-228, 231
    naturalistic 197, 205, 227-248
    preference-based 190, 197, 203-226
training (of staff) 95-97, 128-129, 245, 249, 250, 255-260
transitions 180, 188-189
treatment plans (see also person-centered planning) 73, 124, 135, 160, 172
turnover (of staff) 62-64, 251
work enjoyment (of staff) 251-252, 262-264, 266-267, 269-270, 272-277